Unsex'd Revolutionaries
Five Women Novelists of the 1790s

Women had been writing long before the French Revolution, but the reactionary character of the 1790s infused their work with a public importance and an urgency. The decade was one of intense argument and reflection on the role of women in society. Eleanor Ty studies the ways in which five women writers of the 1790s politicized the domestic or sentimental novel in response to oppression and exclusion. Influenced by radical post-revolution thinkers, Mary Wollstonecraft, Mary Hays, Helen Maria Williams, Elizabeth Inchbald, and Charlotte Smith wrote fiction that questioned existing social, economic, legal, and cultural practices as they related to women. In particular, they dealt with historically specific gender issues such as female education, the rights and 'wrongs' of woman, and the duties of a wife.

Using historical and feminist psycho-linguistic studies as a base, Ty explores some of the complexities encountered in the writings of these five women. Through their challenge to Edmund Burke's patriarchal ideas, they discovered strategies of writing based on the maternal or female aesthetic.

For these 'unsex'd revolutionaries,' sentimental or domestic fiction was not just about courtship, love, and romance. Their writings interrogate the structures of society, and criticize and make relevant the connections between the personal and the political, the domestic and the public sphere.

ELEANOR TY is Assistant Professor in the Department of English, Wilfrid Laurier University. She is editor of *The Victim of Prejudice* by Mary Hays.

Theory/Culture

General Editors:
Linda Hutcheon and Paul Perron

Unsex'd Revolutionaries

Five Women Novelists
of the 1790s

ELEANOR TY

UNIVERSITY OF TORONTO PRESS
Toronto Buffalo London

©University of Toronto Press Incorporated 1993
Toronto Buffalo London
Printed in Canada

ISBN 0-8020-2949-3 (cloth)
ISBN 0-8020-7774-9 (paper)

Printed on acid-free paper

Canadian Cataloguing in Publication Data

Ty, Eleanor Rose, 1958–
    Unsex'd revolutionaries: five women novelists of the 1790s

    (Theory/Culture)
    Includes index.
    ISBN 0-8020-2949-3 (bound) ISBN 0-8020-7774-9 (pbk.)

    1. Feminist fiction, English – History and criticism. 2. English
fiction – 18th century – History and criticism. 3. Women in literature.
I. Title. II. Series.

PR858.W6T9 1993   823'.6099287   C93-093724-4

This book has been published with the help of a grant from the Canadian Federation for the Humanities, using funds provided by the
Social Sciences and Humanities Research Council of Canada.

For my mother

Contents

viii   Contents

Acknowledgments

This book has benefited greatly from dialogues with friends, teachers, and students. I am grateful for the guidance and help of those who read all or parts of the manuscript in its various stages: David Blewett, Joan Coldwell, James King, Gary Kelly, Donald Goellnicht, Frances Armstrong, Darrell Laird, and Brigitte Glaser. I received encouragement and advice from Marlene Kadar, Kenneth Graham, and Kevin Cope. For their support, friendship, and stimulating conversations through the years, I wish to thank Sylvia Bowerbank, Nancy Copeland, Heather Jones, and members of the McMaster University Women's Issues Group during 1982–6. Above all, my thanks are due to Linda Hutcheon, whose ability to connect the rigour of the professional and the theoretical with the warmth of the personal I shall always admire.

The anonymous readers for University of Toronto Press, as well as editors Ron Schoeffel and Ken Lewis, provided me with helpful comments for revision. Wilfrid Laurier University's generous book preparation grant facilitated the completion of the work. Finally, I owe much to my family, Dave and Jason, for their love and patience.

Preface

This book studies the way in which five women writers of the 1790s politicized the domestic or sentimental novel. Influenced by the radical thinkers of the decade following the French Revolution of 1789, Mary Wollstonecraft, Mary Hays, Helen Maria Williams, Elizabeth Inchbald, and Charlotte Smith wrote fiction that questioned existing social, economic, legal, and cultural practices as they related to women. In particular, they dealt with historically specific gender issues such as female education, the rights and 'wrongs' of woman, and the duties of a wife. What is most interesting about these authors to a twentieth-century reader is the way they manipulated and changed the function and scope of the domestic novel in the process of challenging the patriarchal order.

In attempting to respond to Edmund Burke's and other conservatives' notion of the benevolent patriarch, these novelists discovered strategies of writing that are based on the maternal, or on what I perceive to be a kind of female aesthetics. The notion of an essential difference between women and men is a subject of current debate, particularly in the light of post-structuralist feminist theory; nevertheless, in the late eighteenth century, and to a lesser extent in the present, women's positioning in linguistic, social, familial, and ideological structures differed, and differs, fundamentally from men's. This difference results in distinct means of imaging reality and using symbolic language. While these five women novelists may not have been consciously attempting to find a different method of recording their 'experience,' their fictional works, while typically tendentious and polemical (as were many other novels of the 1790s), nevertheless manifest a noticeable divergence from those of their male counterparts, and certainly from those of the conservative writers of the time. Sometimes their fiction shows a tendency to 'literalize' the figurative, or to translate the metaphoric into the real. At other times these women reveal their disillusionment with, and mistrust of, the patriarchal system, as they create protagonists who choose to live outside what we have come to call the Law of the Father. Techniques such as repetition and replication become powerful ways in their narratives of recreating and reinforcing woman's sense of oppression, and of communicating the urgency of the female plight.

My argument begins with a historical and cultural overview; but because history and culture are irrevocably linked to language and its structures for their transmission and dissemination, I have used Lacanian-inspired psycho-linguistic feminist theories to explain some of the complexities encountered in the writings of these five eighteenth-century women. Feminist critics have pointed out that the dominant figure in our 'androcentric' Western civilization is male, and they have sought to redress the balance by focusing on female figures and female-centred relationships. When I chose to study five relatively unknown writers of the 1790s, I knew that I was making an ideological statement about their importance in the English literary canon. I found, not wholly to my surprise, that certain significant patterns emerged as I studied their novels. The number of mother-daughter relationships in these books, for instance, is unusually high. This motif obviously points to the five authors' concern with female identity and bonding. It may also indicate a desire to rebut Burke's elevation of the paternal figure, which is based on the Law of the Father. Their implicit disagreement with his ideals inspired them to create alternative visions for themselves based on the maternal.

The common meeting place for the works in this study – which uses both historical and feminist psychoanalytic approaches – is the family. Burke's insistence on the patriarch as the head of the household is challenged by these five women writers, who realized that the situation at home was in itself a representation of the political and social scene. Twentieth-century French feminists who challenge the Law of the Father have also been rewriting the story of the Freudian family by pointing out the exclusion of the female from what Lacan calls the symbolic order. Though the works of the five 'unsex'd revolutionaries' – to use a derogatory epithet of their day – were not called feminist novels at the time, they do deal with marginalization, oppression, and exclusion of the female, concerns that surface in feminist writing today. For these writers of the 1790s sentimental or domestic fiction was not just about courtship, love, and romance, but also about inter-rogating the structures of the society, criticizing and making relevant the connections between the personal and the political, the domestic and the public spheres.

A Note on Methodology

Though I have sometimes treated more than one novel by the same author, I have not attempted a chronological survey of any one writer. This book does not offer a broad, historical study of the period,[1] but instead examines how specific issues of subjectivity and identity, mother-daughter relations, and the politics of gender are handled in selected novels written by five women of the 1790s. In highlighting these concerns as well as these particular novels, I wish to focus attention on subjects that are not usually included in discussions organized under the universal heading of 'man.' In the Western liter-ary tradition the stories of female development are usually subsumed within those of 'individual' development, or else they are inscribed in someone else's narrative. My effort to listen to mothers' and daughters' versions of the construction of self in a male-dominated society is an endeavour to understand the other side of what Ellen Pollak calls the 'myth of passive womanhood' which prevailed in seventeenth- and eighteenth-century England.[2] The enterprise follows and is indebted to the works of critics such as Jane Spencer, Janet Todd, Dale Spender, Mary Poovey, Mary Anne Schofield, Cecilia Macheski, Ann H. Jones, and Katherine Sobba Green,[3] who have similarly concentrated on giving voice to eighteenth-century women. Until very recently these women writers had been rendered silent by the unavailability of their texts in modern editions and their exclusion from the academic curric-ulum.

Readers who are familiar with what Nancy Miller has termed 'femio-centric' novels[4] of the eighteenth century may perhaps wonder at the telling absence of Defoe, Richardson, and Fielding in my discussions. These writers, particularly Richardson, are known for their attempts to capture 'feminine' sensibility and are thought to have expressed the 'feminine' unconscious in their fiction. However, as Miller points out, the 'plots of these femiocentric fictions are not female in impulse or origin, nor feminist in spirit' (149). These texts code femininity in 'paradigms of sexual vulnerability' (Miller, xi), and though they may portray psychologically complex female characters, they do not question the hierarchical relationship between the sexes, or the necessity of women's submission to the patriarchal order. As one critic observes, Richardson 'addresses himself to ... serious problems affecting women, but always with the ultimate complacency of a man who regards women as soft, gentle creatures to be guided and guarded by men.'[5] Although these earlier writers and the women novelists of the 1790s all employ the figure of the woman in distress as a staple of their works, there are differences in the aims as well as effects of this use. In Richardson's novels there is a strong sense of an over-arching structure, what could be called a belief in the patriarchal arrangement and in a supreme being who ultimately redeems female suffering or the woman in distress. This assumption enables one to view the heroine Clarissa, for example, as a figure who rises above her earthly trials. When Clarissa announces to Lovelace, 'I am setting out with all diligence for my father's house,'[6] readers are aware of the metaphoric and religious implications of the statement. By contrast, in the fiction published in the 1790s by these five radical women, female affliction originates and is rooted in the social, institutional, and secular world. There is far less transcendence and distancing afforded by the spiritual or the figurative.

In this study I argue that dissimilarities in the construction of female and male subjects in our society result in women writers' using language and representing their quotidian life in different ways than men. Implicit in this contention is the belief that there is a critical divergence between male- and female-authored texts, not because women and men are biologically different, but because they are 'en-gendered' through culture, which has customarily divided the sexes into two. Diana Fuss notes that a constructionist position, which 'insists that essence is itself a historical construction,' is 'a helpful one in that it reminds us that a complex system of cultural, social, psychical, and historical differences, and not a set of pre-existent human essences, position and constitute the subject.'[7] But, we must also note, in another critic's terms, that 'sexual difference is ontological, not accidental, peripheral, or contingent upon socio-economic conditions; that one be socially constructed as a female is an evidence, that the recognition of the fact may take place in language is clear, but that the process of construction of femininity fastens and builds upon anatomical realities is equally true. One is born and constructed as a woman.'[8] It is this construction of woman that the women writers of the 1790s are interrogating in their novels and that I examine in the chapters to follow.

The construction of the subject is a topic that has been much discussed by contemporary theorists. Because subjectivity is linked to language, I have found feminist thinkers such as Julia Kristeva and Luce Irigaray, who have made links between gender, discourse, and the unconscious, particularly useful. Though both theorists are influenced by Lacan and are often categorized together as proponents of '*l'écriture féminine*,'[9] it is important to note distinctions between their ideas. Kristeva advances the notion of the 'semiotic,' which, with its origins in the pre-verbal and pre-Oedipal, serves to disrupt the conscious acts of speech, or the symbolic processes. Like Jean Wyatt I will argue that semiotic energy is 'countercultural' because when it 'invades language, it distorts the signifying chain.'[10] Though women do not have a monopoly on the semiotic, Kristeva's emphasis of its marginalized position makes the notion attractive to many feminist critics. Luce Irigaray, however, believes that woman 'does not exist yet'[11] because in Western philosophy the female 'imaginary' has not yet been established. As Margaret Whitford explains: 'Using language ... presents a woman with the choice between remaining outside the signifying system altogether (in order to stay with her mother) or entering a patriarchal genealogy in which her position as object is already given.'[12] Irigaray envisions a speaking position for women that would incorporate the 'maternal-feminine in language,' rather than one that 'presupposes woman as universal predicate.'[13]

What the two French feminists have in common is the investigation of the means and bases of signification in the Western world, and the implications of such for the non-dominant groups in that culture. Women writers who use symbolic language have to contend with 'categories and divisions that pretend to be neutral while organizing thought in hierarchical structures that support male dominance.'[14] As Wyatt says, 'both reading and writing require an engagement with linguistic structures that carry patriarchal values. Using language means submitting to forms of logic that are also forms of authority and control; it means being interpellated into the structures ... of patriarchal discourse' (4). Kristeva's and Irigaray's theories suggest ways in which writers can subvert and challenge this discourse, thereby putting into question fundamental assumptions of Western epistemology.

In a similar manner, though the studies of both Nancy Chodorow in *The Reproduction of Mothering* (1978) and Carol Gilligan in *In a Different Voice* (1982) were done in this century and in North America rather than Britain, I feel that their findings are nevertheless relevant to the women writers of England nearly two centuries ago. Chodorow argues that because of mothering practices in our culture, girls remain unconsciously connected to their mothers well past infancy. Though science and technology have 'progressed' immensely, the social and psychological development of women today is not very different from that of their eighteenth-century counterparts. As Margaret Homans argues, 'We are all the inheritors of the same literary tradition, through which cultural values and myths are transmitted, stretching from the classics and the Bible to Milton ... Moreover, the dominant ideology of family structure in industrialized society has not, in its main outlines, changed very much.'[15] Many of the contradictions in self-representation, in subjectivity, found in earlier women's writings are still being played out today. Just as Freud's modern observations of his patients can cast some light on the character of Oedipus, so I think Chodorow's and Gilligan's views and conclusions can prove helpful in a discussion of texts written in the 1790s.

American thinkers like Chodorow and Gilligan differ from French feminists like Kristeva and Irigaray because their theories of female psycho-sexual development are based on sociological rather than linguistic and/or philosophical studies. However, their findings are similar in their stress on the maternal and in their emphasis on the mother-daughter connection. Margaret Homans has successfully employed Irigaray's and Gilligan's theories to suggest that women's relationship to literal and figurative language differs from men's.[16] In this study I have also used both the French and American feminist theories to support my readings, since I see the boundaries between them as more fluid than some critics suggest.[17] I have tended not to make absolute distinctions, for instance, between the notion of the repressed semiotic and that of the continuous attachment to the mother which results in girls using symbolic language differently than boys. Of greater interest is the instability created by this non-traditional discourse, which I see as potentially revolutionary.

Finally, the sequence of the chapters – which are not offered chronologically according to the publication dates of the novels – may need some explanation here. I have started with Mary Wollstonecraft's work because, of the five writers, she is the best known and the one most often cited as the speaker of women's rights in the 1790s. I have followed this chapter with readings of Hays's novels since Hays regarded herself as a friend and disciple of Wollstonecraft. Next to Wollstonecraft, Hays wrote the most lucid tracts on feminism in the decade. Though Williams, Inchbald, and Smith sympathized with the French revolutionaries and were very much aware of women's problems, they did not make published statements about the rights and 'wrongs' of woman in the same way. Their novels are equally compelling but are in many ways more subtle expressions of female discontent.

'A degree of exertion, produced by some want, more or less painful, is probably the price we must all pay for knowledge,' wrote Mary Wollstonecraft in a letter during her travels to Scandinavia in 1795.[18] Wollstonecraft's observation, which arose from her own experience as an author, applies as well to the other writers of this study. Their 'want,' which very likely was 'more or less painful' judging from their novels, caused them to wish for change for themselves and for the women about whom they wrote. The contemporaneity of the issues they raised, the powerful narratives, and the richness and complexity revealed about women's lives certainly make the novels worthy of our 'exertion' and investigation as readers and critics some two hundred years after they were published.

Unsex'd Revolutionaries

Five Women Novelists of the 1790s

Introduction

Our unsexed female writers now instruct, or confuse, us and themselves,
in the labyrinth of politics, or turn us wild with Gallic frenzy.

Rev. T.J. Mathias, *Pursuits of Literature* (1797)

Excuse me, therefore, if I have dwelt too long on the atrocious spectacle
of the 6th of October, 1789, or have given too much scope to the reflections which have arisen in my mind on occasion of the most important
of all revolutions, which may be dated from that day – I mean a revolution in sentiments, manners, and moral opinions.

Edmund Burke, *Reflections on the Revolution in France*

Revolutionary Context of the 1790s

In 1798 the anti-Jacobin poet, topographer, and theologian Reverend
Richard Polwhele (1760–1838) published *The Unsex'd Females: A Poem*,
which denounced the followers of Mary Wollstonecraft as unnatural
and 'unsex'd' women resigned to 'Gallic freaks' and 'Gallic faith.'[1]
Among the vindicators of the 'Rights of womankind' cited by Polwhele
are Anna Laetitia Barbauld, Mary 'Perdita' Robinson, Charlotte Smith,
Helen Maria Williams, Ann Yearsley, Mary Hays, Angelica Kauffman,
and Emma Crewe. On the opposite side of the spectrum, headed by
Hannah More, are mild and sweet models of 'female genius' such as
Mary Wortley Montague, Elizabeth Carter, Anna Seward, Hester Thrale
Piozzi, Fanny Burney, and Ann Radcliffe. This book focuses on five
writers whom Polwhele would classify as belonging to the monstrous

or 'unsex'd' category, but it is important to keep in mind that his distinctions are oversimplified and exaggerated. A number of recent scholars have pointed out that the two camps, whose views seemed diametrically opposed, in fact shared many concerns and employed comparable techniques to propagate their beliefs.[2]

That Mathias and Polwhele after him should have chosen this relatively uncommon word to describe the female radicals of the 1790s is significant. The *Oxford English Dictionary* defines 'unsex' as a transitive verb meaning 'to deprive or divest of sex, or of the typical qualities of one or the other (especially the female) sex.' One of the earliest uses of the word is found in Shakespeare's *Macbeth* (1605) in Lady Macbeth's villainous invocation: 'Come, you spirits / That tend on mortal thoughts, unsex me here, / And fill me, from the crown to the toe, top-full / Of Direst cruelty!' (1.5.42–4). Implicit in the three quotations is the suggestion that it is unnatural for women as the frail or gentle sex to harbour brutal thoughts, to want to be the equals of men, or to meddle in politics, all of which make them perverse or unacceptable examples of their kind. Polwhele sees the female intellectuals as creatures devoid of their 'natural' sex, as dangerous models precisely because of the element of sexual politics involved. Interestingly enough, there were already 'feminist'[3] thinkers such as Mary Astell with her *A Serious Proposal to the Ladies* published in 1694,[4] and notorious female writers such as Aphra Behn, Eliza Haywood, and Delariviere Manley a century earlier.[5] But what made the women of the 1790s seem particularly threatening to the anti-Jacobins was the outspoken claiming of their 'rights' shortly after and coinciding with the events in France that culminated in the revolution, which Edmund Burke saw as 'the most important of all revolutions.'[6]

According to Burke's account of the revolution, the political is intimately linked to the familial. For Burke the day of 6 October 1789, more so than the storming of the Bastille on 14 July 1789, marked a crucial date in history, as it was the day the French king and the National Assembly were forced to transfer from Versailles to the Tuileries in Paris. One of the most often cited passages in Burke's *Reflections* is his graphic description of the king and the queen being yanked out of their bed by a 'band of cruel ruffians and assassins, reeking with blood.'[7] In his presentation of the political act as a sexual act of violation – the queen flees 'almost naked' to seek the protection of her husband – he is making an explicit link between the public and the domestic realms. The 'vast and multi-faceted series of events in France' are described in terms of a 'unitary family drama,' emphasizing the vulnerability and destruction of patriarchal rule and authority by crazed ruffians, ideologues who seek 'to create a new society.'[8] For Burke the family becomes a microcosmic state, a basic political unit in its own right. Duty to the patriarchal family is the first step towards a love of society, country, and mankind. His *Reflections* warns England against levellers who would subvert the aristocratic concepts of paternalism, loyalty, chivalry, and the hereditary principle. As J.G.A. Pocock points out, he was 'defending a complex governing order – monarchic, clerical, aristocratic, commercial – against the inroads of the revolutionary intellect.'[9] Developing further the idea that the seduction of a wife or daughter is the first step towards the undermining of authority, Burke's *A Letter to a Member of the National Assembly* (1791) blames Rousseau's *Confessions* and his *Nouvelle Héloïse* for encouraging servants and upstarts such as dancing masters, hairdressers, fiddlers, and valets to betray their masters. According to Burke, revolutionaries 'endeavour to subvert those principles of domestic trust and fidelity which form the discipline of social life.' This could lead to 'every considerable father of a family' losing 'the sanctuary of his house.'[10]

Though they did not all write prose tracts against Burke's influential pamphlets, the five women writers in this study – Mary Wollstonecraft, Mary Hays, Helen Maria Williams, Elizabeth Inchbald, and Charlotte Smith – were, in varying degrees, all reacting to the conservative, patriarchal position promoted by Burke, and by the anti-Jacobins towards the end of the decade. While most of them were classified as members of Wollstonecraft's band by Polwhele, the five novelists did not, in fact, belong to any organized literary group or salon, but they were connected in various ways. After reading Wollstonecraft's *A Vindication of the Rights of Woman*, Hays commented that the book was 'a work full of truth and genius' and asked the publisher Joseph Johnson to introduce her to the celebrated author.[11] She is later credited with bringing together Wollstonecraft and Godwin by giving a small party in her lodgings.[12] As a critic for the *Analytical Review* Wollstonecraft was very likely responsible for the reviews published in that journal of Smith's *Emmeline*, Williams's *Julia*, and Inchbald's *A Simple Story*.[13] Though she did not have any personal contact with the other writers, Smith had certainly read Wollstonecraft by 1798, as she cites her in connection with reform laws affecting married women in the preface to her *Young Philosopher*.[14]

What the five did have in common was a belief in what Burke had feared, that following the example of the overthrow of government in France 'a revolution in sentiments, manners, and moral opinions' was possible in their own country.[15] As Ronald Paulson and others have explained, the original meaning of 'revolution' was astronomical, referring to the rotation of bodies: a circular motion returning to its point of origin. Thus the 'Glorious' Revolution of 1688 removed a usurping tyrant in order to restore ancient liberties. The five radical writers were revolutionaries in this sense: they believed in succession and restoration of rights which were 'natural' in the same way as the rotation of heavenly bodies was natural. Hence, these women were viewed by Burke as responsible for social upheaval and political insurrection.[16] There were many others who shared the conviction that England was on the verge of a new millennium, a new age more liberal and egalitarian than the one they were living in. To varying degrees, these people influenced and interacted with the five women writers in question. For instance, Wollstonecraft and Hays read the works of the rational dissenters Richard Price (1723–91) and Joseph Priestley (1733–1804); and they admired the defender of the 'Rights of man,' Tom Paine (1737–1809). Except for Smith they were all part of the London circle of middle-class writers, artists, and intellectuals who clustered around the bookseller and publisher Joseph Johnson. Others in the group included Henry Fuseli, William Godwin, Anna Laetitia Barbauld, William Blake, Joel Barlow, Maria Edgeworth, Erasmus Darwin, and John Horne Tooke. Blake challenged the establishment with his poetry and art and may have picked up some of Wollstonecraft's ideas on the emancipation of women. Not only did his mythologized historical narratives *The French Revolution* and *America* celebrate the two actual revolutions, but his work during the years 1790–4, including *Visions of the Daughters of Albion, Europe,* and *The First Book of Urizen,* all anticipated the end of an old world and the coming of a new dawn.[17] In addition, his *Marriage of Heaven and Hell,* attacking the established church and other institutions, and the Swedish philosopher and mystic Emmanuel Swedenborg (1688–1772), in particular, proclaims the rebel figure Satan as the true hero of Milton's *Paradise Lost* (pl. 6), and finishes with the political piece 'A Song of Liberty.'

Another intellectual who looked forward to change was Richard Price, who preached in 'A Discourse on the Love of Our Country,' delivered on 4 November 1789, that 'civil governors are properly the servants of the public, created by it, maintained by it, and responsible to it: and all the homage paid [them], is due to [them] on no other account than [their] relation to the public.'[18] This sermon, though not intended to advocate the abolition of the monarchy, attracted the attention of Burke, who criticized Price for quitting his 'proper character' and assuming a role that did not 'belong' to him.[19] Believing that a pulpit was not a place for politics, he declared: 'No sound ought to be heard in the church but the healing voice of Christian charity.'[20] Joseph Priestley, Mary Wollstonecraft, and Tom Paine were quick to answer Burke's rhetorical arguments with pamphlets and public 'letters' addressed to him. Priestley, in his *Letters to the Right Hon. Edmund Burke, Occasioned by His Reflections on the Revolution in France* (Birmingham 1791), chastises Burke for his hypocrisy and eloquently defends 'the great revolution that has taken place in France, as well as ... that which some time ago took place in America.'[21] Condemning monarchies in general, Priestley writes:

> The generality of governments have hitherto been little more than a combination of *the few*, against *the many*; and to the mean passions and low cunning of these few, have the great interests of mankind been too long sacrificed. Whole nations have been deluged with blood, and every source of future prosperity has been drained, to gratify the caprices of some of the most despicable, or the most execrable, of the human species. For what else have been the generality of kings, their ministers of state, or their mistresses, to whose wills whole kingdoms have been subject?[22]

Like the other revolutionary sympathizers he was not afraid to criticize what he believed to be the rule of the despotic few and looked forward to a new and better future: 'How glorious, then, is the prospect, the reverse of all the past, which is now opening upon us, and upon the world.'[23] The fearless spirit in which he criticized the government may have indirectly inspired women writers like Wollstonecraft and Hays, who at this time were beginning to formulate their thoughts on the inequality of men and women in the eyes of society and the law, and who saw an analogy between political tyranny and the situation in the household.

Wollstonecraft's most explicit reply to Burke came in the form of her *A Vindication of the Rights of Men, in a Letter to the Right Hon. Edmund Burke; Occasioned by His Reflections on the Revolution in France.* She accused Burke of being ruled by emotion rather than reason; but Wollstonecraft, who, I want to argue subsequently, was never totally at ease with what Lacan and Kristeva call the symbolic language of the Father,[24] was similarly passionate and full of volatile emotion as she wrote from 'the effusions of the moment' (Advertisement).[25] Composed in less than thirty days, Wollstonecraft's book vehemently challenged Burke on a number of points. While Burke believed that patrimony with its orderly transmission of property was one of the stabilizing principles of society, Wollstonecraft denounces 'hereditary property' and 'hereditary honours' as the primary causes of the retardation of civilization's 'progress,' arguing that 'man has been changed into an artificial monster by the station in which he was born.'[26] Appealing to 'nature' and reason, Wollstonecraft contends: 'The only security of property that nature authorizes and reason sanctions is, the right a man has to enjoy the acquisitions which his talents and industry have acquired; and to bequeath them to whom he chooses.'[27] The emphasis on an individual's abilities rather than on his birth or family becomes one of the rallying cries of the supporters of the French Revolution. Wollstonecraft and Hays were later to apply these principles of *egalité* and individualism to women as well. In response to Burke's melodramatic depiction of the events of 6 October 1789, Wollstonecraft counters with a legitimate objection, that of the more urgent needs and 'remediless evils' of the poor, which he ignores. However, she gives an equally sentimental vision of their pathetic condition, calling them the 'loathsome sight of human misery,' and rhetorically comments: 'What were the outrages of a day to these continual miseries?'[28] Even though the *Vindication* fails to avoid most of the problems that Wollstonecraft sees in Burke's *Reflections*, it still stands as an impressive and powerful document. The instant fame and recognition it gave Wollstonecraft also bolstered her confidence and belief in herself as a writer.

By far the most popular and sustained response to Burke was Paine's *Rights of Man* (1791–2). Like the other radicals Paine was opposed to the old system of government based on heredity: 'All hereditary government is in its nature tyranny. An heritable crown, or an heritable throne ... have no other significant explanation than that mankind are heritable property.'[29] Replying to criticism that *Rights of Man* is a 'levelling' system, he maintains that the 'hereditary monarchical system' is a 'system of mental levelling ... Kings succeed each other, not as rationals, but as animals. It signifies not what their mental or moral characters are.'[30] Part 1 of *Rights of Man* was 'one of the most widely read pamphlets of all time,' partly because of the 'simplicity of [Paine's] revolutionary doctrine and the lucid directness with which he expressed it.'[31] Based on the French 'Declaration of the Rights of Man and of Citizens,' which Paine includes in translation, his own doctrine speaks on behalf of all people: 'There never did, there never will, and there never can exist a parliament, or any description of men, or any generation of men, in any country, possessed of the right or the power of binding and controlling posperity to the "end of time" ...'[32] In 1797 T.J. Mathias attested to the pamphlet's popularity when he observed that 'our peasantry now read the *Rights of Man* on mountains, and moors, and by the wayside.'[33] Like Wollstonecraft, Paine reacted to Burke's pathetic depiction of the French king and queen, accusing Burke of degenerating 'into a composition of art,' 'tragic paintings,' and 'theatrical representation' manufactured to produce 'a weeping effect'[34] rather than adhering to factual details. His own work, emphasizing fact and common sense, using a 'vulgar' and plain rather than a decorous and refined style, appealed to a great mass of the common people.[35]

Towards the second half of the decade pamphlets expressing revolutionary sympathy declined for several reasons. The dissenting preacher Richard Price died in 1791, and in the second half of 1792 Pitt's administration began a series of moves to stop the spread of radicalism through the printed word. Paine left for France in September 1792, but in December he was tried and sentenced in his absence for seditious libel. Robespierre's Reign of Terror (1793–4) in France made many English people who had supported republicanism lose faith in the redeeming possibilities of the revolution. In 1794 many London radical leaders, including Thomas Holcroft, John Horne Tooke, and Thomas Hardy, were arrested for high treason. There were, however, still a few defenders of the revolutionary cause. One of three defendants tried in November 1794 was John Thelwall (1764–1834), who emerged as a leading figure of the group during 1793–6. In 1796 ex-mercer, ex-tailor, unqualified lawyer, and minor poet Thelwall produced his most important political pieces, which stirred Coleridge's admiration.[36] In *The Tribune, a Periodical Publication, Consisting Chiefly of the Political Lectures of J. Thelwall* (1796) he pleads with his middle-class audience on behalf of the truly poor: 'Oh citizens, reflect, I conjure you, that the common class of mankind and you are one! that you are one in nature! that you are one in interest! and that those who seek to *oppress the lower*, seek to *annihilate the intermediate orders*.'[37] Like Wollstonecraft and Paine, Thelwall sought to minimize the differences between the classes and appealed to the spirit of 'humanity.' Responding to Burke's *A Letter to a Noble Lord on the Attacks Made upon Him and His Pension* (1796), he wrote *Sober Reflections on the Seditious and Inflammatory Letter of the Right Hon. Edmund Burke*, accusing the conservative writer of artfully exciting 'groundless terror' and causing the public to misinterpret the actions of the 'true sons of moderation and good order' by 'making them accountable for actions they were never consulted upon, books they never read, and sentiments they never heard.'[38]

In general, however, the fervent tone of radicalism had changed by the middle years of the 1790s. The revolutionary spirit became diffused and manifested itself sometimes indirectly in literature of various forms. William Wordsworth, who is not now known primarily for his association with the radicals of the 1790s,[39] was aligned with them by at least one contemporary critic because of his *Lyrical Ballads* and its 'Preface.' Francis Jeffrey, editor of the *Edinburgh Review* and its most prolific review writer, linked the Wordsworthian ballad with Paine's *Rights of Man*, the implication, Butler suggests, being that 'the influence of Wordsworth is likely to be similarly in the direction of "levelling" proper social distinctions.'[40] Other male writers of the period were more overtly partisan in their works. William Godwin, Robert Bage, and Thomas Holcroft, referred to by contemporary and present-day critics as 'Jacobin'[41] novelists because of their opposition to tyranny and oppression, and their belief, as Gary Kelly puts it, that 'reason should decide the issue in human affairs and human government, not power based on money, age, rank, sex, or physical strength,'[42] wrote fiction which thematized their concerns and beliefs. Because of the deliberate use of politics in their fiction, these male writers of the decade are comparable to the five revolutionary women writers in question. Godwin, Holcroft, and Bage did desire social change and had aims similar to those of Wollstonecroft, Smith, or Hays. But their novels were less concerned with gender inequalities than they were with inequalities of class.

Perhaps the most influential of these novels on the women writers is Godwin's *Things As They Are; or, The Adventures of Caleb Williams* (1794),[43] which has been read as an extension of the arguments found in his *Enquiry Concerning Political Justice*, as well as a 'Romantic study of individual psychology.'[44] One of the most relevant tenets for the radicals of the 1790s was the Godwinian philosophy that 'the characters of men originate in their external circumstances.'[45] For if, as Godwin believed, 'the actions and dispositions of mankind are the offspring of circumstances and events, and not of any original determination that they bring into the world,'[46] then an active manipulation of one's situation could bring about an improvement. Hence one's birth was no longer the sole determinant of one's place in life. In his novel, through the creation of the polished, elegant, and wealthy gentleman Ferdinando Falkland, who has secretly committed a murder, Godwin repudiates Burke's belief in the benevolence and goodness of the country squire. For instead of using his prestigious position to protect and bestow kindness on his tenants and his servants, he abuses his power over the poor and the weak, relentlessly pursuing and tormenting his employee Caleb, who has found out his guilty deed. Written to expose the inadequacy and corruption of the legal and political system which favours the rich, Godwin's novel demonstrated that truth is an equivocal matter in the hands of those with authority. The chivalric code of honour and the ideal of gentleman's conduct extolled by Burke in his *Reflections on the Revolution* are shown to be insufficient guarantees of justice for a man with an obscure birth such as Caleb Williams. The novel served as a model for Wollstonecraft's *Wrongs of Woman* and may have inspired parts of Hays's *Victim of Prejudice.*

In a similar effort to censure the affluent and elevate the ordinary man, Thomas Holcroft's *Anna St. Ives* (1792) depicts a heroine torn between the love of an aristocratic rake, Coke Clifton, and a sincere but low-born reformer, Frank Henley.[47] Anna's belief that reason can triumph over passion leads her to select Clifton as her suitor, but he soon shows his Lovelacean villainous nature by attempting to 'ruin' her before their nuptials. Though based on a sentimental plot, Holcroft's novel does not end in tragedy, as Richardson's *Clarissa* or Mary Hays's *Victim of Prejudice* does. Instead the emphasis is on the transformations possible through the virtuous and benevolent examples of Anna and Frank. Mary Wollstonecraft criticized the novel's idealized heroine and perceived Anna's actions to be 'improbable and unnatural.'[48] Indeed, Anna is often described in exaggerated terms of perfection by both her admirers. Frank describes her showing 'angelic sensibility' at the sight of his wound and says that 'she has a soul alive to all the throbs of humanity' (15), while Clifton calls her 'the pearl of pearls! The inestimable jewel! The unique!' (92). I would suggest that Holcroft's characterization of Anna and his subsequent solution to her dilemma are indications of the way Holcroft is distinguishable from the five women novelists who are the main focus of my book. While *Anna St. Ives* contains some proto-feminist passages[49] which make Holcroft's intentions seem comparable to those of Wollstonecraft or Hays, these concerns of gender are, on the whole, subservient to his more important theme of revolutionary reform. The potentially menacing and very disturbing masculine power of Clifton is deflected too easily by the kindness and forgiving nature of Anna, and more than one critic has commented on the novel's rather facile and fabular characterization as well as ending.[50] Holcroft, like Bage, was sympathetic to the plight of contemporary women but did not see the need to make the issue of women's rights a primary consideration in his fiction.

The tone and degree of radicalism of Bage's novels are closer to those of Inchbald and Smith than to those of Wollstonecraft or Hays. Though usually associated with the revolutionary 'Jacobins' of the 1790s, Robert Bage was actually a product of an earlier generation of thinkers. Born in 1728 Bage was already in his sixties during the French Revolution. In his last two novels, *Man As He Is* (1792) and *Hermsprong; or, Man As He Is Not* (1796), he explores some of the political and social issues of the day, but his attitude is often good-humoured and gently satiric rather than didactic and earnest. His wit, rambling style, and picaresque form have often been compared to Smollett's,[51] but critics are not in agreement as to whether his humour, in fact, acts as a mask for his radicalism or whether it demonstrates a 'civilised tolerance and understanding of the relatively of ideas.'[52] In *Hermsprong*, the novel in which he is most influenced by the revolutionary ideas of the 1790s, the character Lord Grondale is an example of an unreasonable tyrannical father because he attempts to force his dutiful daughter Caroline Campinet into marriage with the physically deformed and mean-spirited Sir Philip Chestrum.[53] He is aided by the Reverend Mr Blick, a servile clergyman of the established church who is willing to sacrifice moral principles for the worldly interest of his patron. As in the case of Godwin's *Caleb Williams*, this scenario could be read as a reaction against Burke's ideal of the benevolent landlord and patriarch, as both father-figures are here shown to be self-interested rather than generous and noble. Another element linking Bage with the reformer Holcroft is the outspoken character of Hermsprong, who is initially introduced as a mysterious American lately come from France who heroically saves Caroline from falling over a cliff. The potential radical nature of his alliance with Caroline is undercut towards the end when he turns out to be Sir Charles Campinet, son of Lord Grondale's elder brother and rightful heir to the estates, rather than an obscure stranger with good intentions.

Feminist views are presented by the hero in *Hermsprong*, but the only female character who dares agree openly with and act according to Hermsprong's idea that women have not had the liberty of mind and spirit they deserve is Caroline's 'foil,' her friend Maria Fluart, who is vivacious and forthright. It is Maria Fluart who dares challenge the 'duty' that Caroline believes she herself unquestionably owes her father. When asked if she would give serious consideration if a lord were to lay his rank, title, person, and fortune at her feet, Maria coyly replies: 'Why, my lord, these are very serious things, no doubt; one should like to tread upon some of them' (111). Had Maria Fluart been the heroine, and the implications of her many witty remarks been more seriously considered, *Hermsprong* would indeed have been one of the most radical novels of the 1790s. However, as it stands, with the fortuitous and sentimental death of the villain father at the end, it remains an entertaining display of a variety of undeveloped but conceivably extremely revolutionary ideas.

Female Novelists and the Revolutionary Crisis

By describing the female revolutionary sympathizers as 'unsex'd' the Reverend Richard Polwhele was voicing his, and perhaps, many late-eighteenth-century people's opinion of the inappropriate behaviour of these women. What he was opposing was not female authorship per se, as he extolled the chaste British matrons such as Montague, Carter, and Chapone, among others, for being able to 'refine a letter'd age' and 'diffuse / The moral precepts of the Grecian Muse.'[54] What he objected to in the 'unsex'd' females was either one or both of two things: their support of the French people's desire for a republican government, and hence their meddling in politics; and/or their sexually liberated notions. Republicanism and licentiousness have tended to be conflated as one fault, largely because of the example of Mary Wollstonecraft, whom Polwhele castigates as his principal target, but not all the women he cites as part of Wollstonecraft's band were listed because of their lasciviousness. For instance, in Polwhele's own notes to the poem he praises Charlotte Smith's skills as a writer but laments her political interests:

> The sonnets of Charlotte Smith have a pensiveness peculiarly their own: ... It is a strain of wild, yet softened sorrow, that breathes a romantic air, without losing, for a moment, its mellowness ... There is so uncommon a variety in her expression, that I could read a thousand of such Sonnets without lassitude ... As a novel-writer, her *Ethelinde* and *Emmeline* place her above all her contemporaries, except Mrs. D'Arblay and Mrs. Radcliffe. But why does she suffer her mind to be infected with the Gallic mania?[55]

Unlike Polwhele's comments on Wollstonecraft, Robinson, Williams, Kauffman, or Crewe, his criticism of Smith does not mention sexual lewdness. Polwhele simply objects to her 'Gallic mania,' or so he says. Yet if he was only protesting against a writer's political opinions, why are reformers such as Godwin and Holcroft not labelled 'unsex'd' males? Clearly the underlying concern for Polwhele is gender, a problematic issue for a woman trying to be a writer at the time.

While women had been writing long before the revolution in France, the reactionary decade of the 1790s brought a sense of public importance and urgency to the works they now produced. After the connection Burke made between the stalwart patriarchal home and the strength of the nation, concerns normally thought to be private and domestic – women's education, their choice of husbands, female conduct, sexuality, and manners – became politicized as general topics of interest. There was an increasing awareness that every major aspect of woman's experience was closely related to that of the man in the public arena and that, in fact, 'women's lives already serve[d] a political agenda.'[56] Not all women writers, of course, believed in changing the status quo. The period of the 1790s could be described in terms of what Showalter calls the three distinct stages of development in women's literary history: the feminine phase, in which women 'internalize' the male culture's assumptions about female nature; the feminist phase, in which women are able to 'dramatize the ordeals of wronged womanhood'; and the female phase, when women 'turn ... to female experience as the source of an autonomous art.'[57] The relationship between 'lived experience' and its representation in language and a text is admittedly vexed and complicated. Various post-structuralist theorists have questioned the humanist assumption that women's 'experience' is directly available and communicable through women's texts.[58] Because language is male-centred, some argue that women's ideas and images of themselves are already bound by pre-existent structures and ideologies. Nevertheless, I think that the socially and historically produced concerns of these women writers, as depicted in their fiction, give an indication of the possible subject-positions open to women of the late eighteenth century, 'what they could say or not from within the discursive field of femininity in which they were located.'[59] I wish to explore how the female novelists of the 1790s, who believed that they were able to write about 'things as they are' based on their lives and 'experiences,' contested, rebelled against, but also inadvertently participated in the perpetuation of the existing cultural, social, and linguistic categories of woman and assignments of gender.

Female involvement with politics, ideology, and partisan arguments is perhaps most evident then in the novels women published in the 1790s. Jane West, one of the most prolific writers for the conservative side, warned in 1799 that the title of a work no longer announces its intention: books of travels are converted into vehicles of politics and systems of legislation. Female letter-writers teach us the arcana of government, and obliquely vindicate ... manners and actions at which female delicacy should blush ... Tracts on education subvert every principle of filial reverence ... the novel ... is converted into an offensive weapon, directed against our religion, our morals, or our govenment, as the humour of the writer may determine his particular warfare.[60]

West herself, writing sometimes as the retired old woman Mrs Prudentia Homespun, subscribed to the ideological notion of female subservience to male authority, making this a central theme in many of her works. She is a good example of a woman writer from Showalter's 'feminine' stage, one who is dominated by and speaks from the position of the Father. Lacanian-inspired feminist criticism would suggest that for West 'sexual identity is ordered by phallocentric difference'[61] and that the dominance or the privileging of the phallus is taken for granted.[62] West, like many other women who supported the Burkean paradigm of the domestic monarch, accepts that as a woman she cannot physiologically possess the phallus and its accompanying power, and thus constructs an identity from the position of Other which is subservient to the male. Josette Féral argues that a woman 'cannot assume ... identification with the Father except by denying her difference as a woman, except by repressing the maternal within her – and she is impelled to do this by society, a society which, moreover, constitutes itself only through its repression of the mother.'[63] Hence we find that while there are possible strong maternal figures in West's novels, they constantly defer to the husbands and fathers as representatives of authority.

For example, in *The Advantages of Education; or, The History of Maria Williams* (1793) there is no obvious paternal model, but the heroine's mother, with her experience and good sense, gives her daughter this advice before her nuptials:

a wife must not always expect the behaviour of a lover, even from an affectionate husband ... shew him that you are his helpmate, not his incumbrance ... convince him that you have fortitude to bear the common ills of life, as well as patience to endure its common provocations ... Humility, which inspires a lowly mind and moderate desires, is the surest road to content.[64]

The lesson to be learned here is one that West later makes even more explicit in her conduct books: female deference and respect to the husband, who is the acknowledged 'monarch' of the family. In *Letters to a Young Lady* (1806) she similarly asserts:

> Without wasting our time in a philosophical analysis of the peculiar construction of our intellects, or the physical organization of our bodies, we may rest assured that we are endowed with powers adequate to the design of our creation; namely, to be the helpmate of man, to partake of his labours, to alleviate his distresses, to regulate his domestic concerns, to rear and instruct the subsequent generation ...[65]

While it is true that even the radical Wollstonecraft, advocating better education for women, assumed that this instruction would make women better wives and 'helpmates,' the difference between the two writers is that West, unlike Wollstonecraft, ignores the very real possibility of the abuse of power by these figures of authority. In addition, her heroines do not dare challenge the male prerogative as, for instance, Wollstonecraft's character Maria would.

In *A Tale of the Times* (1799) West begins with an idealized model of a paternalistic society. The heroine's father, Sir Anthony Powerscourt, is depicted as a 'prudent monarch' who acts in the best interest of his daughter and the community at large. He is portrayed as a benevolent country gentleman, a 'conscientious guardian' rather than a 'self-accountable owner,' a 'protector' and 'friend' rather than master of his tenants: 'his hospitable doors were open to indigence; his delicacy was never hurt by the simplicity of rustic manners' (1:28). The subsequent 'ruin' of his daughter's marriage and happiness is blamed largely on the 'free notions of the age' (2:278). The arch-villain of the story, Edward Fitzosborne, is associated with revolutionaries and 'sophists,' whose belief in such doctrines as 'human actions ought to be free' ends up destroying the important 'bonds of society' (2:272, 273). Like other post–French Revolution conservatives West equates domestic discord with national chaos, arguing that in 'dissolving domestic confidence and undermining private worth,' one paves the 'way for universal confusion' (2:275).

In *Letters to a Young Lady* West again makes a specific link between the domestic and the political realms, echoing Burke's ideas: 'No nation has preserved its political independence for any long period after its women became dissipated and licentious. When the hallowed graces of the chaste matron have given place to the bold allurements

of the courtesan, the rising generation always proclaims its base origin'
(1:56–7). In other words, the preservation of women's chastity, and
hence family sanctity, became equated with the defence of the country.
Allusions to the disruptive effects of radical women intellectuals occur
frequently in the book. For example, West claims that she prefers a
'common' woman who 'suffers the passing scene to flit by her without
much anxiety, or much reflection,' to the 'petticoat philosophist, who
seeks for eminence and distinction in infidelity and scepticism, or in
the equally monstrous extravagances of German morality' (1:18).
Believing in English society with its clearly defined hierarchical structure, West regrets to see 'these solid excellences ... bartered for German principles, illustrated by French practice' (1:193). We could say
that West speaks from and for the Law of the Father, as she subscribes
to the version of the cultural myth that believes in the elevation of
masculine authority and the necessary subordination and repression
of feminine desire.

Another conservative writer who became a novelist after the reactionary debate of the 1790s was the evangelical crusader and Sunday school
educator Hannah More. More's only novel, *Coelebs in Search of a Wife*
(1809), was another fictional work which took up and defended the
Burkean model of the patriarchal household with an added emphasis
on Christian doctrines. In Showalter's terms More would be writing in
the 'feminine' stage, as she expresses and internalizes male culture's
assumptions about female nature. Again and again the text maintains
that one of the essential qualities of a 'proper' lady[66] is her subordination. The extent of this female self-effacement can be seen in the lack
of both the female name and signature in *Coelebs*. The novel, designed
to edify its mainly female audience, was published anonymously, with
a preface attributed to a 'Coelebs.' In the novel itself the 'heroine,'
Lucilla, the ideal wife whom Coelebs finally finds, does not appear on
or speak for more than a few pages of the two-volume (over 800-page)
opus. More adopts not only a masculine point of view in terms of
narrative technique, but also what Irigaray calls the specularizing
tendency of the 'male imaginary,' which focuses on itself as the centre
or 'sun.'[67]

As Coelebs leaves his home in search of the perfect wife whose
whole character should be devoted, and he quotes Milton, 'To study
household good, / And good works in her husband to promote,'[68] he
meets many unsuitable girls who are either too frivolous, not religious
enough, too learned or 'accomplished' in useless arts, or unable to
cook. Interestingly enough, Coelebs and his reader do not often get

even to meet the daughters, as the defective conduct of the mother is usually sufficient to frighten off Coelebs.[69] The superiority and judiciousness of patriarchal authority are reinforced in the novel as Coelebs's 'choice' of partner turns out to be one whom his father had desired from the beginning. Ironically what confirms the correctness of the selection in the fastidious bachelor's mind is that Lucilla, too, looks to Milton's Eve, demurely tending her garden, as the most 'beautiful model of delicacy, propriety, grace, and elegance' (2:284). Neither Coelebs, Lucilla, nor More as the narrator mentions the paradoxical nature of Eve's character in *Paradise Lost.* As we know, Milton's Eve, who is full of 'softness' and 'sweet attractive grace,' as Coelebs notes, is also the one whose curiosity about the serpent's knowledge leads to the Fall. More's suppression of the self-willed, disobedient, and unsettling side of Eve indicates the inadequacy and the one-sidedness of her ideal. Eve/Lucilla is only 'perfect' for a man when one deliberately omits or silences an essential part of her nature or her 'desire.'

Indeed, for More, self-restraint is a necessary part of the ideology of the ideal woman. Lucilla maintains the 'silence of delicate propriety' in Coelebs's presence (1:190) and informs him: 'In general I hold it indiscreet to speak of the state of one's mind' (2:107). The circumspect heroine illustrates the doctrines More set forth in her *Strictures on the Modern System of Female Education* (1799):

> An early habitual restraint is peculiarly important to the future character and happiness of women. They should when very young be inured to contradiction ... They should be led to distrust their own judgement, they should learn not to murmur at expostulation; but should be accustomed to expect and to endure opposition.[70]

More believes that 'a girl who has docility will seldom be found to want understanding sufficient for all the purposes of a useful, a happy, and a pious life' (*Strictures,* 1:159). In her novel an anti-heroine such as Lady Bab Lawless is shown to be too vivacious, gay, and open; and Amelia Rattle, who has learned French and Italian and is starting German, is too confident of her accomplishments and too forward in her opinions. Only Lucilla is praised for her 'well bred' attention and 'intelligent' silence (1:323). However, as one critic has pointed out, 'silence so unbroken cannot be distinguished from insipidness or imbecility.'[71] As Irigaray contends, 'femininity' is a 'role, an image, a value, imposed upon women by male systems of representation. In this masquerade of femininity, the woman loses herself, and loses herself by playing on her femininity. The fact remains that this masquerade requires an *effort* on her part for which she is not compensated.'[72] In attempting to create an ideal modest domestic woman, More has created only a flat, dull, and rather unimpressive shadow of a character. Irigaray would criticize this type of woman as one who is merely 'chosen as an object ... of desire by masculine "subjects"' (*This Sex*, 84).

Other female novelists, including Jane Austen and Fanny Burney, who were writing and publishing during the 1790s were not as adamant about defending the Burkean patriarchal ideal as West and More were.[73] While these writers have been called 'conservative' and placed on the anti-Jacobin side of the 'war of ideas' because they did not seem to support the French Revolution, their attitudes and relations to established power are actually more complex than an unqualified endorsement. For the most part, while they did not question the view that compliance with patriarchal notions of female subservience was necessary, these writers often illustrated in their fiction the difficulties and high psychic cost of this female surrender. There were many who were sympathetic to the rights for which radicals such as Wollstonecraft and Hays were fighting, but novelists such as Ann Radcliffe, Mary Ann Hanway, Maria Edgeworth, Amelia Opie, Elizabeth Hamilton, and Mary Brunton were reluctant to declare their political affiliation with a cause which was becoming notorious. Fanny Burney had noted in her journal of June 1795 that 'politics were, all ways, left out ... they were not a *feminine* subject for discussion.'[74] But it was more than mere feminine diffidence or fear of impropriety which kept some women silent. Towards the end of the century 'feminism' was associated with being anti-English and with sexual licentiousness. After the Treason Trials of 1794, after Robespierre and his Reign of Terror, and the increasing patriotic fervour caused by the Napoleonic invasions, supporters of the French Revolution and its optimistic ideals dwindled and became extremely unpopular. In addition, Godwin's well-intentioned but ill-timed *Memoirs of the Author of a Vindication of the Rights of Woman* (1798), in which he presents a sensitive but factual account of Wollstonecraft's life, including her infatuation with the already married painter Henry Fuseli, her affair with the American speculator and former officer Gilbert Imlay, the birth of her illegitimate daughter, Fanny, and her two unsuccessful attempts at suicide, gave the conservative side an opportune and tangible example of the negative moral effects of the 'vindicators of woman.' The *Anti-Jacobin Review* of 1798 took advantage of Wollstonecraft's infamous reputation and, with malicious glee, listed her in the index under the word 'prostitution.'

Perhaps to avoid being labelled and ridiculed as a follower of Wollstonecraft, then, many of these writers developed narrative techniques and methods of representation which enabled them to explore highly charged political topics without censure. Rather than using polemics and confrontation, they employed more indirect means of examining the legitimacy of masculine authority, the prescribed ideal of the docile female, or the proper kind of education for women. One could say that they were using what Irigaray calls a 'hysterical' discourse, miming their male master's language, often suppressing their own desire, and yet, at the same time, in many ways subverting the Law of the Father through contradictoriness and multiplicity of text.[75] An indication of their participation in the current debate is their use of a series of sensitive words appropriated from the radical discourse of the progressives. From the French *philosophe*, the revolutionaries used 'philosophy' and 'philosopher' to denote one who was able to think and judge for him/herself, but in anti-Jacobin terms the words became equated with a system of outrageous and 'newfangled theories privileging private judgment and justifying the chimerical and hedonistic pursuit of personal happiness.'[76] Other key words included 'reason,' 'necessity,' 'feeling,' 'freedom,' and 'liberty,' all of which became volatile terms in the debate of the 1790s. Women writers often deliberately employed this vocabulary equivocally, inviting their readers to question the too obvious distinctions or binary oppositions which Burke outlined in his argument.

One writer who participated in this battle of ideas is Maria Edgeworth, who is best known today for her *Castle Rackrent* (1800) and her treatise *Practical Education* (1798), which was influenced by her father, Richard Lovell Edgeworth. However, in *Belinda* (1801), her first three-volume novel, she deals with a subject in which writers of both the conservative and the progressive sides were interested – the proper education and mode of conduct for a young lady.[77] While the behaviour of her prudent and moral heroine, Belinda Portman, conforms, as her name suggests, to the ideal deportment of 'femininity' recommended by More and West, the disgraceful conduct of Belinda's guardians simultaneously puts into question the Burkean concept of the wisdom and judgment of authority figures. Edgeworth does not highlight gender issues in the novel in the same way that Wollstonecraft and Hays do, for her undesirable examples are both female and male. But she deliberately confuses readers' allegiances between the conservative and the radical sides. Both Belinda's preceptors, Lady Delacour and Mrs Stanhope, are negative models for her: the former's dissipated life causes Belinda to see 'things in a new light' and judge 'for herself upon what she saw and felt,'[78] while the latter's unscrupulous scheming and matchmaking mortify the heroine. Even the Percivals of Oakly-Park, who are portrayed as the epitome of domestic happiness with their belief in rational thinking and a 'companionate marriage,'[79] give Belinda the wrong advice about her choice of partner. The Percivals counsel Belinda to trust duty and reason rather than passion and the impulse of 'first love' (233), but end up mistaken in their recommendation of the gambling Mr Vincent. Hence, while Edgeworth's novel seems to advocate prudence, duty, and submission, the lesson it supplies is the reverse of one furnished by a novel of education. Instead of learning to yield, Belinda learns to escape authority and to rely instead on her own discernment.

Edgeworth contrasts Belinda with Virginia, the character who embodies conventional 'feminine' virtues of docility and compliance and the girl whom Clarence wishes to educate as a wife for himself. Schooled in isolation and virtual ignorance, Virginia demonstrates the 'simplicity of her taste, and the purity of her mind' when she prefers a 'moss rosebud' to 'a pair of diamond earrings' (337). However, the inadequacy of this ideal soon becomes evident to Clarence, who realizes that what he wants in Virginia is a 'wife' not a 'mistress' (340), and that though innocent, Virginia is 'insipid,' 'ignorant,' and 'indolent' (344). Hence, while Virginia possesses the qualities Hannah More believed would be 'sufficient for a useful, a happy, and a pious life,' Edgeworth demonstrates the limitations of this model. Paradoxically the most memorable and liveliest characters in the novel are the outrageous, shocking ones. As Lady Delacour reforms and becomes a gracious and meek wife, we sense a loss of the vitality, wit, and energy of her character. When one sees the result of female docility and submission in Virginia, one cannot help but be entertained by and even admire the caricatured character Harriot Freke, the 'champion for the Rights of Woman' (208), modelled on Wollstonecraft and possibly Hays, who charges around protesting against female 'delicacy' and enslavement. Whimsical, free-spoken, dashing, and eccentric, Harriot Freke, with her ideas of liberty, may not be such a 'freak' when one considers the alternatives and ideologies with which she had to contend.

Other female novelists similarly made problematic the Burkean belief in patriarchal authority through seemingly 'innocent' types of fiction. Mary Darby Robinson, who is often associated with the circle of English Jacobins because of her friendship with William Godwin, wrote novels using Gothic, fairy-tale, and romantic elements, the kind of stories that made one reviewer call her work 'trash.'[80] While Polwhele had condemned her novels because they contained 'the doctrines of Philosophism' (*Unsex'd Females*, 17), they did not openly confront ideological or feminist issues in the same way Wollstonecraft's fiction did. In fact, in the preface to *Vancenza; or, The Dangers of Credulity* (1792) she disclaims 'the title of a Writer of Novels,' because a novel 'often conveys a lesson' she 'did not wish to inculcate.'[81] *Vancenza*, set in a twelfth-century castle, features an orphan girl, Elvira, who falls in love with Prince Almanza. The novel seems to have all the ingredients of a medieval romance. However, in the conclusion Robinson reveals her distrust of the kind of power a patriarchal ruler wields. Papers hidden behind a secret panel prove that in fact the prince and Elvira are siblings because the heroine's mother was seduced by Almanza's father many years ago. This dramatic disclosure is an instance of a female writer's actualization, or what Margaret Homans calls literalization, of a woman's fear of the will of the father. Because this notion of literalization is an important one, I want to give a brief explanation of it here. On the basis of Nancy Chodorow's mothering theories,[82] Homans argues that a daughter's relation to language is different from that of a son. Along with the symbolic language which she learns, she 'retains the literal or the presymbolic language that the son represses at the time of this renunciation of his mother.'[83] She therefore speaks two languages at once.

This retention of the pre-symbolic language, according to Homans, has 'profound implications for the differential valuations of literal and figurative, and for women writers' relations to them' (13). Homans associates representational language with the figurative, as it is 'symbolic language alone that can approximate the bridging of the gap between child and mother opened up by the ... prohibition of incest' (7). Because of the mother's association with nature, and with the Other, the son tends to 'view the mother as literal, she whose absence makes language both necessary and possible' (13). For the daughter, however, who is 'only partially within the symbolic order, the whole question of the literal and figurative will be more complex' (13). The daughter 'will perhaps prefer the literal that her brother devalues' (13), or she 'might simply not find the opposition of literal and figurative as telling and important as the son might, for it maintains a boundary not sacred to her – the boundary of the prohibition of incest with the mother' (14). In the case of Robinson's *Vancenza* the fear of violation by the father is literalized, though in some ways made distant by the generational gap between the heroine and her mother. Homans has also suggested that 'the gothic literalizes the romantic imagination, and it is this literalization that produces its terror' (86). In *Vancenza* we see Robinson's ambivalent feelings about the beneficence of male power, because what seems like a fairy-tale plot becomes a story of the abuse of male prerogative. The theatrical twist to the age-old plot of 'prince charming' rescuing the orphan girl re-examines the validity and justification of Burkean monarchical rule.

Robinson presents another bizarre plot in *Walsingham; or, The Pupil of Nature* (1797). This novel features a hero of sensibility whose frequent complaints of 'sorrow' remind us of Goethe's *Werther*, which is in fact quoted several times.[84] The author's sympathies with the revolutionaries are not stated directly, but she does allow her hero, while in prison, to read books by Beattie, Pratt, Murphy, Charlotte Smith, and Burney (2:298). In addition, though it was unfashionable to do so by the end of the decade, she continues to refer to Rousseau and his *La Nouvelle Héloïse* (3:229, 329), and thereby probably earned Polwhele's criticism. The shocking twist in this plot is the revelation that Sir Sidney, whose adventures and amatory interest for Isabella we have been following, is in fact, a woman, rather than a man. She has been posing as a man only in order to receive an inheritance designated for a son. Robinson's seemingly far-fetched plot was probably conceived as a result of her stage experience as an actress, for she had frequently dressed in man's clothing and played male parts.[85] In creating such an elaborate scheme for her protagonist, she implicitly questions the custom of patrilineage and the system of primogeniture privileging the eldest son of the family, both of which Burke had extolled and defended in his *Reflections on the Revolution in France*. The plot is another instance of literalization of the symbolic by a woman writer, this time involving the female fantasy of obtaining male authority, economic power, and social mobility.

Another female author who is better known as a Gothic novelist than as a polemicist is Ann Radcliffe. Like Edgeworth and Opie, Radcliffe seems to be writing on the side of the anti-Jacobins or the conservatives, but her romances can be read as attempts to subvert or challenge the notion of the benevolent patriarchy and the ideological construction of the docile, delicate eighteenth-century woman. Paulson notes that 'by the time *The Mysteries of Udolpho* appeared, the castle, prison, tyrant, and sensitive young girl could no longer be presented naïvely; they had all been familiarized and sophisticated by the events in France.'[86] As some critics have noted, one achievement of Radcliffe is that she invented in a fictional language a set of conventions within which 'respectable' feminine sexuality might find expression.[87] While the heroine in *The Mysteries of Udolpho* (1794), Emily St Aubert, never violates the codes of sensibility, propriety, and softness, Radcliffe nonetheless expresses and explores female sexual feelings in a subversive, disguised form. She projects female desire into two male figures in the creation of the 'chaste' lover, Valancourt, and the 'demon lover,' Montoni. As Emily struggles physically with the terrors of Udolpho castle, she is also battling with her subconscious emotions of attraction and repulsion to good and evil, gentleness versus violence, rationality versus madness, compliance versus force, freedom versus authority. While she has already declared her preference for the force of order and benevolence early on in the novel by choosing Valancourt, her frequent encounters with Montoni in the dark passages or bedrooms of the castle enable her to flirt with the malevolent and dark side of herself. One could say that the Gothic, with its dreamlike, nightmarish landscapes, its inarticulate and dark fears, and its depiction of a chaotic, disruptive universe, highlights the features of what Julia Kristeva has described as the 'semiotic' order, with its pulses, drives, and preverbal yearnings.

In *Revolution in Poetic Language* Kristeva distinguishes between what she calls the 'semiotic' and the 'symbolic' as 'two modalities' inseparable within the 'signifying process that constitutes language.'[88] The semiotic is linked to the pre-Oedipal primary processes, drives, energies, pulsions, which are gathered up in the 'chora,' which Kristeva emphasizes is not a sign or a position but is 'analogous only to vocal or kinetic rhythm' (25, 26). These drives, 'already ambiguous, simultaneously assimilating and destructive,' connect and 'orient the body to the mother' (27). Ruptures, discontinuity, flux, heterogeneity, emotional and bodily drives, are characteristic of the semiotic. The symbolic, however, is associated with linguistic acquisition, with the rational Law of the Father. For Kristeva subjectivity is a continuing 'process' in which both the semiotic and the symbolic struggle to maintain an equilibrium. The symbolic is established only through a repression or marginalization of the semiotic, and while this process is present in both sexes, woman occupies a 'privileged position' in a sense. As Féral explains:

> Having remained close to the maternal body in spite of the repression which society forces upon her, she inscribes herself naturally within the semiotic and occupies a privileged position within the dialectic unit-

ing/opposing the semiotic and the symbolic ... She possesses a 'spasmod-
ic force' ... which allows the subject to renew the bonds with what is
repressed within her, with the repressed that is always the mother ...[89]

Radcliffe, and the five women authors of this study, have never been
totally absorbed by the Law of the Father and are working out their
relation to symbolic language in their writing. Their works often show
qualities Kristeva associates with the semiotic. Kristeva herself constantly focuses on literature in her discussions of subjectivity because, as
Paul Smith notes, 'literature is the place where the legalistic or fixatory
structures of the social ... confront the repressed or marginalized
processes of language and subjectivity ... the text comes to constitute
something like a borderline or an interface between the demands of
social and subjective existence.'[90] The women writers of the 1790s use
their novels to test and transgress boundaries between self and other,
between the socially acceptable and the marginalized, between excess
and control. Their uneasiness with the masculine symbolic realm is
manifest in their distrust of conventional literary forms, in their restrained use of teleological means of closure in their novels, or in their
refusal to privilege the phallus.[91] In *Udolpho* it is significant that the
most interesting passages are those that take place in the realm characterized by flux, fluidity, and confusion, or the semiotic, rather than in
the clear and reasonable world outside where all apprehensions have
a linguistically expressible, rational explanation.

In addition to letting her seemingly 'innocent' heroine flirt with
socially prohibited dark forces, Radcliffe, like Robinson, Edgeworth,
and Austen in *Northanger Abbey*, invites her readers to re-examine the
Burkean ideal of the benevolent patriarch by showing how this figure
of authority can in fact become a tyrant and abuse his position. When
Emily's guardian and uncle, Montoni, wields his legal and social power
for self-interest rather than for the good of those under his care, one
is led to put less faith in the model of goodness, sincerity, and pastoral
simplicity exemplified by St Aubert and his care of La Vallée. By
having the paternal figure become the despot who 'imprisons' the
helpless heroine in his castle, Radcliffe, like Wollstonecraft in *Wrongs
of Woman*, literalizes female powerlessness and dependence. At the
castle in Udolpho, Emily discovers that her bedroom door 'had no
bolts on the chamber side, though it had two on the other.'[92] The
situation with the doors that cannot be locked seems to be a literalization of the vulnerability of the female body. With Radcliffe, as with
other novelists, the heroine's physical surroundings mirror what the

author feels are the real dangers to the female self. However, the essential difference between the more 'moderate' writers and the radical novelists of the 1790s is in the willingness of the latter to carry out the implications of their perceptions to the fullest. Wollstonecraft, Hays, and Inchbald would not have let their heroines be rescued quite as fortuitously as did Radcliffe, who thereby diminished somewhat the political ramifications of her novel.

Finally, Elizabeth Hamilton and Amelia Opie are two writers who used satire and forms of burlesque to voice their opinions about the impact of revolutionary ideals. In her novel *Memoirs of Modern Philosophers* (1800) Hamilton says the narrative is intended to expose the 'dangerous tendency' of not the whole but only those parts of Godwin's theory in *Political Justice* which might 'be converted into an engine of mischief, and be made the means of ensnaring innocence and virtue.'[93] While the cruel caricatures of 'modern philosophers' such as Hays, Wollstonecraft, and Godwin, and the mockery of their belief in the perfectibility of human beings and in 'general utility,' put Hamilton firmly on the side of the anti-Jacobin thinkers, the novel does not endorse the sanctity of paternal control as wholeheartedly as do the works of West or More. As in Edgeworth's *Belinda* and later in Mary Brunton's *Self-Control* (1810–11), parental or pseudo-parental judgment is shown to be sometimes faulty. Captain Delmond is as much to blame as Julia for her conversion to Jacobin philosophy and subsequent 'ruin' by the rhetorician Vallaton because he 'laid no restraint upon her choice' of reading material, and taught her to consider religious doctrines as mere 'vulgar prejudice' (1:145, 149). Upon his deathbed he confesses his error: 'I encouraged her ... to substitute the laws of honour for the laws of God; and to consult the dictates of her mind instead of the morality of the gospel' (3:53). As one character laments, 'how shall the children of a fool come by the information necessary to point out the line of duty, or to fix the principles of filial piety in the heart?' (3:55). While Hamilton ultimately does not answer this question, she does render problematic the belief that a father is the best moral guide of his children.

In transforming the intelligent but passionate Mary Hays and her heroine Emma Courtney into the short, disfigured, squinting, ugly, and obnoxious Bridgetina Botherim, Hamilton is adopting a masculine means of controlling a disruptive female figure. Hays's character possesses what Irigaray would later call a woman's 'insatiable (hysterical) thirst for satisfaction' (*Speculum*, 229). Her reluctance to make female desire secondary to that of the male, whose wishes reflect more closely that of society, endangers the eighteenth-century ideological construct of the docile, submissive woman contented with her domestic sphere. Through exaggeration and caricature this questing subject is changed into the stereotypical shrew/hag/old maid figure who is familiar to literary conventions and therefore easily dismissed as non-threatening. Categorization of the character into a type that fits into the symbolic realm results in containment of a potentially disturbing and chaotic force. This happens to Julia Delmond to a certain extent, too. Instead of allowing her to become a full subject and portraying the conflict between the duties to her family and the new 'philosophy,' Hamilton turns her into the clichéd seduced victim whose only possible end is death.

However, as recent theorists argue, the use of parody may suggest, not so much the inadequacy of its predecessor, as a desire to re-function the form to its own needs. In *A Theory of Parody* Linda Hutcheon contends that parody is 'a form of imitation, but imitation characterized by ironic inversion, not always at the expense of the parodied text.'[94] As *para* in Greek can also mean 'beside,' Hutcheon points out that 'there is a suggestion of an accord or intimacy instead of a contrast' (32). The critical distance signalled by irony 'can be playful as well as belittling; it can be critically constructive as well as destructive' (32). Hamilton's text, which replaces the seriousness and ardour of Godwin's and Hays's proposals with buffoonery and pathos, can be read as a reworking rather than a condemnation of 'modern philosophy.' While the idea of perfectibility is carried to an extreme, as Bridgetina Botherim even denounces 'sleeping' as a 'torpid and insensible state, from which it will be the glory of philosophy to free the human race' (2:22), the novel does reveal that there are many social ills that need to be changed. One of the touchstone characters, Mr Sydney, even admits that he admires and applauds the 'zeal' with which Mr Myope (the Godwin figure) espouses 'the cause of the poor and oppressed' (3:290). Thus, the gaps and inconsistencies within the text show the author's uneasiness with the doctrines she supposedly espouses.

Another way in which the conservative ideal is subverted is through the incorporation and reproduction of the parodied material. By her extensive quotation of *Political Justice* and *Emma Courtney*, albeit in a ridiculous context, Hamilton repeats and incorporates revolutionary ideals, ultimately directing her readers back to the parent texts. For example, Bridgetina Botherim's speeches are very often direct appropriations of Godwin's work, complete with footnotes by Hamilton. At

one point, when Bridgetina makes up her mind to follow a man she
admires to London, she defends her plan by saying:

> My scheme ... is too extensive for any but a mind of great powers to
> comprehend. It is not bounded by the narrow limits of individual happi-
> ness, but extends to embrace the grand object of general utility. Your
> education has been too confined to enable you to follow an energetic
> mind in which passions generate powers, and powers generate passions
> ... to general usefulness. (2:237)

Hamilton, of course, is mocking Godwin's notion of 'general utility'
here. In the context of the novel Bridgetina is laughable to the point
of absurdity because she applies Godwin's theory to her failed *amour*.
Yet, despite the comedy, melodrama, and foolishness, there is something noble about Bridgetina's speech, something attractive about her
goals. It is true that she acts rashly, but she is also full of energy and
ambition compared to the other rather insipid, but obedient girls in
the story. The ambivalent effect of the passage here is an instance of
what Mikhail Bakhtin would call 'heteroglossia' or 'double-voiced
discourse,' in which the discourse serves 'two speakers at the same
time and expresses simultaneously two different intentions: the direct
intention of the character who is speaking, and the refracted intention
of the author.'[95] Without directly committing herself to the revolutionary cause, Hamilton is able to repeat and thereby promulgate some
of its tenets, although in a comic fashion. Godwin's text is 're-func-
tioned' or produced to suit Hamilton's ideological and political purposes. The quotation shows how *Memoirs of Modern Philosophers* perches
precariously between dependence and independence, between mockery and admiration of the parent texts and their philosophies.

In *Adeline Mowbray; or, The Mother and Daughter* (1804) Amelia Opie
writes a 'treatise against free love,'[96] or the dangers of cohabitation
without the sanction of marriage, based on the life of Mary Wollstonecraft. The heroine, who has wholeheartedly imbibed the liberal notions
of the books she has perused, declaims 'against marriage, as an institution ... absurd, unjust, and immoral' and declares 'that she would
never submit to so contemptible a form' (1:73). Her refusal to be
bound by any other ties than 'those of love and reason' (1:100) to her
lover Glenmurray causes her to suffer through a series of social, economic, and psychological deprivations. By the end of the novel, however, she changes her opinion formed in youth and concludes that
marriage 'has a tendency to call forth and exercise the affections, and

control the passions' (3:207), and is a 'wise' and 'sacred institution' (3:209). While this renunciation of her conviction seems to make the novel an anti-Jacobian tract against the new 'philosophy,' several other elements in the text reveal a contradictory view, an underlying sympathy for revolutionary advocates.

For example, Opie exposes the foolishness of society's preconceptions by showing its hypocrisy. While Adeline Mowbray's marital status is unknown, people profess an admiration of her character. But they later retract their praises and condemn her when they find out that she is not married. The same Adeline who was described as a 'blessed' and 'pitying angel' because of her charity is labelled 'wicked' and 'fallen' (2:117; 1:211). One cannot help but agree with Adeline, who thinks: 'How strange and irrational are the prejudices of society! Because an idle ceremony has not been muttered over me at the altar, I am liable to be thought a woman of vicious inclinations' (2:95). Thus, while Opie seems to be ridiculing Adeline's false notions, she reveals at the same time the inadequacy and folly of conventional moral judgment.

Moreover, while advocating the institution of marriage, Opie demonstrates its deficiencies at the same time. In the novel marriage affords women neither security nor protection from the fickle nature of men, nor from the possibility of their abusing their prerogative and paternal authority. Adeline's widowed mother marries Sir Patrick O'Carrol, who only 'wanted [her] wealth' and the 'chance for giving him possession of the daughter's person' (1:71). His attitude towards women is reminiscent of that of a despotic, irresponsible husband in Charlotte Smith's *Desmond*, a novel published as a direct response to the French Revolution:

> In his dealings with men, Sir Patrick was a man of honour; in his dealings with women, completely the reverse: he considered them as a race of subordinate beings, formed for the service and amusement of men; and that if, like horses they were lodged, fed, and kept clean, they had no right to complain. (1:71)

In her portrait of the arrogant, insensitive mate Opie uses words such as 'subordinate' and 'right,' which are echoes of the language used in the volatile period of the revolution. In addition, she makes explicit the link between her anti-hero, Sir Patrick, and the character in Smith's *Desmond*. Both male characters employ a metaphor that associates women with horses, implying that they, like animals, are kept merely for the use of man. Thus, while the novel seems to suggest that marriage is a social necessity, it also shows its inadequacies.

This seemingly contradictory tendency to speak on behalf of marriage and then undercut it makes *Adeline Mowbray* an example of the kind of writing that is characteristic of those women who were caught between two camps during the 1790s. In the twentieth century Luce Irigaray has advised women to attempt to subvert the existing patriarchal order through confusion: 'Make it impossible for a while to predict whence, whither, when how, why ... something goes by or goes on: will come, will spread, will reverse, will cease moving' (*Speculum*, 142). While there may not have been a concerted effort on the part of women novelists to create this type of puzzlement, the effect of the ambivalent writing I have described is, nevertheless, a kind of questioning, or even subversion. Opie, like Edgeworth, Radcliffe, and Hamilton, weaves between the Burkean and the radical beliefs, not offering her readers a single, comfortable, solid position but presenting multiple views on the subject. Like much of the writing of the women in this study, her text reveals her uneasiness with the masculine symbolic order, or what Lacan would call the Law of the Father. The inconsistencies and disparity between avowed doctrine and its thematization are indications of the troubled subjectivity and the complex position from which these women, marginalized as they were in eighteenth-century society, could respond and write. As Felicity Nussbaum points out: '... eighteenth-century women, as a gendered category, had little access to philosophical discourse, to equal wages, or to equality under the law – all of which distinguished their lived experience, in differing degrees, from some classes of eighteenth-century men or from twentieth-century women of privilege.'[97] It is appropriate now to turn to the group of female novelists to whom the conservative writers were reacting, and against whom there were so many satires produced and written at the close of the decade. The fiction of Mary Wollstonecraft, Mary Hays, Helen Maria Williams, Elizabeth Inchbald, and Charlotte Smith, written in response to the revolutionary climate in England in the 1790s, illustrates how the domestic, the lived, and the quotidian become political, exemplary, and ideological.

CHAPTER ONE

Female Confinement Literalized
The Wrongs of Woman; or, Maria

While the heroine of Mary Wollstonecraft's first novel, *Mary, a Fiction*, suffers from a vaguely defined form of spiritual deprivation, the protagonist of her second and last novel, *The Wrongs of Woman* (1798), is besieged by physical, economic, and emotional distresses. As the title suggests, the book is a conscious attempt to fictionalize and thematize Wollstonecraft's ideas about the injustices or 'wrongs' from which women suffer. Though the work is influenced by a male author's novel, William Godwin's *Things As They Are; or, The Adventures of Caleb Williams* (1794), it is one of the clearest instances of what Margaret Homans calls 'literalization' by a woman writer. I want to argue that because Wollstonecraft is a daughter, whose relation to her mother was one of literality, her writing is strengthened by the use of the non-symbolic or the literal language combined with the rational and the symbolic discourse of the Father.

As in *Mary, a Fiction* and in *Letters Written during a Short Residence in Sweden, Norway, and Denmark,*[1] *Wrongs of Woman* is characterized by a number of competing discourses. Several scholars have pointed out that the narrative contains at least two voices and have emphasized their contradictory nature. Sara Harasym, for example, contends that there 'is a sharp contrast between Maria's first-person autobiographical memories and the third-person narrative discourse which criticizes and censors Maria's actions,' but that ultimately 'Maria's melancholic, fatalistic memoirs usurp the political statements of the text.'[2] Similarly, Mary Poovey says that as the narrator, Wollstonecraft emphasizes the 'pernicious effects of sentimentalism' and presents Maria's 'incorrigible romanticism ... ironically,' but that 'the narrator herself repeatedly lapses back into sentimental jargon and romantic idealism.'[3] While I agree with both these critics that there are contrasting tendencies in the narrative, I do not think that the narrator's use of sentimental language necessarily suggests a failure on Wollstonecraft's part. Janet Todd's defence of the autobiographical elements in the novel also applies to the romantic idealism in the work: it is 'a feature of the female novel of sensibility, a feature contained by the genre and therefore expected by readers, who had already noted in previous fiction the autobiographical complaints of Charlotte Smith and the personal pain of Mary Hays.'[4] My own view is that Wollstonecraft attempts to use several forms and many voices, as she negotiates between what Julia Kristeva calls the semiotic and the symbolic world of the Father.

Kristeva's twentieth-century notions of the semiotic provide a useful means of approaching Wollstonecraft's work. Associated with the pre-Oedipal primary processes, the semiotic is impelled by 'oral and anal' drives – bodily desires, life versus death instincts – and is discontinuous, unstable, and structured around the maternal.[5] Sentimental fiction, which is to a great extent dependent on the eighteenth-century notion of 'sensibility,'[6] is similarly characterized by extreme emotion, spontaneity, agitation, and instability. It has a penchant for bodily distresses and for death scenes; and it is often associated with the feminine. Sensibility and, in turn, sentimentalism seem to be a deliberate valorization of the qualities Kristeva associates with the semiotic. While Nancy Chodorow does not use the word *semiotic* in her discussion of women's mothering, she does assert that because of a mother's identification with her daughter, girls tend to retain more of the pre-Oedipal world of the mother and 'grow up more connected to others' externally and internally.[7] Aside from growing up female, certain elements in Wollstonecraft's life may also have contributed to her distrust of the world dominated by the Father. Born in 1759 Mary was the second of seven children. Her father, unsuccessful at farming, consoled himself for his failures by drinking to excess and tyrannizing his timid wife. Virginia Woolf views this early experience as a crucial one that distinguishes the writings of Wollstonecraft from someone like Austen: 'If Jane Austen had lain as a child on the landing to prevent her father from thrashing her mother, her soul might have burnt with such a passion against tyranny that all her novels might have been consumed in one cry for justice.'[8] While the relationship between Wollstonecraft and her mother was not a particularly strong one, Wollstonecraft did form very close ties with other women: with her sister, Eliza, and with her friend Fanny Blood in her early years. I believe that, like many women in our culture, Wollstonecraft does not wholly embrace the world of the Father and does not use symbolic language in the way male writers do. In her novel one form of discourse is always competing with the other, but this tendency to allow both languages to speak does not weaken Wollstonecraft's 'main object,' which is to exhibit 'the misery and oppression, peculiar to women, that arise out of the partial laws and customs of society.'[9] In fact, it is the juxtaposition of the romantic and symbolic with the literal and the real that creates the powerful tension of the novel.

In the preface Wollstonecraft maintains that the story 'ought rather to be considered, as of woman,' than of an individual' (73), and that the wrongs, though 'necessarily various,' are directed to women of all classes (74). *Wrongs of Woman* illustrates the universality of sexual oppression through the use of multiple voices and echoing narratives. Repetition reinforces the heroine's observation: 'Was not the world a vast prison, and women born slaves?' (79). This metaphor is literalized in the novel, as the heroine, Maria, is incarcerated in a madhouse[10] by her husband so that he can control her property. While Charlotte Smith in *Desmond* and Mary Hays in *Emma Courtney* used figurative language to write about the fetters that bound women and the 'magic circle' in which they were confined, Wollstonecraft realized and made concrete this metaphor of imprisonment. The Gothic castle, which in Radcliffe's *Udolpho* merely suggested patriarchal tyranny, now becomes an explicit thematization of masculine oppression.

Beginning *in medias res*, as Poovey notes,[11] *Wrongs of Woman* opens with Maria in her 'mansion of despair ... endeavouring to recall her scattered thoughts' (75). Like the rebel Satan in Milton's *Paradise Lost* Maria wakes 'by degrees to a keen sense of anguish' in the midst of the 'groans and shrieks' of her hell-like prison. Taking advantage of the vogue for Gothic romance, with its use of tyrant father-figures, ancient castles, and imprisoned heroines, Wollstonecraft describes Maria's chamber as a 'dreary cell,' with a 'small grated window' overlooking a 'huge pile of buildings' fallen to decay: 'the ivy had been torn off the turrets, and the stones not wanted to patch up the breaches of time ... left in heaps in the disordered court' (76–7). Recalling Burke's analogy of the husband as the monarch of the household, Wollstonecraft deliberately employs post-revolutionary language in her novel. The heroine calls herself the 'victim' of an 'act of atrocity' by 'her tyrant – her husband' (76). Finding it difficult to 'move her manacled arms,' she 'raved of injustice' to the 'master of this most horrid of prisons' (76, 77). Published in the 1790s, these terms would instantly call to mind the events of the French Revolution: the Bastille, the deposition of the tyrant king, the rebellion of the victims. Following Smith's *Desmond*, which had implicitly linked Verney, the tyrannical husband, with French aristocrats, Wollstonecraft now literalizes the symbolic association.

As in Gothic fiction the horrors of the real and the physical are reinforced by the psychological: 'the retreating shadows of former sorrows rushed back in a gloomy train, and seemed to be pictured on the walls of her prison, magnified by the state of mind in which they were viewed' (75). But the emphasis is on the effect of physical, tyrannical force on the helpless: 'The gates opened heavily, and the sullen sound of many locks and bolts drawn back, grated on my very soul, before I was appalled by the creeking of the dismal hinges, as they closed after me' (184). Marilyn Butler notes that 'Godwin and Mary Wollstonecraft were drawn to the Gothic, because it had developed powerful images for conveying the idea of an oppressive, coercive environment ... for exploring ... the clash between the victimized individual and the social institution.'[12] Borrowing from the conventions of the Gothic was particularly effective as it was a form of literature which used nightmarish and dreamlike landscapes, the figures of the subconscious imagination, to give form to amorphous fears and semiotic impulses. Wollstonecraft could project and literalize her worst anxieties about patriarchy and the abuse of authority into this type of a novel. Her fears about woman being stifled and disempowered become real as Maria is 'buried alive' (185) in the madhouse, and exists in a 'tomb of living death' (101). In prison she meets women who act as if they were 'slaves' to their husbands.

As well as allowing one to dwell on the spectacles of one's terrors,[13] Gothic fiction offers a depiction of polar characters of good and evil, and in this respect too it served Wollstonecraft's purposes. Elizabeth MacAndrew explains:

> The characters of this literature find themselves teetering with terrifying vertigo on the edge of this abyss or they leave the craggy moral landscape to grope through dank subterranean corridors of evil into which only an occasional ray of the sunlight of virtue can filter. And these characters are, on the one hand, sensitive, tearful, one-sided depictions of man's virtuous potential transported whole from the Sentimental novel and, on the other, towering villains caught in the fearful psychomachia of evil.[14]

Because of the conventions of the genre Wollstonecraft's Maria would be associated with its innocent, sensitive, and virtuous heroines. In contrast, the use of 'tyrant' as an appellation for the husband suggests that Wollstonecraft intended him to be equated with the despotic, evil villains of Gothic fiction who deprive the victims of their right to liberty and frequently of their property. The Gothic atmosphere and opposing sets of characters intensify the arguments Wollstonecraft had already articulated elsewhere.

Earlier, in her *Vindication of the Rights of Woman*, for example, Wollstonecraft had complained of women's dependence on men. According to Wollstonecraft, not only were women 'dependent on men in the various relations of life' because of their 'apparent inferiority with respect to bodily strength,' but 'the only way women [could] rise in the world' was 'by marriage.'[15] In *Wrongs of Woman* Wollstonecraft shows that this dependency can cause a kind of imprisonment, making women victims of emotional and physical abuse. Maria's story exposes the injustices perpetrated on women of the middle class which were legal under the judicial system of the late eighteenth century. Once married, Maria realized that she 'had been caught in a trap, and caged for life' (144), as she loses control of her property, her person, and even her child. Her husband, George Venables, 'appeared to have little relish for [her] society,' except when he needed money for his 'fraudulent speculations' (145, 155). After enduring his frequent bouts of drunkenness and his fondness for 'wantons of the lowest class' (146), Maria articulates the injustice of the 'double standard' of sexual morality in society:

A man would only be expected to maintain; yes, barely grant a subsistence, to a woman rendered odious by habitual intoxication; but who would expect him, or think it possible to love her? ... whilst woman, weak in reason, impotent in will, is required to moralize, sentimentalize herself to stone, and pine her life away, labouring to reform her embruted mate. He may even spend in dissipation, and intemperance ... her property, and by stinting her expences, not permit her to beguile in society, a wearisome, joyless life; for over their mutual fortune she has no power, it must all pass through his hand. (154)

Though she possessed a small fortune, Maria discovers that 'marriage had bastilled [her] for life' (155). Instead of being able to enjoy 'the various pleasures existence affords,' she felt 'fettered by the partial laws,' so that 'this fair globe was to [her] an universal blank' (155).

Wollstonecraft deliberately appropriates political language here to describe Maria's state in order to link the personal to the institutional and social. For Wollstonecraft there is little or no separation between the domestic and the political, between the literal and the symbolic. While Maria's story is the story of one individual, it illustrates that as long as the 'fair globe' is 'fettered by the partial laws' of man, for women 'the world' will always be 'a vast prison' (79) as Wollstonecraft argues. Literalization and choice of terms and images here give Wollstonecraft's arguments more power and more poignancy: repeated use of various metaphors of confinement which become real – trap, cage, bastille, fetters – create a cumulative effect of psychological constriction and claustrophobia in the narrative.

The purpose of these metaphors is to criticize and show the limitations of eighteenth-century property laws relating to married women. These stated, as William Blackstone bluntly puts it, that 'the husband and wife are one, and the husband is that one.'[16] Lawrence Stone says of the domestic arrangement of the time, 'whatever is hers is his,' including the children, who 'belonged solely to the husband.' Some of the difficulties Maria experiences arise from contemporary laws governing property. Stone discusses the lack of options for a woman:

> If she should desert him, however severe the provocation, she could take nothing with her, neither her children nor her property. Her husband could, if he chose, compel her to return. Or he could at any time seize any income she might earn, or any means of support given to her by others.[17]

In the novel the injustice of these laws urges Maria to become a speaker for the rights of woman. She challenges the marital laws which 'force women ... to sign a contract, which renders them dependent on the caprice of the tyrant, whom choice or necessity has appointed to reign over them' (195). She also argues for the right of a wife who leaves a husband to be treated as a human being, not a criminal: '... she must be allowed to consult her conscience, and regulate her conduct, in some degree, by her own sense of right' (197). Maria herself claims 'a divorce, and the liberty of enjoying, free from molestation, [her] fortune' left to her by her uncle (198).

The revolutionary implications of Maria's propositions, which the judge dismisses as 'new-fangled notions' and 'French principles' (199), may be best understood when compared to the solutions devised by other women novelists who treated the same problem before and after

Wollstonecraft . One early forerunner of the Maria plot is found in Eliza Haywood's *The History of Miss Betsy Thoughtless* (1751), which features a heroine married on the rebound to an inconsiderate and spiteful man. Betsy Thoughtless's husband, Mr Munden, 'considered a wife no more than an upper-servant, bound to study and obey, in all things, the will of him to whom she had given her hand.'[18] His stinginess makes him grudge his wife even her pin-money. Like Wollstonecraft's Venables he, too, surreptitiously agrees to let his patron lord receive sexual favours from his wife, so that he can advance financially and socially. Betsy's brief separation from her husband is more successful than Maria's. However, instead of carrying out the consequences of this separation to the fullest, Haywood resorts to a facile, sentimental resolution at the end of the novel. Repentant, the heroine is reunited with her sick husband, and upon his death becomes free to marry her true love, Charles Trueworth.

Similarly, in Charlotte Smith's *Desmond* (1792) the death of Verney, the gambling, irresponsible husband of Geraldine, frees her to marry the worthy suitor, Desmond. While Smith does make some radical suggestions through her association of the tyrannical husband with French aristocrats and supporters of the king, she does not go as far as Wollstonecraft in explicitly questioning the authority of the household monarch. Unlike Maria, Geraldine accepts her lot and obeys her husband without argument even while she realizes that he, like Venables, is willing to sell her person to pay for his debts. Wollstonecraft differs from these other writers in her willingness to confront Burke and his ideal of the benevolent patriarch, and in her courage to challenge one of the most fundamental beliefs of the Judaeo-Christian tradition – that of the duty of wives to submit to their husbands.

Indeed, this challenge to rebel rather than to submit was refuted by conservative writers after Wollstonecraft. In a digressive tale in *Coelebs in Search of a Wife* Hannah More tells the exemplary story of a pious woman, Mrs Carlton, who married not out of love but to oblige her father. Mr Carlton neglects her and spends all his time and their fortune on and with his friends. Instead of complaining or chastising him, Mrs Carlton prays for him, acts as if nothing is wrong, cooks him his favourite dish, and wears a dress he admires. Eventually her fidelity is rewarded as he repents, sees the folly of his actions, and comes to appreciate his wife. Mr Carlton remarks: 'Even at the time that I had most reason to blush at my own conduct, she never gave me cause to blush for hers.'[19] More's lessons of patience and submission to the masculine will, be it God or man, can be contrasted with Wollstonecraft's defiance of male authority. While Maria is ultimately defeated in court, as the judge tells her that 'it was her duty to love and obey the man chosen by her parents and relations' (199), the mere fact that Wollstonecraft chose to resolve an unhappy marriage in her fiction by radical alternatives such as separation and divorce while others were advocating submission is extraordinary.

Aside from the physical incarceration of the middle-class heroine, another way *Wrongs of Woman* thematizes woman's oppression is through the claustrophobic and restrictive structure of the novel. Static compared to the works of other eighteenth-century writers such as Defoe, Fielding, Smollett, Burney, or even Austen, which are characterized by activity, bustle, and movement of some sort, Wollstonecraft's last novel confines reader, writer, and narrator in a dungeonlike private madhouse. All three are forced to listen to story after story of injustice and atrocity told by various female voices. Rather than having a single, linear plot structure which advances towards a teleological end, the plot of *Wrongs of Woman* moves in a circular, weblike fashion, re-confronting the same problem in different ways through the narratives of women of different classes.

For instance, juxtaposed to Maria's first-person narrative is the account of Jemima, Maria's prison warden. Jemima's story, unlike Maria's, is anti-romantic and 'decidedly *un*sentimental' as Poovey points out.[20] An illegitimate child born of a poor servant girl, Jemima's whole life has been a series of exploitations by men, particularly of her sexuality. Luce Irigaray has observed that

> women are marked phallically by their fathers, husbands, procurers. And this branding determines their value in sexual commerce. Woman is never anything but the locus of a more or less competitive exchange between two men, including the competition for the possession of mother earth.[21]

Raped and impregnated by her master at sixteen, Jemima is used by one man after another. She says: 'I was ... born a slave, and chained by infamy to slavery during the whole of existence, without having any companions to alleviate it by sympathy, or teach me how to rise above it by their example' (106). The categorization of herself as a slave echoes the observation made earlier by Maria: 'Was not the world a vast prison, and women born slaves?' (79). In Jemima's case the metaphor is actualized: like a slave she works because she has absolutely no choice. She also has no control of and no right to her own body.

Brought up in poverty, without affection and without education, Jemima seems to have survived only by sheer will-power and her animal-like instincts. She describes herself as 'the filching cat, the ravenous dog, the dumb brute' (105). Significantly her self-comparison to lower forms of life, her dumbness, emphasizes her distance from the rational, linguistic world of the Father. Deprived of education, of meaningful language, hence, full participation in symbolic discourse, she is condemned to the world of bodily and instinctual drives, forever coping with hunger, pain from beatings, or from an abortion, and lack of adequate shelter. One myth that Wollstonecraft seems to be correcting is that of the 'fortunate orphan' – the most famous one being Fielding's Tom Jones – who, though born without social sanction, manages to become integrated into the community by some chance or good fortune at the end of the novel. Jemima, by contrast, remains an outcast throughout her life: she is 'an egg dropped on the sand; a pauper by nature, hunted from family to family, who belonged to nobody' (106). This figure of the outcast recurs frequently in the fiction of this period: it is used by Godwin in *Caleb Williams*, by Hays in her first two novels, and later by Wollstonecraft's daughter Mary Shelley in her most famous work, *Frankenstein*.[22] Because of their radical ideas these writers were marginalized in different ways by society and seemed to live intimately with the trope of exile and exclusion.

As Hays did in *Emma Courtney* and was later to repeat in *Victim of Prejudice*, Wollstonecraft shows that under the existing social system, women had virtually no means of becoming self-sufficient and self-supporting except through servitude and prostitution. In order to subsist Jemima first works as a servant, becomes a kept mistress, and then a washerwoman. She comments on the 'wretchedness of situation peculiar to [her] sex': 'A man with half my industry, and, I may say, abilities, could have procured a decent livelihood, and discharged some of the duties which knit mankind together; whilst I, who had acquired a taste for the rational ... the virtuous enjoyments of life, was cast aside as the filth of society' (115–16). Jemima's account of her adult years dispels any romantic illusions one may have about the life of a prostitute. Whereas in such novels as Defoe's *Moll Flanders* and *Roxana* or Cleland's *Fanny Hill* the mistresses of pleasure are depicted as enjoying their trades and gaining financial success at least for a while, Wollstonecraft's narrative shows only the 'wretchedness and depravity,' the misery, of a life based on the brutal sexual appetites of man (109). Jemima tells Maria and Henry Darnford: 'I ... yielded to the desires of the brutes I met, with ... detestation ... I have since read in novels of the blandishments of seduction, but I had not even the pleasure of being enticed into vice' (109). Jemima's tale is the literalization of the repression of female desire in its extreme form. As the object of masculine pleasure she lives perpetually in what Irigaray calls 'unrealized potentiality' a 'being that exists for/by another.'[23]

While the narrative of Maria and its parallel diegesis, that of Jemima, are the main focus of the novel, several other stories echo the notion of the world as a 'vast prison' for women (79). Wollstonecraft uses repetition as a structural device, using the voices of other female characters in the novel to weave her argument back and forth. Within Maria's narrative are the tales of the women she encounters, which reinforce Wollstonecraft's point that the history of Maria's oppression is to be considered that of all women rather than that of an individual.

Early on in her captivity Maria listens to the singing of 'a lovely maniac, just brought into an adjoining chamber' (88). Maria is frightened by the woman's 'unconnected exclamations' and 'fits of laughter, so horrid,' and finds out that the wretch 'had been married, against her inclination, to a rich old man, extremely jealous; ... and that, in consequence of his treatment ... she had, during her first lying-in, lost her senses' (88). Though the story may seem melodramatic, it is similar to the short married life of Wollstonecraft's sister, Eliza. Wedded in October 1782 to Meridith Bishop, Eliza had a baby and then suffered 'an acute post-partum breakdown.'[24] Mary persuaded Eliza to run away from her husband, and the couple never reunited. In *Wrongs of Woman* the story of the 'maniac' serves as an example of the extent of psychological damage that can result from parental greed and the use of a daughter as a commodity for exchange and for self-aggrandizement. In *A Vindication of the Rights of Woman* Wollstonecraft writes: 'Parental affection, is, perhaps, the blindest modification of perverse self-love ... Parents often love their children in the most brutal manner, and sacrifice every relative duty to promote their advancement in the world' (150). She believes that parental affection, 'in many minds, is but a pretext to tyrannize where it can be done with impunity' (150–1). The story of the creature who, unlike Maria, actually does go mad is only one of the many variations, slightly intensified, of how women become, in Irigaray's words, an 'exchange value' among those with power (*This Sex*, 31).

Another story of woman's oppression is recounted to Maria when she seeks shelter from her husband. The lady who owns the shop where Maria conceals herself does not believe that Maria can ever get

away, because 'when a woman was once married, she must bear everything' (170). Maria observes her:

> Her pale face, on which appeared a thousand haggard lines and delving
> wrinkles, produced by what is emphatically termed fretting, inforced her
> remark ... She toiled from morning till night; yet her husband would rob
> the till, and take away the money reserved for paying bills; and, returning
> home drunk, he would beat her if she chanced to offend him, though
> she had a child at the breast. (170–1)

Despite this maltreatment the woman still considered 'her dear
Johnny' to be 'her master' (171). Using the slave metaphor again,
Wollstonecraft has Maria comment: '... no slave in the West Indies had
one more despotic' master (171).

While the narrator does not link them together, there are many
similaritics between the haberdasher lady's and Maria's narratives. Like
a despotic ruler George Venables, Maria's husband, extorts large sums
of money from Maria for his gambling debts. Like Johnny, Venables
is a habitual drinker and meets Maria regularly at the breakfast table
with a 'squalid appearance' and a squeamish stomach 'produced by
the last night's intemperance' (147). Her description of Venables
'lolling in an arm-chair, in a dirty powdering gown, soiled linen,
ungartered stockings, and tangled hair, yawning and stretching himself' (147) is reminiscent of the second plate of Hogarth's *Marriage à
la Mode*, as Gary Kelly notes.[25] While Venables does not beat Maria, he
does persecute Maria emotionally and sexually, and his persecutions
are allowed by the law and contemporary customs. The story of the
haberdasher lady then, is a *mise-en-abyme*, or a microcosm of the central
issues of the novel. The compressed narrative, the tale within the tale,
reinforces, restates, and echoes the heroine's plight. Lest her readers
think that Maria's story is unusual, or the product of a specific social
class, Wollstonecraft deliberately repeats the problems over and over
with various female characters.

Maria hears of yet another tale of female oppression when she once
more searches for new lodgings. Like the haberdasher lady the landlady has accepted her oppression and can only reiterate maxims traditionally taught to women: 'Women must be submissive ... Indeed what
could most women do? Who had they to maintain them, but their
husbands?' (176–7). While Wollstonecraft has the landlady reproduce
the lessons of the conservative moralists, she shows how female docility
and compliance can actually encourage abuse under eighteenth-

century property laws. The landlady and her husband's story seems to be a replication of Maria's and the haberdasher lady's:

> My husband got acquainted with an impudent slut, who chose to live on other people's means – and then all went to rack and ruin. He ran in debt to buy her fine clothes ... and ... signed an execution on my very goods, bought with the money I worked so hard to get; and they came and took my bed from under me ... I sought for a service again ... but he used to follow me, and kick up such a riot when he was drunk, that I could not keep a place; nay, he even stole my clothes and pawned them; and when I went to the pawnbroker's, ... they said, 'It was all as one, my husband had a right to whatever I had.' (177)

As the intradiegetic listener, Maria's reaction to the tale – 'Why should I dwell on similar incidents' (178) – signals to the reader the appropriate response to the text. We are meant to see, and draw our own conclusions from, the similarities between the landlady's story and Maria's narrative. Although their social situations are different, they face the same kind of problems of emotional, economic, and even physical abuse. For this reason Maria concludes that when one is 'born a woman,' one is 'born to suffer' (181).

In the memoirs addressed to her daughter she writes: 'I feel ... acutely the various ills my sex are fated to bear – I feel that the evils they are subject to endure degrade them so far below their oppressors, as almost to justify their tyranny; leading at the same time superficial reasoners to term that weakness the cause, which is only the consequence of short-sighted despotism' (181). The repetition and replication of similar plots in the women's narratives prove the commonality of female experience under a historically specific set of circumstances. The cumulative effect of the tales is a powerful repudiation of the Burkean paradigm of the benevolent patriarch, as well as of Rousseau's notions of feminine softness as a model of conduct. Docility and pliability in females lead only to what many men call 'weakness' in women and do not promote happiness in either sex, contrary to what a conservative like Hannah More would argue.

After dealing with the histories of these diverse women, Wollstonecraft then comes back almost full circle to her heroine's plight. Viewed in the context of these other narratives, Maria's, and perhaps even the narrator's, reactions and their 'romantic expectations' are more understandable.[26] Eighteenth-century marital and property laws did not leave women with many means towards independence. An enlightened marriage was still one of the easiest ways of achieving happiness under these laws, as Jane Austen would later point out. Hence, Wollstonecraft was hesitant about ruling out the possibilities of her heroine's realizing personal satisfaction through a companionate relationship. While one critic feels that Maria's efforts at composition produce only a 'romantic' and 'escapist' narrative, and that her art is an 'expression' or perhaps even a cause of her 'political impotence,'[27] I believe that, read in conjunction with the various female histories, Maria's memoirs are an effective personal testament against the misapplication of male power in the domestic sphere.

If the novel betrays a tendency to succumb to sentimentality and romantic idealization, it is perhaps because, as Irigaray suggests, women need to write from the position of mimics first, before they can be their own subjects. According to Irigaray:

> There is, in an initial phase, perhaps only one 'path,' the one historically assigned to the feminine: that of *mimicry*. One must assume the feminine role deliberately. Which means already to convert a form of subordination into an affirmation, and thus to begin to thwart it ... To play with mimesis is thus, for a woman, to try to recover the place of her exploitation by discourse, without allowing herself to be simply reduced to it. It means to resubmit herself – inasmuch as she is on the side of the 'perceptible,' of 'matter' – to 'ideas,' in particular to ideas about herself, that are elaborated in/by a masculine logic, but so as to make 'visible,' by an effect of playful repetition, what was supposed to remain invisible: the cover-up of a possible operation of the feminine in language. (*This Sex*, 76)

In replicating some of the beliefs of the male-dominated society through the voices of these female characters, Wollstonecraft is using what Irigaray calls 'mimesis' as a technique. She has her characters 'assume the feminine role deliberately,' but the effect is that they challenge the logic of their exploitation through her literalization of metaphors of confinement and subjection. In depicting the various 'wrongs' suffered by women – rape, assault, forcible confinement, deprivation of children, poverty, – Wollstonecraft makes visible and physical the horrors of subordination which symbolic language and patriarchal culture tend to cover up or to ignore.

Finally, biographical evidence as well as the numerous fragmentary endings to *Wrongs of Woman* reveal the difficulties Wollstonecraft experienced while trying to imagine a forceful practical solution to the issues she had raised.[28] For Poovey, Wollstonecraft's problem came from her belief in 'individual feeling,' or the 'myth of personal autonomy': Wollstonecraft 'continued to envision social change and personal fulfilment primarily in terms of individual effort, and therefore did not focus on the systemic constraints exercised by such legal and political institutions as marriage.'[29] In my view Wollstonecraft's attachment to what Poovey calls 'individual feeling' not only springs from her post-Renaissance liberal humanist background, but also arises from a number of other sources. Firstly, the literary convention of the Jacobin novel of the 1790s often demonstrated the individual's capacity to effect social change; and secondly, as I have tried to argue, Wollstonecraft writes as a daughter, who, according to Chodorow's and Kristeva's theories, tends to be attracted to both the rational symbolic discourse as well as the pre-Oedipal semiotic one. As a woman novelist Wollstonecraft has not wholly embraced the Law of the Father; hence, we see her not wholeheartedly trusting the objective, rational discourse of the courts or the third-person voice of the narrator. During her defence, for example, Maria has a factual account of her life and the injustices she has suffered read from a paper she wrote. However, this effort to speak solely from the symbolic discourse is thwarted as she appeals to her own 'sense of justice' and to the sympathy of the jury, rather than relying on written laws (197). Hoping to persuade her listeners that she has been victimized, she adopts the role of the sentimental heroine and calls herself a 'forlorn and oppressed woman' (198). She is the virtuous, wronged martyr of sentimental fiction: 'I pardon my oppressor – bitterly as I lament the loss of my child, torn from me in the most violent manner' (197). In addition to using a detached voice, and the legal jargon of the justice system, Wollstonecraft also pleads her case by employing a language that appealed directly to emotions, to one's sensations and sensibility, to the semiotic bodily drives.

Within the novel itself this use of the language of feeling seems not to have succeeded. Maria's appeal to the masculine court is rejected: the judge alludes to 'the fallacy of letting women plead their feelings, as an excuse for the violation of the marriage vow' (198). However, given that Wollstonecraft was writing a sentimental novel, a genre that was most commonly read by women in the late eighteenth century the employment and manipulation of emotions to strengthen argument do not seem mistaken or ineffective. I am suggesting that what attracted Wollstonecraft as a daughter would have also seemed inviting to her women readers. Wavering between the linguistic and the semiotic, her writing, with its flirtation with symbolic representation and with literalization, would have captivated her intended audience. Her use of language may seem inconsistent; but, as Irigaray says, 'Contradictory words seem a little crazy to the logic of reason, and inaudible for him who listens with ready-made grids, a code prepared in advance ... One must listen to her differently in order to hear an *"other meaning" which is constantly in the process of weaving itself, the same time ceaselessly embracing words and yet casting them off to avoid becoming fixed, immobilized.*'[30] Thus Wollstonecraft's conflation of public, symbolic discourse with private, emotional, semiotic language can be viewed as a strength rather than a weakness of her fiction. The style further links the thematic connections between the political and the domestic, between the individual and the social. The many instances of literalization of metaphors in the novel serve to reinforce and make powerfully real the many arguments against female oppression.

CHAPTER TWO

Breaking the 'Magic Circle'
From Repression to Effusion in
Memoirs of Emma Courtney

In the preface to her first novel Mary Hays contends that 'the most interesting, and the most useful fictions' are those that delineate 'the progress' and trace 'the consequences of one strong, indulged passion or prejudice.'[1] That *Emma Courtney* was to be about the perils of a woman's excessive passion is evident from Hays's defensive attitude towards her heroine:

> I meant to represent her, as a human being, loving virtue while enslaved by passion, liable to the mistakes and weaknesses of our fragile nature ... the errors of my heroine were the offspring of sensibility; and ... The result of her hazardous experiment is calculated to operate as a *warning*, rather than as an example. (xviii)

While Hays's avowed intent was to teach through a negative model, what actually happens is that the lesson is often lost or sublimated as the reader gets enticed into the novel. The moral, which has to do with the consequences of indulged passion, becomes increasingly contradictory and ambiguous. In fact, the unstated but undoubtedly calculated thesis of the work seems to be the fatal repercussions of repression on the eighteenth-century middle-class woman.

Female repression or limitation occurs on three levels in *Emma Courtney*: firstly, restraint in speech and language; secondly, professional restrictions; and lastly, sexual repression. Emma's excessive response to her specific situation shows the dangerous effects of these forms of limitation on an intelligent woman of the 1790s. As Wollstonecraft was to do in *Wrongs of Woman*, in her two novels of the decade Hays makes use of the sentimental novel with its standard conventions – acute sensibility, the distressed heroine, exhibitions of pathos, a plot of sudden reversal[2] – as a medium for her feminist dialectics. In contrast to conservative writers such as Jane West and Hannah More, who advocated compliance and restraint in women, Hays like Wollstonecraft argues that these artificially instilled qualities only serve to create havoc in a female subject. Forced into a culturally produced rather than natural subject-position, a woman, such as Emma Courtney in fiction or Mary Hays herself in real life, became a potentially catastrophic site of ideological struggle. Caught between her need to conform to the feminine ideals of submission and silence, and her desire to participate in the traditionally designated 'masculine' modes of activity and expression, an eighteenth-century woman often became an emotional and mental outcast, fitting into neither sphere. Thus, while the novel seems to be about one woman's struggle with her passion – a fairly common subject of sentimental fiction – it is actually a public statement about sexual politics.

In her two prose tracts written in the revolutionary decade Hays similarly verbalizes her disapproval of the passivity, docility, and submission required of a middle-class woman. Disagreeing with the conservative thinkers who believed that these were desirable qualities in women, Hays maintains that subordination and lack of proper education kept women in 'a state of PERPETUAL BABYISM.'[3] In her *Appeal to the Men of Great Britain in Behalf of Women* (1798) she writes: 'Women ... ought to be considered as the companions and equals, not as the inferiors – much less as they virtually are, – as the slaves of men' (127). Like Wollstonecraft and Smith, Hays took advantage of the currency of the revolutionary language to speak of woman's plight.[4] In *Letters and Essays* (1793), for example, Hays protests against what she calls 'mental bondage,' contending that the 'female mind' is 'enslaved,' and the 'understandings of women ... chained down to frivolity and trifles.'[5] Using post-revolution are rhetoric, she argues that 'the modes of education, and the customs of society are degrading to the female character, and the tyranny of custom is sometimes worse than the tyranny of government' (*Letters and Essays*, 11). Published just shortly after the fall of the Bastille, *Letters and Essays* deliberately uses such politically suggestive words as *bondage, chains, tyranny,* and *slavery.*

For Hays, women are not naturally inferior, but they, like 'any race of people' or 'any class of rational beings' who are 'held in a state of subjection and dependence from generation to generation by another party,' are liable to 'degenerate both in body and mind' (*Appeal,* 69). This belief is a version of the Godwinian notion that people are products of their external circumstances rather than of their birth.[6] Again comparing gender relations to political activity, Hays says that men maintain their authority 'by the same law by which the strong oppresses the weak, and the rich the poor' (*Appeal,* 28). She asks 'man' to examine his conscience and to judge whether he holds his 'empire by force alone; or if it is founded on the eternal and immutable laws of nature, and supported by justice and reason' (*Appeal,* 28). Assuming that the 'men' to whom the *Appeal* is addressed are enlightened, Hays frequently implores them to use their judgment and sense of justice to reassess their treatment of women.[7]

While in her prose tracts Hays relies on 'reason' to convince the audience of her arguments, in her novels she counts on sentiments and sensibility to arouse sympathy in her readers for her cause. Both *Emma Courtney* and *Victim of Prejudice* are deliberately dramatic and emotional, full of sensational events, plots, and characters. These elements intensify Hays's rational arguments, illustrating and thematizing graphically the reasonable and logical contentions found in her essays. The pathos and extreme emotion that are characteristic of the genre become harnessed for a dialectical purpose. As in Wollstonecraft's fiction metaphors are frequently 'literalized,' as Hays translates a linguistic construct or a figure of speech and makes it real.

One of the androcentric practices *Emma Courtney* seems to be questioning, for example, is the objectification and the silencing of women. In the *Appeal* Hays similarly questions:

> Since ... the beneficent Creator of all, has dealt out to his children of this world his portions of intelligence, and all his benefits, with so impartial an hand, that we are not only entitled, but irresistibly impelled to claim equality in his paternal inheritance; why should women be excluded from having, and giving their opinions, upon matters of importance to themselves? (154)

In her novel she demonstrates one possible tragic effect of women's exclusion from linguistic practice, from the symbolic order of the Father. Speech and silence become crucial themes that run through the text. In Emma's youth, for instance, authority and defiance of that authority are shown through a manipulation of language. While as a child Emma had grown up 'in joy and innocence,' running 'like the hind,' frisking 'like the kid,' and singing 'like the lark,' in her adolescent years at boarding-school, this freedom is curtailed: 'I was obliged to sit poring over needle work, and forbidden to prate; – my body was tortured into forms, my mind coerced, and talks imposed upon me, grammar and French, mere words, that conveyed to me no ideas' (14). As punishment for bad behaviour Emma 'was constrained to learn, by way of penance, chapters in the Proverbs of Solomon, or verses from the French testament' (15).

While Hays does not relate Emma's problems to gender here, the needlework and the torturing of her body 'into forms' suggest that these restrictions were specifically designed for females. Language is paradoxically forbidden and imposed on women as a means of conformity and discipline. Emma cannot 'prate,' but she has to learn verses written by authoritarian patriarchs. However, here as in her later years, Emma soon learns to 'turn everything upside down,' as Irigaray says.[8] Writing from a mode of 'forbidden speech' or hysteria,[9] she revenges herself by satirizing her 'tyrants in doggrel rhymes' (15). While this scenario may seem childish and insignificant, it is an early indication of the rebellious way in which Emma deals with social and linguistic restraints. In her adult years Emma similarly seeks to escape power and cultural constraints through writing in an unorthodox manner.

Emma's relationship to the two most important male figures in her life – to her father and to her beloved Augustus – is similarly signalled by the absence and thereafter effusion of speech. Both seem to be negative illustrations of the Burkean ideal of the benevolent patriarch as they provide Emma with neither protection nor support. Mr Courtney, for example, refuses 'the title of father' because 'his conduct gave him no claim to the endearing appellation' (28). As an only parent, he does not supervise Emma's education, but is content merely with 'occasional remarks and reflections' to her (19). On his deathbed, where 'a gloomy silence' reigned, he delivers a long lecture to Emma in preparation for her life of poverty and dependence. Emma is not allowed to answer and 'make[s] no comment on the closing scene of his life' (30). Her dealings with her parent illustrate in a very literal manner woman's exclusion from the symbolic world of the Father. Even when matters relate directly to her upbringing or her future, Emma is never consulted or permitted to speak for herself.

At the Morton household wherein Emma is consigned by her father, she is also besieged by problems of speech and communication. Here she cannot seem to make herself understood. The women of Morton Park are full of superficial language: Mrs Morton's voice is 'loud and discordant'; Sarah Morton is 'loquacious' and sarcastic; while Ann is described as a 'prattler' (33, 53). Emma's intentions are misread twice by the family. When Emma offers to assist Mrs Morton in the education of her children, she is accused of possessing 'vanity' (35). When she shows her appreciation for Mr Francis's conversation and friendship, she is charged with exhibiting indecorous 'partial sentiments' for him (42). The only person whom Emma finds a kindred spirit is the neighbour, Mrs Harley, whose address is 'engaging,' and with whom Emma reads, walks, and talks (54). Because Mrs Harley is the only one whom Emma can speak and converse properly with, it is not surprising that her affection for this woman of 'cultivated understanding' is soon transferred to her son, Augustus Harley.

Even before meeting him, Emma calls Augustus 'the St. Preux, the Emilius of [her] sleeping and waking reveries' (59). Because Emma has been largely excluded from meaningful speech and communication up to now, she seems to expend all her repressed energies in her letters to Augustus. Augustus becomes the dubious recipient of numerous letters from Emma informing him of her 'pure' affection (80) for him. Just as Emma had 'revenged' herself as an adolescent by writing forbidden and disruptive 'doggrel rhymes,' she now rebels against her restrictive environment by pouring out her innermost wishes in her epistles. In a rather unprecedented manner for an eighteenth-century middle-class woman, Emma ventures to confide her sentiments to Augustus, disregarding '*rules* sanctioned by usage, by prejudice, by expediency' (80). She tells him: 'Remember, *that you have once been beloved, for yourself alone*, by one, who, in contributing to the comfort of your life, would have found the happiness of her own' (81). Emma's radical declaration may be somewhat limited since, as Janet Todd points out, 'what the heroine wants is the conventional romantic ending albeit brought about by unromantic means: marriage to Harley proposed by herself.'[10] However, while her goal may be conventional, I believe that the importance of Emma's proposal lies elsewhere.

In expressing her ardour, Emma is not only asserting the existence of female desire, but also challenging the objectification and silencing of women. By professing her feelings, she ceases to be merely the 'object of transaction' in a cultural exchange, as Irigaray puts it (*This Sex*, 85), but becomes a subject initiating desire. Historically, her choice of Augustus is significant because it supports the Godwinian and Jacobin emphasis on individual merit rather than on birth, fortune, and heredity. Emma stresses that she loves Augustus for himself alone, and not for his ancestral name or family. In fact, she is aware of the 'tenure,' or the peculiar terms specifying that he remain single, upon which he retains his fortune (81). Willing to sacrifice economic considerations and social position, Emma argues that her love is one that results from the 'laws of nature' (89). It occurs 'when mind has given dignity to natural affections; when reason, culture, taste, delicacy, have combined to chasten, to refine, to exalt ... to sanctify them' (89). Quoting Rousseau, she contends that 'moral, mental, and personal qualifications' can make even a 'union between a prince and the daughter of an executioner' suitable (103). Like Holcroft in *Anna St. Ives* Hays is implicitly suggesting an opposition to rank based on class and promoting instead distinctions based on individual merit, a revolutionary notion which would have horrified a conservative thinker such as Burke.

Ironically the effect on Augustus of Emma's announcement of her love is to render him silent. In fact, there is a perverse kind of gender or role reversal in the novel upon which Hays does not comment. As Emma acquires more powers of speech, the men around her seem to become more inarticulate or ineffective. Augustus repeatedly evades Emma's queries on the state of his heart and postpones replying to her letters. Her plea for 'one hour's frank conversation' with him is ignored (99), and Emma, like the reader, is left uncertain of his response to her passion until almost the end of the novel. Like Wollstonecraft, Hays was hesitant or perhaps unwilling to allow herself and her readers the possibility of escape through sheer romantic fantasy. Instead she resorts to the sentimental, possibly because of her own thwarted romances in real life, or perhaps because she felt the tragic ending would serve the purposes of her dialectical novel better. Emma's experiment does not bring her connubial felicity but illustrates how the silencing and the repression of females lead to tragedy and misplaced affections. It may be, as Irigaray suggests, that writing as a 'hysteric,' that is, forced to mime and reproduce a language that is not her own but 'masculine language,' Hays could not yet write adequately about herself and her needs (*This Sex*, 136, 137). Irigaray argues that by 'virtue of the *subordination* of feminine desire to phallocratism,' the full power of woman is still 'kept in reserve' and 'paralysed' (*This Sex*, 138).

Aside from verbal and linguistic repression, Hays shows how an eighteenth-century woman suffers from limitations in her choice of profession. Self-educated, intelligent, and energetic, Emma finds that a single woman with no fortune had virtually no means of subsisting independently in the 1790s in England. 'Dependence' is what Emma wishes to avoid, and it becomes a key word that runs through the novel. The career alternatives opened to Emma were either marriage or forms of servitude,[11] against which she exclaims:

> Cruel prejudices! ... hapless woman! Why was I not educated for commerce, for a profession, for labour? Why have I been rendered feeble and delicate by bodily constraints, and fastidious by artificial refinement? Why are we bound, by the habits of society ... Why do we suffer ourselves to be confined within a magic circle, without daring ... to dissolve the barbarous spell? (31).

This plea for a means of self-support is a direct transcription of Hays's arguments in her *Appeal to the Men of Great Britain*, where she complains that men have been 'monopolizing trades' such as tailoring, hairdressing, millinery, mantua- and stay-making which women could easily do (200–1). In the *Appeal* she also uses the same metaphor of the 'magic circle,'[12] this 'prison of the soul' out of which women 'cannot move, but to contempt or destruction' (111). In *Emma Courtney* Hays illustrates the convictions she had articulated in her prose: while Emma was 'active, industrious, willing to employ [her] faculties in any way,' she 'beheld no path open ... but ... the degradation of servitude' (164). This tangible example of the 'iron hand of barbarous despotism' (164) thematizes graphically in fiction the implications of the 'magic' circle or social limitation on women's lives.

That this 'magic circle' is a result of social and cultural conditioning rather than of nature is demonstrated in the novel. Hays begins by having the heroine 'trace' the events of her life, as Emma is convinced 'of the irresistible power of circumstances, modifying and controuling our characters, and introducing, mechanically, those associations and habits which make us what we are' (6). Echoing Godwinian philosophy, Hays then shows how economic and social circumstances, education, and background mould Emma into the 'victim of ... a distempered imagination' that she becomes (77). In her childhood and adolescent years Emma is 'interpellated' by the literature that she happens to read.[13] 'Attached' to books, she says, '... stories were ... my passion, and I sighed for a romance that would never end' (12). Unaware of gender distinction, she acted the part of both the male and female protagonists of the stories: the 'valiant knight – the gentle damsel – the adventurous mariner – the daring robber' (12), even identifying with the 'grecian heroes' in the *Lives* of Plutarch (21). As she gets older however, she falls prey to sentimental fiction: 'I subscribed to a circulating library, and frequently read, or rather devoured – little careful in the selection – from ten to fourteen novels a week' (17). These novels, and the '*Héloïse* of Rousseau,' the 'dangerous, enchanting work' which Emma peruses with 'transport' (25), make her believe that she is a heroine of sensibility. Full of self-pity,[14] she often describes herself in clichéd sentimental terms, calling herself, for example, 'a poor, a friendless, an unprotected being,' and a 'deserted outcast from society – a desolate orphan' (35, 74). Paradoxically, while her reading has made her yearn for heroism and romance in her youth, it also makes her eager to adopt the subject-position of the suffering female victim depicted in the novels.

Most significantly, however, Emma's education and her reading make her aware of women's economic and mental imprisonment, their confinement within the 'magic circle.' Hays's heroine proves to be antithetical to the conservative ideal of the docile, submissive woman content with her domestic sphere, an ideal proposed by writers such as More and West. Emma realizes that she suffers from intellectual and spiritual deprivation: '... my mind panted for freedom, for social intercourse, for scenes in motion, where the active curiosity of my temper might find a scope wherein to range and speculate' (31). For her, the kinds of things women were supposed to be interested in were not rewarding. She complains of the 'insipid routine of heartless, mindless intercourse ... domestic employment, or the childish vanity of varying external ornaments' (85) which are 'insufficient to engross, to satisfy, the active, aspiring mind' (86).

Insightfully, Hays contends that this limitation of woman's sphere can cause psychological damage and eventually destroy intelligent women. In *Appeal to the Men of Great Britain*, she says that women as well as men possess a 'passion to distinguish themselves, – this rage to excel' but 'when applied to woman it commonly receives the denomination of vanity' or 'pride' (77). Because of the denial of this impulse women are driven to do foolish things:

> Driven and excluded from what are commonly esteemed the consequential offices of life; denied... any political existence; and literary talents and acquirements, nay genius itself ... nothing in short being left for them, but domestic duties, and superficial accomplishments and vanities – Is it surprising, that instead of doing as men bid them ... that spoiled by prosperity and goaded on by temptation and the allurements of pleasure, they give a loose rein to their passions, and plunge headlong into folly and dissipation ... to the utter extinction of thought, moderation, or strict morality? (*Appeal*, 81–2)

In *Emma Courtney* this argument is repeated by the heroine:

> While men pursue interest, honor, pleasure, as accords with their several
> dispositions, women ... remain insulated beings, and must be content
> tamely to look on, without taking any part in the great, though often
> absurd and tragical drama of life. Hence the eccentricities of conduct,
> with which women of superior minds have been accused ... the despairing
> ... struggles of an ardent spirit, denied a scope for its exertions! The
> strong feelings, and ... energies ... forced back, and pent up, ravage and
> destroy the mind which gave them birth! (86)

What happens to Emma is a literal transcription of this contention:
instead of being able to direct her strong energies to a useful channel,
Emma becomes strongly infatuated and obsessed with an admirable
man with a doubtful past.

While Augustus Harley is not a villain, he is rather like Wollstonecraft's Darnford in *Wrongs of Woman* in that he is a hero largely created
by the heroine's imagination. Part of his attraction stems from the fact
that he is the son of Emma's friend, but part of it arises from his
willingness to assist Emma 'in the pursuit of learning and science ...
astronomy and philosophy ... languages ... criticism and grammar, and
... composition' (71). In other words, he widens Emma's mental hor-
izons and encourages her development in a way that no one else had
before. Subsequently, at a dinner party, Emma listens with admiration
to a discussion on the slave trade in which 'Mr. Harley pleaded the
cause of freedom and humanity with a bold and manly eloquence,
expatiating warmly on the iniquity as well as impolicy of so accursed
a traffic' (115). Like Emma, Augustus, too, is an advocate of 'freedom
and humanity.' She feels a sympathy between them, a 'union between
mind and mind,' but also knows that her emotions are aided by her
'imagination, ever lively,' which 'traced the glowing picture, and
dipped the pencil in rainbow tints!' (103).

The fact that Augustus, who seems to shun Emma throughout the
novel, actually reciprocates her feelings and admits that he has loved
her adds a touch of irony to the lesson of restraint that Hays seems to
be inculcating in her readers. All along, Hays cautions that Emma's
conduct '*is not what I would recommend to general imitation*' (89). Emma
seems to be exposing and humiliating herself by her constant harassment of Augustus with detailed proofs of her affection and with her
queries: 'Had he, or had he not, a *present, existing engagement?*' (109).
At the height of her passion she even offers herself to him without the

sanctity of marriage: 'I breathe with difficulty – *My friend* – *I would give myself to you* – the gift is not worthless' (126). This sensational declaration of the heroine's willingness to give herself physically to a man is made even more shocking by Emma's admittance of the existence of sexual desires. Emma's reading has not only enriched her mind, but has also made her aware of her sexuality, as she explains: 'I am neither a philosopher, nor a heroine – but a *woman, to whom education has given a sexual character*' (120). As one critic remarks, Emma longs for the 'twin sources of masculine power; knowledge and sex.'[15] To eighteenth-century readers women who wished to meddle in 'masculine' spheres of learning were already considered freaks or 'unsex'd,' but women who desired both erudition and passion were virtual monsters.[16]

It is not coincidental that Foucault credits the eighteenth century with the beginning of the production of sexuality, when 'specific mechanisms of knowledge and power centering on sex' were formed.[17] Foucault argues that among a number of developments at this time were the 'hysterization of women's bodies' and the 'socialization of procreative behavior' (104). Both the character Emma Courtney and the author Hays are affected by the period's fear of woman's sexuality and the overt way in which Hays attempted to discuss it. Because it was widely known that *Emma Courtney* was based on her unrequited love for William Frend, the Cambridge mathematician and rebel, who had advocated many of Godwin's beliefs, Hays became the target of a number of censures. Frequently the attacks on Hays's ideas were accompanied by unjust invectives against her person. In a letter to Robert Southey dated Saturday, 25 January 1800, an irascible Samuel Taylor Coleridge wrote:

> Of Miss Hays' intellect I do not think so highly as you, or rather, to speak sincerely, I think, not contemptuously, but certainly very despectively thereof [*sic*]. – Yet I think you likely in this case to have judged better than I – for to hear a Thing, ugly & petticoated, ex-syllogize a God with cold-blooded Precision, & attempt to run Religion thro' the body with an Icicle ... If do not endure it![18]

Another assault came from Charles Lloyd, who satirized Coleridge and the excessive, uncontrolled sensibility of the English Jacobins in his novel *Edmund Oliver* (1798). In the work Hays appears as Lady Gertrude Sinclair, a passionate girl of very advanced principles who is throwing herself at a revolutionary who turns out to be a hypocrite.[19]

As in Hamilton's *Memoirs Modern Philosophers, Edmund Oliver* replicates passages from *Emma Courtney* verbatim, which, though meant to satirize, also created more publicity and certainly reinforced Hays's notoriety. That Hays's novel and her person should inspire a number of writers to depict her in their works, albeit negatively, is an indication of the disruptive power of her revolutionary ideas. In addition, in *Emma Courtney* itself, the heroine's declaration of her passion causes some to believe that she is hysterical. Harley refuses to acknowledge her sexual desires, while Mr Francis believes that her conduct is a sign of 'moon-struck madness' (142).

Hays's novel created an outrage and became a target for satires because she used her fiction to transgress the boundaries allocated to women by the male-dominated culture. Her heroine's declaration openly challenged the notions of female propriety and modesty as prescribed by the conservatives. What Irigaray says of women's sexuality applies to Hays's Emma Courtney: '... what they desire is precisely nothing, and at the same time everything ... Their desire is often interpreted, and feared, as a sort of insatiable hunger, a voracity that will swallow you whole' (*This Sex,* 29). Indeed, fear is undoubtedly one of the reasons why *Emma Courtney* inspired the number of parodies and caricatures that it did. Hays's insistence on the moral aspects of her tale does not, in fact, lessen its revolutionary implications. While Emma complains that she is 'hemmed in on every side by the constitutions of society' and that she perceives 'the magic circle, without knowing how to dissolve the powerful spell' (86), she does succeed in breaking this 'magic circle' in many ways. Emma reverses eighteenth-century courtship conventions by infringing on the masculine right to selection, openly acknowledges her sexual longing, breaks out of silence, and becomes a subject rather than an 'specularized' object of male desire. Her repentant covering letters to Augustus, Jr, at the beginning and end of the memoirs do not, ultimately, negate her achievement or the power of her tale. The virtues that she tries to instil in the young Augustus – 'vigor' of the mind, 'self controul,' the 'dignity of active, intrepid virtue' – are very worthy, but the didactic lessons seem pale and lifeless in comparison to the narration of the potency and frenzy of forbidden and 'contemned love' (198–9).

Another way in which the sense of women's limitations and imprisonment within the 'magic circle' is reinforced is through the circular and repetitive structure of the narrative. Emma's sexual and intellectual frustrations, her feelings of being a 'miserable, oppressed, and impotent woman' excluded from expanding her 'sensations' (146), are reflected in the novel's textual confinement of the reader. As Emma writes and rewrites the same argument, as she repeatedly confronts Augustus with identical proofs of her sincerity and affection based on reason, it is difficult not to be exasperated by her seemingly futile efforts. Emma's narrative, with its tedious, but very real and urgent, supplications, encircles and confines the reader just as she is in fact 'hemmed in' by her lack of alternatives or choices. I suggest that rather than lose patience with the heroine, Hays wishes that her readers would cease to tolerate the social and cultural institutions or structures that are responsible for her plight. As in Wollstonecraft's *Wrongs of Woman* repetition, inactivity, and confinement are designed to instigate revolt and reaction in the reader.

Finally, the ambiguous and rather hasty resolution of *Emma Courtney* betrays Hays's ambivalent feelings about the power of emotions and passion. According to Lacanian myth, Hays, like Wollstonecraft, is writing from the position of the daughter. Her text therefore reveals both a strong penchant for what Kristeva calls the semiotic realm, and a desire to conform to the symbolic world, with its emphasis on language and reason. In 'From One Identity to an Other' Kristeva says that 'semiotic processes prepare the future speaker for entrance into meaning and signification,' but points out that 'language as symbolic function constitutes itself at the cost of repressing instinctual drive and continuous relation to the mother.' Poetic language is useful because it signifies 'what is untenable in the symbolic, nominal, paternal function.'[20] Critic Patricia Elliot suggests that 'as such, poetic language reveals the process through which subjects are constituted, a process repressed by a rationality that assumes the conscious ego to be master in its own house.' She notes that 'from Kristeva's perspective this rationality marks another instance of sacrifice ... in the process of establishing coherent social and symbolic identities.'[21] Through Emma, Hays reveals the cost of this sacrifice, and by implication, the need for change in the construction of women's identity. As Catherine Belsey puts it, 'It is this contradiction in the subject – between the conscious self, which is conscious in so far as it is able to feature in discourse, and the self which is only partially represented there – which constitutes the source of possible change.'[22]

Near the end of the novel Emma believes herself cured of 'the morbid excess of a distempered imagination' and marries a second-rate suitor, Montague, because she owed him 'life, and its comforts, rational enjoyments, and the opportunity of usefulness' (172). However, this peaceful relationship based on 'a rational esteem, and a grateful affection' (171) is quickly destroyed when Emma accidentally encounters Augustus before his expiration. After Augustus's deathbed confession that Emma's 'tenderness early penetrated [his] heart' and that he has loved her all along (180), Emma becomes ill and in her delirium 'incessantly call[s] upon the name of Augustus Harley' (182), thereby negating her assertions that she is now completely ruled by reason rather than passion.

Indeed, even as she terminates her memoirs with the entreaty to young Augustus to learn from 'the errors of [her] past life' (198), and to escape 'from the tyranny of the passions' (199), she also says in a rather contradictory manner: 'The social affections were necessary to my existence, but they have been only inlets to sorrow – *yet still, I bind them to my heart!*' (198). Her half-hearted repentance and her romantic narrative do not actually condemn pure passion as much as the conventions of society which do not tolerate its expression. Though she claims that her 'affections' have only brought her 'sorrow,' she is nevertheless unwilling to let them go. Clinging to her feelings, she fails in her attempts to follow the advice of her philosopher friend, Mr Francis. In fact, the weak and rather impotent authority of Francis's admonition is another indication of Hays's distrust of the Law of the Father. Francis, the paternal figure, points out to Emma that her conduct has been 'moon-struck madness, hunting after torture' and that 'disappointed love' cannot be catalogued as one of the 'real evils of human life' (142), but his sagacious counsel is wasted on the ardent Emma. Emma refuses his abstract rationalism and insists that her sorrow is real: 'That which embitters all my life, that which stops the genial current of health and peace is whatever be its nature, a real calamity to me' (144). For Emma, reasoning powers cannot take the place of or compete with emotional strength. She maintains that 'my reason was the auxiliary of my passion, or rather my passion the generative principle of my reason' (145). As with Wollstonecraft, Hays was attracted to both of these forces and tried to work out in her fiction the place of each in a woman's life.

Similar to a Gothic novel such as Radcliffe's *Mysteries of Udolpho*, *Emma Courtney* ends with a sense of order, sanity, and normality after having taken the reader through what seems to be a world of uncertainty, doubts, heightened emotions, and tensions. Both Emily St Aubert and Emma Courtney appear to be 'cured' of excessive sensibility after their experience in the dark maze of agitation, passion, and imagination. However, despite the moralistic beginning and ending of Hays's novel, the tendency of the whole work is still towards feeling, sensation, and the free expression of one's sentiments. As in *Udolpho* the most exciting and innovative parts of the novel are those that deal with the excesses, the effusions of passions, the mystery of the unknown. The strong middle part of the work, where the heroine gives 'loose rein' to her passion, to her emotional and bodily drives, her 'semiotic' self, subverts and undermines the lesson of good sense that the narrator tries to teach. It is as if Hays felt compromised by the demands of the critics and the conservative writers into tacking a moral onto her powerful tale depicting female desire.

In addition to the tension between the moral and the effect of the work, another revolutionary aspect of Hays's novel is in its unusual conclusion. In the final scene of *Emma Courtney* we do not see the conventional heterosexual couple ending the novel but a tableau of a mother and child dyad. Like Wollstonecraft's in *Mary, a Fiction,* Hays's resistance to the Burkean notion of paternal authority is shown in her refusal to let her heroine submit to the name of the Father. Instead Hays resorts to the maternal and places her hopes on the youth of the next generation. While Emma had identified herself with the sentimental heroine in her younger years, in her middle age she is very much a female survivor, outliving both the prevaricating Augustus and her weak-willed husband. Though she is still affected by her memories, the 'long forgotten emotions' (198), she looks forward to a new and better society in which 'men begin to think and reason; reformation dawns, though the advance is tardy' (199). This belief in the Godwinian notion of the perfectibility of humankind, though laudable, was difficult to sustain; and, by her next novel, Hays became more pessimistic about the ability of society to reform.

CHAPTER THREE

The Mother and Daughter
The Dangers of Replication in
The Victim of Prejudice

Despite its contradictory message towards freedom of expression and excessive feeling *Emma Courtney* maintained the hope shared by the radical intellectuals of the 1790s that the example of the French Revolution would bring about change in England. By the time Mary Hays wrote her second novel, *The Victim of Prejudice* (1799), however, this glimmer of hope was fast disappearing. Hays was much more pessimistic in her attitude at the close of the revolutionary decade, and this outlook resulted in a novel less idealistic and more sombre in tone than her first one. In spirit and intent *Victim of Prejudice* is closer to Wollstonecraft's *Wrongs of Woman* in that it presents a catalogue of possible 'wrongs' or acts of social injustice perpetrated on the eighteenth-century middle-class female.

Using elements of the sentimental and the Gothic novel, Hays sets out to disprove and dispel the Burkean myth of the benevolent country squire as an adequate miniature head or 'monarch' of the residents of his estates. Sir Peter Osborne, the representative patriarch, is the complete opposite of the Burkean ideal and is devoid of any sense of kindness or generosity towards his tenants. In fact, he deliberately takes advantage of his authority to gratify his selfish desires for seduction and revenge. Other issues Hays attempts to deal with in her second novel are the objectification of women in a male-dominated society, and their lack of social and economic power. As in *Emma Courtney* the theme of dependence becomes important and is fictionalized in the work. Indeed much of *Victim of Prejudice* is a transcription of the feminist contentions found in her prose writings, *Letters and*

Essays and, especially, *An Appeal to the Men of Great Britain*. Literalization occurs at various levels in the novel: the metaphor of the confinement of women in the 'magic circle' becomes a physical reality;
horrors and nightmares discovered in ancient papers are enacted and
become 'real'; and finally, a woman's sense of helplessness, most often
imagined in the form of sexual violation and its consequences, materi-
alizes and becomes literal.

Similar in tone and ideology to Godwin's *Things As They Are; or, The
Adventures of Caleb Williams*, by which Wollstonecraft's *Wrongs* was also
influenced, Hays's *Victim* attempts to expose the corruption of such
man-made institutions as the court and legislative systems which favour
persons of wealth and rank. Jane Spencer says that '*The Victim of Prejudice* is a study of the obstacles in the way of female independence, the
ideal that animated Wollstonecraft in *The Rights of Woman*.'[1] But the
novel also deals with the complexities of mother-daughter relations,
and with more general concerns such as social prejudices which tend
to distinguish worth according to birth, reputation, and fortune and
blind people to an individual's personal merit.[2] Like Caleb Williams
the heroine sees herself as a victim of society, describing herself rather
sentimentally but nevertheless appropriately as a 'child of misfortune,
a wretched outcast from [her] fellow beings.'[3] Using language borrowed from the revolutionary decade of the 1790s, she addresses her
memoirs to the 'victim of despotism, oppression, or error, tenant of a
dungeon,' her successor in her prison cell, whom she calls 'fellow
sufferer' (1:ii, iii). While Emma Courtney is metaphorically confined
in her 'magic circle,' Mary Raymond, the 'victim' of a 'barbarous prejudice' (2:230), is incarcerated in a literal prison as she writes her
autobiography.

According to Mary's reconstruction of her life, her history has been
like a fall from paradise to a dungeon or hell. Treated like a beloved
daughter by her benevolent guardian, Mr Raymond, Mary grows up
with a 'robust constitution, a cultivated understanding, and a vigorous
intellect' (1:6). Like Emma she has had a liberal education, learning
the rudiments not only of 'French, Italian, and Latin,' but also 'geom-
etry, algebra, and arithmetic' (1:8). She has been taught to 'triumph
over the imperious demands of passion, to yield only to the dictates of
right reason and truth' (1:65–6). However, as in *Emma Courtney*, theory
and knowledge of how to act do not necessarily lead to success in
practice. These lessons fail to save her from the cruelty and persecutions of the Gothic-like villain, Sir Peter Osborne, who happens to
catch Mary stealing a cluster of grapes from his greenhouse one day.

Admiring her innocence and beauty, Osborne tauntingly calls her 'a true daughter of Eve' (1:28) because of her transgression. This appellation becomes ironically appropriate because shortly after her theft of the forbidden fruit, Mary is expelled from her Edenic idyll, loses her 'innocence' in both the physical and mental senses, and becomes subjected to the continual harassment of the powerful Sir Peter. Instead of extricating her from her difficulties, Mary's learning has only made her aware of the peculiar social conditions which contribute to her plight.

Another irony of this appellation is that it links the then virginal Mary with the temptress figure of Eve. It is perhaps not coincidental that two of the most prominent women of the Bible are seen to be fused in the character of Mary. In Osborne's limited understanding all women are stereotyped as both the mother and the whore. Mary unwittingly becomes the object of Osborne's desire and never gets a chance to articulate her wishes or speak as a subject. He only sees her as his specularized 'other,' projecting his desire onto her, and refuses to treat her as the individual she is. His stereotypical and automatic categorization of her is a form of victimization which becomes a literalization when, through his manipulations, she is later reduced to a 'daughter of Eve,' or a figure of temptation in the eyes of men.

Aside from being the object of desire, Mary also represents the oppressed and the defenceless. In her next encounter with Osborne she receives lashes from his whip while trying to shelter a hare from him. Mary is linked to the little animal lexically: she describes it here as a 'panting victim' while she later depicts herself as a 'helpless, devoted victim,' 'panting, half-breathless with emotion' (1:46; 2:128). Implicitly Hays suggests that the aristocratic Osborne desires to sport with her much in the same way he does with the hare, chasing it and eventually killing it in the guise of adventure. According to the Burkean ideal of the benevolent patriarch, as lord of the manor and of the surrounding estates, Osborne should be the benefactor and protector of his tenants. However, Hays shows the inadequacy of this ideal as Sir Peter abuses his privileges of power and peerage, giving in to his lascivious needs, to his 'sport,' rather than considering the good of the community, of which Mary is part.

Earlier, in her *Appeal to the Men of Great Britain*, Hays had expressed her reservations about giving power to men merely on the basis of their gender: 'As matters now stand, it is very difficult to decide, where authority should in prudence begin, or where it ought in justice to end.'[4] Protesting against 'things as they are,' she asks: '... in forming the laws by which women are governed ... have not men ... consulted more their own conveniency, comfort, and dignity, as far as their judgement and foresight served them than that of women?' (158–9). In *Victim of Prejudice* she demonstrates how 'having no hand in forming [the laws],' women become the 'sufferers' (*Appeal*, 159). Mary is not the only 'victim' in the novel: she seems destined to repeat or replicate the sensational and melodramatic life of her mother. At one time admired and beloved by Mr Raymond, the Mary of the first generation was also a 'victim of the injustice, of the prejudices of society' (1:162). Seduced and abandoned by a man whom she had trusted, she became a prostitute out of desperation. Then, after giving birth to her illegitimate daughter, she murdered her lover in a tavern brawl and later died on the scaffold for her crime. Like her daughter, the mother blames society for her destruction: '*Law* completes the triumph of injustice. The despotism of man rendered me weak, his vices betrayed me into shame, a barbarous policy stifled returning dignity, prejudice robbed me of the means of independence ...' (1:168). In the eyes of the world the degrading circumstances surrounding Mary's birth are enough to exclude her from respectable society. Her education and accomplishments, her dignity and character, signify nothing. Mary laments: 'While the practice of the world opposes the principles of the sage, education is a fallacious effort, morals an empty theory, and sentiment a delusive dream' (1:78).

Despite her determination not to fall prey to seduction like her mother, the second Mary ends up with an equally tragic fate. The younger Mary's worst nightmares are literalized in the novel, which is thereby given an unreal, Gothic-like quality. As she peruses the memoirs of her mother, Mary becomes the intradiegetic reader, or the reader within the narrative, whose reactions to the tale gauge our own. She is unable to transcend the imprisoning web of the narrative, and becomes enmeshed by the words. She feels 'a sense of oppression, almost to suffocation,' after reading her mother's story and goes out into the 'dark and stormy' night in order to relieve herself of her anguish (1:175). Literally trying to wash away her pain, she stays out in the howling wind and rain, but finds herself unable to escape the narrative:

> I recalled to my remembrance the image of my wretched mother: I beheld her, in idea, abandoned to infamy, cast out of society, stained with blood, expiring on a scaffold, unpitied and unwept. I clasped my hands in agony; terrors assailed me till then unknown; the blood froze in my veins; a shuddering horror crept through my heart ...(1:176)

Because Mary was abandoned as an infant, the image that she sees here of her mother is an imagined rather than a recollected one. The terror that she experiences is not only for her mother's experiences in the past, but also for herself, as she feels the danger of replicating her mother's life in the future.

Replication and literalization are made more explicit in yet another instance. After her rape Mary sees her 'wretched mother' in 'visionary form':

> One moment, methought I beheld her in the arms of her seducer, revelling in licentious pleasure; the next, saw her haggard, intoxicated, self-abandoned, joining in the midnight riot; and, in an instant ... covered with blood, accused of murder, shrieking in horrible despair ... Then, all pallid and ghastly, with clasped hands ... and agonizing earnestness, she seemed to urge me to take example from her fate! (2:95–6)

The ghostly, Gothic-like nightmare of her mother ends with Mary clasping her parent 'in a last embrace' (2:96). It is as if Mary subconsciously desired to be linked with her mother and her disgrace. This realization of something that happened a generation ago seems to be a physical and mental manifestation of the desire to return to the marginalized and outcast maternal.[5] Like Wollstonecraft, Hays demonstrates the ambivalence a woman feels, for the world dominated by the Father. For these female writers the emphasis of maternal figures, dreams, and nightmares, of the disruptive, suggests a move in the direction of the pre-Oedipal mother-child relation, even if this move frequently entails danger, death, or exclusion from the symbolic order.

This mother-daughter link and the subsequent literal re-enactment[6] of the first Mary's written memoirs create much of the tension and sense of foreboding in the novel. As Mary imagines her mother 'abandoned to infamy, cast out of society, stained with blood ... unpitied and unwept' (1:176), she is also ironically prescribing and envisioning her own future in many ways. Except for the murder of her seducer Mary's life follows that of her mother's, as she is systematically seduced, abandoned, and cast out of society. That Hays understood the consequences that arise from a return to the maternal is revealed when she associates it with betrayal and exclusion from the male symbolic order. Attractive as the mother-daughter connection may seem to be, its cost is undeniably high. Through a replication of the mother's life in the daughter's, Hays shows how challenging the patriarchal system can lead to some form of female punishment in contemporary eighteenth-century culture. The attempts of both the first- and the second-generation Mary to rebel, oppose, and curtail masculine will and desire only create further constraints in their lives. Yearning for more space and freedom, they become physically and spiritually more constricted and circumscribed. In her depiction of the failure of the maternal Hays recognized that the refusal to yield to the Father's law brings about marginalization and isolation under the specific historical and social circumstances in which she and her heroines lived.

Furthermore, the seduction and abandonment of Mary Raymond is not only a transcription of events that have already transpired within the text, but also a replication, or what Margaret Homans would call a 'literalization,' of a more figurative earlier text. The device of the kidnapped heroine was common enough by the 1790s;[7] however, the details of Mary's ravishment and violation closely parallel that of a mid-century novel, *Clarissa*. There is evidence to suggest that Hays was rewriting Samuel Richardson's *Clarissa* from a feminist perspective. Earlier, in an essay entitled 'On Novel Writing' published in the *Monthly Magazine* of September 1797, Hays expressed her disagreement with Samuel Johnson, who believed that fictional narratives should exhibit 'perfect models of virtue.'[8] She cites and criticizes Richardson's *Clarissa* as an example of a character who is depicted too perfectly: '... the character of Clarissa, a beautiful superstructure upon a false and airy foundation, can never be regarded as a model for imitation. It is the portrait of an ideal being, placed in circumstances equally ideal, far removed from common life and human feelings' ('On Novel Writing,' 180). According to Hays, Richardson's novel violates principles of 'truth and nature' and abounds with 'absurd superstitions and ludicrous prejudices' ('On Novel Writing,' 180). Preferring the 'real' to the ideal, Hays questions: '... why should we seek to deceive ... by illusive representations of life? Why should we not rather paint [life] as it really exists, mingled with imperfection, and discoloured by passion?' ('On Novel Writing,' 180).

Hays's rejection of 'illusive' or figurative representations can be explained with the help of Chodorow, Kristeva, Irigaray, and others as a manifestation of a woman writer's lingering attachment to pre-Oedipal, literal language, as opposed to a son's wholehearted embrace of the symbolic, figurative language associated with the father. In the depiction of women in literature figurative or ideal representations often entail the death or destruction of the real.[9] That Hays was aware of, and uncomfortable with, this notion is revealed in her opposition to iconic representations of good and evil. Arguing that such delineations are not 'consistent with truth and fact,' she writes: 'Human nature seems to be at an equal distance from the humiliating descriptions of certain ascetic moralists, and the exaggerated eulogiums of enthusiasts. Gradations, almost imperceptible, of light and shade, must mingle in every true portrait of the human mind' ('On Novel Writing,' 180). Hence, in *Victim of Prejudice* the heroine is neither the virgin Mary, despite her name, nor the temptress Eve, as Sir Osborne believes. She is not 'wholly or disinterestedly virtuous or vicious' ('On Novel Writing,' 180), but a complex and probable human being.

That Hays intended her readers to think of *Clarissa* as an intertext to her own novel is confirmed by the many similarities between the two works. Like Clarissa, Mary is from an untitled middle-class family and is courted by an aristocrat. Both heroines are transported from their homes by deceit to the London residences of the villain/rakes. Both are raped and dishonoured by their abductors and live long enough to exclaim against their fate in writing, Clarissa in her numerous epistles and Mary in her memoirs. However, even more significant are the differences between the two texts. Hays reworks the Richardsonian material according to her beliefs: her heroine is not a paragon, nor is she placed in ideal circumstances. Radically changing the denouement, Hays does not end her novel with the triumphant death of the heroine, but instead uses the tragic events to illustrate powerfully the injustice of later-eighteenth-century social customs and laws, and the abuse of patriarchal authority. Unlike Richardson, Hays does not shift the focus away from the realistic, brutal consequences of the rape to a more ethereal, spiritual realm; rather, she dwells on the sordid details of the miserable existence of her heroine after her sexual defilement. Hays's Mary, unlike Richardson's Clarissa, does not transcend the physical and the corporeal to become a symbolic representation of Christian fortitude or female virtue, but remains rooted in the social and the real.

Using Gothic elements enabled Hays to increase her heroine's sense of terror and helplessness. Some of these techniques include Osborne's elaborate machinations to get her to his London mansion, confinement in a chamber with the door locked on the outside, and Mary's midnight wandering, in an effort to escape, in the dark halls and corridors of the house on the night of the grand dinner. While these circumstances may remind one of Radcliffe's *Udolpho*, the end result is quite different. For Mary's terrors, unlike most of Emily St Aubert's, are not imagined ones, and her fears of rape become literalized that night. And while Osborne apologizes for his behaviour the next day, maintaining that his action 'had not been premeditated, but was the mere result of accident and a temporary effervescence of spirits' (2:80), he increasingly becomes the obsessive and cruel tyrant who inhabits the imaginations of Gothic maidens like Emily. However, unlike Emily, Mary does not need to resort to fantasy or to the symbolic: her horrors are all too real and literal.

Following the rape Hays uses a stock character of sentimental fiction, that of the suffering heroine, or virtue in distress, to illustrate her beliefs of gender and class inequality. Mary's plight reveals how the existing justice system fails to protect and, in fact, aids in oppressing the wronged in society. Because of her mother's reputation as a whore and murderer, her insufficient knowledge of the city, and her lack of social connections, Mary finds it difficult to convince anyone that she was brutally violated. She threatens Osborne with legal proceedings, but he jeers at her: 'Who will credit the tale you mean to tell? ... Who would support you against my wealth and influence? How would your delicacy shrink from the idea of becoming, in open court, the sport of ribaldry, the theme of obscene jesters?' (2:85–6). As Hays suggests in her advertisement, because of the 'too-great stress laid on the reputation for chastity in woman,' Mary has difficulty in retaining her dignity and self-respect. Paraphrasing Godwin's philosophy, she demands 'liberty,' and proclaims: 'when the mind is determined,' one cannot 'fetter the body' by 'feeble restraints' (1:82, 81). However, her worthy resolutions soon fail: she cannot battle hunger, cold, and poverty with her philosophic ideals. In her struggle to be independent Mary is unable to overcome eighteenth-century gender and class prejudices, and the value system of materialistic and morally corrupt society. Eventually she succumbs to despair, unable to conceive of herself as something other than a victim, or the tragic heroine of sentimental fiction.

While we may be bothered by Mary's stubbornness and her insistence on her freedom at all cost, we cannot help but sympathize with her lack of choice as she desperately clings to the only thing left intact: her self-esteem. Preferring 'disgrace, indigence, contempt' to 'the censure of [her] own heart' (2:110–11), Mary tries to find work as a companion, attempts to teach drawing, aspires to learn engraving, embroidery, even copying, but is rejected in all trades because she is a woman with a tarnished reputation. All the men she encounters view her as only a sexual being, not a serious worker. She complains:

I sought only the base means of subsistence amidst the luxuriant and the opulent ... I put in no claims either for happiness or gratification ... yet, surely, I had a right to exist – For what crime was I driven from society? I seemed to myself like an animal entangled in the toils of the hunter. (2:143)

The metaphor of the hunter and prey is a version of the imagery of imprisonment which radical writers often used.[10] But with Hays, and often with other women writers, this metaphor ceases to be merely figurative and instead becomes literalized in the novel. Mary literally becomes a 'prey' with whom Osborne sports.

As Osborne 'entangles' her in his 'toils,' Mary's freedom increasingly becomes curtailed. The theme of dependence found in *Emma Courtney* is reiterated in Hays's second novel. Mary, like Emma Courtney and Wollstonecraft's Jemima, objects to the fact that she has very limited or virtually no means of existing independently of men. As Hays had pointed out earlier in *Letters and Essays*, 'young women without fortunes, if they do not chance to marry ... have scarce any other resources than in servitude, or prostitution.'[11] Hays continues: 'I never see, without indignation, those trades, which ought to be appropriated to women, almost entirely engrossed by men, haberdashery, millinery, & even mantua-making' (*Letters and Essays*, 84–5). In the *Appeal* she objected to the way girls were brought up: 'Indeed there is something so very degrading in the idea of breeding up women, if allowed to be rational beings at all, merely with the view of catching at a husband' (227). While Emma, out of desperation, eventually succumbs to the enticement of marriage with Montague, Hays's second heroine resists absolutely the traditional solution of marriage. Mary refuses her childhood companion William Pelham's sincere offers of marriage because of her notions of duty and honesty. Later she turns down Mr Raymond's proposal that she wed an honest local farmer and become the 'prettiest dairy-maid in the country' (2:30) because her heart is with William. If Emma Courtney's fault is an over-indulgence of sensibility, Mary Raymond's is an exalted sense of honour and self-righteousness. In many instances Mary seems to glory in anticipation of her suffering. After the rape, for example, she refuses William's affection and financial assistance saying: '... let my ruin be complete! ... Dishonour, death itself, is a calamity less insupportable than *self-reproach*' (2:110–11). While it is undoubtedly true that Osborne's will and the implicit condonation of society are responsible for most of her miseries, her exaggerated sense of heroism and desire for independence also contribute to her agony.

That Hays was influenced by Richardson's *Clarissa* and by Godwin's *Caleb Williams* is evident in her depiction of Sir Peter Osborne. He is as villainous, cruel, and full of stratagems as the wealthy and powerful Lovelace or Ferdinando Falkland. But Hays's anti-hero also shares some affinities with Radcliffe's Montoni from the *Mysteries of Udolpho*. Radcliffe and Hays each recognized and made explicit the link between economic and sexual dependence. Both Montoni's and Osborne's abuses of power involve a deprivation of the heroine's material possessions, a parallel which reveals both female authors' awareness of the close connection between money, property, and power.[12] In *Victim of Prejudice* Osborne places Mary at his mercy by systematically stripping away her every means of self-support. First he forces the Nevilles, with whom Mary is staying, to quit the country, thereby using up the little amount of money Mr Raymond intended for Mary. Subsequently he gives her a choice of a debtor's prison, 'famine and destitution,' or the enjoyment of a 'lavish fortune' and pleasure as his mistress (2:167). As his prey Mary chooses 'desolation, infamy, a prison, the rack, death itself' rather than life with Osborne (2:169). At this point the 'magic circle' that Hays wrote about metaphorically in her first novel and in her prose essays becomes literalized into a real enclosure. Mary is no longer merely figuratively or spiritually confined, but physically imprisoned.

To emphasize the falsity of Burke's ideal of the benevolent patriarch Hays deliberately creates an anti-paternal lord in Osborne. Osborne's relentless pursuit of Mary culminates in his emotional and physical abuse of her while she resides with an elderly servant who is trying to cultivate a farm leased on Osborne's property. As squire of estates Osborne offers no protection or aid to his tenants, but instead takes advantage of his power as 'monarch' of the countryside to pursue his prey further. This time he is humbled, implores Mary's forgiveness, and offers her a '*legal* title to his hand and fortune' (2:204). However, Mary, in her most Clarissa-like heroic manner, refuses his proposal. Without prospects or fortune, she still dares to exclaim: 'Think not that I would ally my soul to your's; my haughty spirit, wounded, but not crushed, utterly contemns you' (2:205). In the spirit of the Richardsonian heroine she claims that she wishes but 'to die decently and alone' (2:206).

The conclusion to *Victim of Prejudice* is melodramatic and sentimental. While Clarissa, true to her tragic form, can will herself to die gracefully within a relatively short time after her violation, Mary lives on for two to three years after her resolution to depart from her 'joyless existence' (2:216). Hays does not even allow Mary to expire with the proper dramatic stage effect of a tragic heroine. Writing from the position of a hysteric, Hays is, to use Irigaray's term, 'miming,' and at the same time questioning, a patriarchal means of resolving the loss of female subjectivity. While she is unable to break out of the literary convention of 'killing off' the fallen woman, the prolonged survival of Mary after her sexual violation reveals a hesitancy in following the prescribed formula. The fact that Mary continues to live and fight for her dignity and self-sufficiency long after her loss of virginity is an indication of Hays's defiance of the popular belief in the male ability to manipulate the female through controlling her body. Mary is not merely a 'specularized' object or mirror which reflects a man's desire or his condition: she does not immediately wither to death after being assaulted and then left by a man.

As a contrast to Mary, Hays presents Mrs Neville as an example of a woman who is nothing but a mirror reflection of a man. The whole episode of Mary's reunion with the Nevilles seems rather odd and out of place located as it is in the concluding chapter of the novel. The Nevilles return to England in time to rescue Mary from her 'deadly torpor' (2:214) and nurse her back to health. However, shortly after, Mr Neville perishes from a fatal illness, followed by his wife, who dies from grief. On her deathbed Mrs Neville confesses to Mary that she has been a 'feeble victim to an excessive, and therefore blameable tenderness' (2:225). The use of the word *victim* here links Mrs Neville to Mary and to her mother, who have also described themselves as victims. However, in contrast to the two Marys, Mrs Neville's victimization has been one in which she willingly participated. She explains:

> My husband was worthy of my affection; but I adored him with a fondness too lavish, an idolatrous devotion, in which every other duty has been at length absorbed ... I modelled to his my temper, my character, my words, my actions, even the expression of my feelings. I had no individual existence; my very being was absorbed in that of my husband ... I was the slave, and am at length become the victim, of my tenderness. (2:226, 228)

Rather belatedly Mrs Neville recognizes the loss of herself as an autonomous subject in her lifelong devotion to her husband. She is nothing but a negative of her husband, a victim of what Irigaray calls the 'feminine,' which 'has never been defined except as the inverse, indeed the underside, of the masculine.'[13]

The differences stand out between Mrs Neville, who has, in Irigaray's words, maintained a 'lack of qualities,' remained 'in unrealized potentiality,' in order to 'ensure ... that the male can achieve his qualifications,'[14] and Mary, who has, conversely, always acted as a subject and has refused the position of Other. But what is more significant is their similarity: both Mrs Neville and Mary in their extreme positions remain in 'unrealized potentiality' and are both 'victims' of society. In introducing the Neville case rather obtrusively in the last chapter, Hays reveals her mistrust of the submissive, dependent, and docile ideal female described by conservatives such as Jane West and Hannah More. In other words, though she is portraying the failure and ultimate demise of the independent woman, she is not endorsing her opposite. In fulfilling the duties of a wife, Mrs Neville, too, has suffered because of social and cultural expectations of that role. For Hays, it is still better to have rebelled and lost, than never to have rebelled at all. While Mary may be bodily confined at the end, her spirit of freedom and desire for self-reliance make her life more memorable than those of a dozen Mrs Nevilles.

In fact, in *Letters and Essays* Hays had maintained with assurance that 'bolts and bars may confine for a time the feeble body, but can never enchain the noble, the free-born mind, the only true grounds of power are reason and affection' (23). However, this bold confidence of the earlier work is curtailed by the time we come to the end of *Victim of Prejudice*. The strong-willed heroine is reduced to a despairing and distressed sentimental sufferer, whose only desire is that 'the story of [her] sorrows should kindle in the heart of man, in behalf of [her] oppressed sex, the sacred claims of humanity and justice' (2:231). Since hope of restitution seems lost to her, she bequeaths it rather wistfully to the reader of her memoirs. This pathetic end of the once energetic heroine seems rather disappointing in the light of Hays's earlier vigorous and spirited attacks on men and the customs of eighteenth-century society. It may be a result of the change in climate by the end of the 1790s. No longer were the revolutionaries as optimistic in their belief in reason and the perfectibility of man as at the beginning of the decade. With Robespierre's Reign of Terror and the Napoleonic invasions, the example of France and the revolution proved to be a negative one. In addition, the death of Wollstonecraft in 1797 and the publication of the *Memoirs* of her life certainly did not aid the feminist cause. Like many other Jacobins, Hays was viewed with hostility and retired from the public sphere shortly after the publication of her second novel.

However negative and sentimental the ending of *Victim of Prejudice* seems to be, the work still stands as a powerful reminder of the difficulties faced by a middle-class woman desiring independence in the late eighteenth century. While Hays did not provide her readers with pat solutions to the problems she has raised, her contribution to social change may lie in her vivid depiction, articulation, and literalization of female constraints and victimization. Her observations about tyrannical governments can be applied to gender subjugation: 'It appears to men that all monarchical, and aristocratical governments, carry within themselves the seeds of their dissolution; for when they become corrupt, and oppressive to a certain degree, the effects must necessarily be murmurs, remonstrances, and revolt' (*Letters and Essays*, 17). Hays believed that 'a benevolent mind cannot view with indifference its fellow-creatures sinking into depravation and consequent misery' (*Letters and Essays*, 16). Perhaps Hays felt that the mere portrayal of women as 'victims' in her novel was a step in the direction of social awakening, if not revolt.

CHAPTER FOUR

Resisting the Phallic

A Return to Maternal Values in
Julia

In the previous chapters we have seen how a woman writer's connection with the pre-Oedipal world, or what Kristeva calls the semiotic, influences her use of language. The unsevered link with the maternal binds both Wollstonecraft and Hays in certain ways to literal meaning. In their fiction which actively engages in feminist politics, this attachment to the literal becomes a strength rather than a weakness as the realization of metaphors and the physical rendering of female fears serve to heighten what the authors saw as the power of the Law of the Father and to demonstrate the dangers of the tyrannical patriarch. In the process of refuting Burke's paradigm of the benevolent ruler, Wollstonecraft and Hays discover alternate narrative strategies which, in our culture, I think are more likely to come from a female than a male pen. Replication, repetition, and the weaving back and forth of the same plots and themes may seem tedious to some, but they are techniques which reinforce woman's sense of helplessness, and her social confinement. They may also reveal the insistence and determination of the writers who created these novels. Helen Maria Williams's novel employs a very different approach and has a different effect because it is neither tendentious nor repetitive. I want to argue, though, that it is similarly politically suggestive. In particular, I want to show how association with the pre-Oedipal results in an appreciation of maternal rather than paternal values, or what is sometimes distinguished as a feminine rather than masculine ethos. Indeed Williams's *Julia*, which appears to be a somewhat innocuous sentimental novel, can be read as a strong statement against patriarchy, and an effort to escape conventional roles designed by society for women,

Before examining the novel itself, I want to look briefly at the second half of *Letters Written in France, in the Summer 1790*, which contains the memoirs of Monsieur and Madame du Fossé. Helen Maria Williams and her sister had met the wife of a French aristocrat, Madame du Fossé, in 1786 while she was exiled in England. To Williams the story of her cruel father-in-law's unrelenting pursuit of his son and the heartless imprisonment of Monsieur du Fossé because of his unwillingness to renounce his wife, who was from a bourgeois family, became an example of French aristocratic tyranny under the old regime. The Baron du Fossé, who 'preferred the exercise of domestic tyranny to the blessings of social happiness, and chose rather to be dreaded than beloved,'[1] is an antithesis to Burke's concept of the benevolent patriarch. Williams seems to be answering Burke's idealistic vision of the caring and protective country gentleman in her portrait of the baron: '... he maintained his aristocratic rights with unrelenting severity, ruled his feudal tenures with a rod of iron, and considered the lower order of people as a set of beings whose existence was tolerated merely for the use of the nobility.' The poor, he believed, were only born for suffering ...' (*Letters from France*, 1:124). The deliberate emphasis of class difference, with words and phrases such as 'aristocratic,' 'feudal,' 'lower order of people,' and 'nobility,' is meant to incite the post-revolutionary spirit of indignation and equality.

Just as Burke had deliberately manipulated his narrative so that the account of the king and queen's removal from their palace on 6 October 1789 reads like a family drama, so Williams writes of the forcible separation of the du Fossé family as a moving melodrama. Believing that his father desired a reconciliation, Monsieur du Fossé prepares to leave his wife and little girl in England:

> At this moment a dark and melancholy presage seemed to agitate his mind. He pressed the child for a long while to his bosom, and bathed it with tears ... he continued clasping his infant in his arms, and at length, tearing himself from her in silence, he rushed out of the house. (*Letters from France*, 1:143)

This sketch, with its use of foreshadowing and its details of the emotions of Monsieur du Fossé, is undoubtedly more fiction than fact. Williams is drawing from the tradition of the novel of sensibility in her depiction of the tearful and distressful farewell of the father to arouse the sentiments of her readers. Similarly when du Fossé is locked up in his 'damp and melancholy cell ... without fire,' Williams laments:

Is it not difficult to believe that these sufferings were inflicted by a father?
A father! – that name which I cannot trace without emotion; which
conveys all the ideas of protection, of security, of tenderness; that dear
relation to which, in general, children owe their prosperity, their enjoyments, and even their virtues! (*Letters from France*, 1:156)

The exclamatory remarks, the excessive language, the strong appeal to
feeling, are all characteristics of sentimental fiction. Clearly Williams
was not unaware of the emotional effect or of the political implications
of such a narrative. Her point is that aristocratic lineage, the dignity
of the title of 'father,' and the sense of paternal duty do not guarantee
kindness, generosity, or even humane behaviour towards those who are
powerless. If a flesh and blood father can commit the kind of atrocities
that the baron inflicts upon his son, how much more must we be
prepared to expect from lords who rule people not related to them by
blood.

Like Burke, Williams made explicit the link between the public and
the private spheres by the correlation between du Fossé's liberation
from his family and the liberation of the French people through the
taking of the Bastille on 4 July 1789. For Williams stresses that it is only
with the 'new constitution of France' that du Fossé feels secure of his
freedom and of his rightful inheritance (*Letters from France*, 1:191). She
views post-revolutionary France as 'a country where iron cages were
broken down, where dungeons were thrown open, and where justice
was henceforth to shed a clear and steady light' (*Letters from France*,
1:193–4).

In the light of this enthusiasm for the French Revolution and for the
emancipation that it represents, it seems peculiar that in her novel,
published in the same year as the first volume of *Letters from France*,
there is only one incidental reference to what must have been current
in the author's mind. *Julia* contains a poem entitled 'The Bastille, a
Vision,' which is the only allusion to the contemporary Continental
event. While the poem does predictably describe the horrors of the
dungeon and praise the fall of the 'threat'ning towers,'[2] it seems, on
the whole, unrelated to the characters or to the plot of the novel.
However, if we were to read *Julia* together with *Letters from France*,
specifically the du Fossé narrative, we begin to see some fascinating
configurations emerge. Julia, whom Mary Wollstonecraft in her review
of the novel criticized as too stoic, with 'principles ... so fixed that
nothing can tempt her to act wrong,'[3] can be seen as acting from a
sense of self-preservation in the light of Williams's objections to patriar-

chy and its possible abuses. In not allowing her heroine to let herself be won over by the name of the Father, Williams reveals her ambivalent feelings about the androcentric bias of her society. The novel can also be viewed as Williams's resistance to traditional expectations of woman, later defined in the novels and conduct books of conservatives such as West and More, which the author may have found restrictive and too prescriptive.

In her fiction Williams depicts the patriarchal society of late-eighteenth-century England in distinctly negative terms. The target of satire in *Julia* is the fashionable upper-class society of London with its preoccupation with wealth, social prestige, and political power.[4] While it is true that both female and male characters who represent what Gary Kelly calls 'aristocratic court culture'[5] are portrayed as vile, self-interested, and predatory, the victims of this mode of life are most often women. Julia, though not a victim herself, is frequently associated with the poor and the helpless. She teaches the children of the neighbouring cottagers to read (1:103), makes a habit of visiting the poor, helps an old soldier who was in her grandfather's company (2:7), and writes verses to defenceless birds. Although to modern readers Julia's lines composed for a linnet after a black cat nearly seizes it (1:69), or her elegy dedicated to a young thrush which had fallen down (2:27), may seem excessively sentimental, even pathetically comic, this kind of poetry was an acceptable kind of 'feminine' composition. Williams was in fact praised by the *Monthly Review* for 'the richness and brilliance of the similes,' and the 'elegant' poetry throughout the work. What she is suggesting with the attribution of these verses to Julia, however, is her heroine's sensibility and compassionate quality.

For Julia is set apart from the society she belongs to by her charity and generosity. While feminine sensibility, the woman of feeling, or sympathy for the weak can all be viewed as stereotypical and hackneyed postures, Williams uses these qualities creatively to achieve the central tension of the novel. Sensibility, which I suggested earlier is a heightening of Kristeva's semiotic because of its characteristics of extreme emotion, spontaneity, agitation, and instability, is pitted against itself in the decision Julia has to make. Julia must choose between her own desires, her impulse and need for love, and that of her cousin Charlotte's. While the two options appear to involve a decision between emotion and reason, they are rendered more complex by Julia's genuine affection for her cousin. In other words, she does not merely act out of a sense of duty but, rightly or wrongly, from a sense of life as dependent upon connection rather than competition.

Using twentieth-century feminist theories such as those of Chodorow and Carol Gilligan, I want to argue that Julia's actions represent a feminine or maternal ethos which is contrasted with the self-seeking patriarchal attitude of most of the characters she encounters.

Both Chodorow and Gilligan maintain that women are more concerned with relationships than men are. For Chodorow, one of the results of women's mothering is that

> externally, as internally, women grow up and remain more connected to others. Not only are the roles which girls learn more interpersonal, particularistic, and affective than those which boys learn. Processes of identification and role learning for girls also tend to be particularistic and affective – embedded in an interpersonal relationship with their mothers. For boys, identification processes and masculine role learning are not likely to be embedded in relationship with their fathers or men but rather to involve the denial of affective relationship to their mothers. These processes tend to be more role-defined and cultural, to consist in abstract or categorical role learning rather than in personal identification.[6]

Largely through interviews and observation of women and men Gilligan similarly finds that 'women not only define themselves in a context of human relationship but also judge themselves in terms of their ability to care.'[7] According to her research, one interesting difference in the way the two sexes visualize relationships is that males tend to use a concept of 'hierarchical ordering, with its imagery of winning and losing and the potential for violence which it contains,' while females construct the world in terms of 'a network of connection, a web of relationships that is sustained by a process of communication.'[8] Gilligan argues that this divergence in images results in women's 'vision that self and other will be treated as of equal worth, that despite differences in power, things will be fair; the vision that everyone will be responded to and included, that no one will be left alone or hurt.'[9] One could question the cultural specificity of Gilligan's theories, but there is evidence to suggest that the distinctions she makes were even more applicable in the 1790s than they are today. For instance, in the eighteenth century, women were believed to have a special capacity for sympathy and feeling. John Gregory gave cautionary advice to his daughters because he felt that women were more easily swayed by their emotions, their ability to care: 'The temper and dispositions of the heart in your sex make you enter more readily and warmly into friendships than men. Your natural propensity to it is so strong, that you often run into intimacies which you soon have sufficient cause to repent of.'[10] I am not suggesting, of course, that all women, whether in the eighteenth or twentieth centuries, are more caring and sympathetic than men, but the fact that Williams deliberately highlights these qualities as traits belonging to female characters is significant.

Using Chodorow's and Gilligan's theories to read *Julia* helps us understand the heroine's altruistic decision, which creates the emotional and psychological dilemma for all three of the main characters. Julia chooses to ignore and decline the love and affection of Frederick Seymour, whom she greatly admires, in order that her cousin Charlotte, who had met and loved him first, may be happy. The knowledge that Seymour had transferred his 'most violent' and 'most unconquerable passion' from Charlotte to herself gives Julia 'the most cruel uneasiness': 'Her heart was too pure to think without horror of supplanting Charlotte in the affections of her lover' (1:118). Chodorow's and Gilligan's theories on women's notion of connectedness and the importance of relationships can aid in explaining why Williams has her heroine determine to 'lock the fatal secret' of the attraction between Seymour and herself in her heart, and to 'hasten' her cousin's 'marriage by every means in her power' (1:119). Writing as a daughter who has remained connected to her earliest bonds, which were established in infancy, Williams tries to work out a conclusion to the familiar love triangle that would entail not competition, winning or losing, but instead connection and non-confrontation. Her solution, which is to have Julia resign Seymour to her cousin, may seem oversentimental and impractical but, in fact, is one that is consistent with the feminist theories of Chodorow and Gilligan.

Moreover, Williams emphasizes the friendship between the two women as an important and positive aspect of the heroine's life. In her study of popular novels in England during 1770–1800 J.M.S. Tompkins notes that one innovative feature of women's novels of this time is the sensitive portrayal of women's bonding. Too often male writers showed 'disbelief ... in the capacity of women for friendship, the serious conviction of thinking men, with which some women agreed, [being] that such a relationship could not survive marriage.'[11] In *Julia* the tie between the two girls is shown to be a strong one, dating back to their childhood years. In leaving London, for instance, Julia 'lamented nothing so much ... as her separation from Charlotte' (1:57). Ironically it is Charlotte's high regard for her cousin which confirms Seymour's admiration for Julia: 'Charlotte, who delighted to display the merits of Julia,' gave Seymour 'the most amiable picture of Julia; described her filial tenderness, her candour, her benevolence, and every amiable quality she possessed, with all the enthusiasm of affection' (1:115). The friendship holds no sense of the animosity or rivalry which is conventionally attributed to two women who vie for the love of one man, but instead is characterized by mutual concern and self-sacrifice.

For feminist readers there are many positive aspects in the close alliance between the two females in the novel. As Ruth Perry points out, 'women's friendship, so essential to psychic survival, and so often the most significant mirror for the self,' is 'constantly undermined, conditioned, distorted, and discouraged in patriarchal culture.'[12] Perry contends that

> if we assume ... women's friendship is a natural outgrowth of shared experience and interest ... then whatever blocks, distorts, or interrupts that friendship might be seen as symptomatic of the way the culture undercuts women's power and self-sufficiency. Women's friendship tests the power of women within a culture. Where women are weak, friendship among them is inhibited; and where they are strong, it flourishes.[13]

While it may seem oversimplified to equate the strong bond between the two women in *Julia* with the force of female power within the culture of late-eighteenth-century England, it is nevertheless a notion worth considering. For Williams depicts Julia very much as Austen depicts Emma, at least according to Perry's reading, that is, as a woman sufficient unto herself, who 'does not have to get married.'[14] Julia possesses a small fortune permitting her independence, and she refuses to marry merely for convenience: 'Her heart, delicate, yet fervent in its affections, capable of the purest attachment, revolted at the idea of marrying where she did not love' (1:188). She finds satisfaction and pleasure instead in her charitable deeds, in nature's beauty, and in reading and composing poetry. In fiction, at least, Williams is asserting the possibility of a woman's attaining a position as full subject without being married or becoming the specularized 'other' of a man.

This figure of the self-reliant female can be viewed as a radical statement on Williams's part. Her refusal to conclude her novel by having her heroine marry a suitable man signals a questioning of conventions, both in the form of the narrative and in the social and cultural expectations of woman. The fact that her heroine finds 'consolation in the duties of religion, the exercise of benevolence, and the society of persons of understanding and merit' and 'refuse[s] many honourable offers of marriage' (2:244–5) demonstrates Williams's unwillingness to let her female protagonist be what Irigaray describes as 'a function of the (re)productive necessities of an intentionally phallic currency, which, for lack of the collaboration of a (potentially female) other, can immediately be assumed to need *its* other, a sort of inverted or negative alter ego – black too, like a photographic negative.'[15] That Julia maintains her liberty and right to decide about her own person points to the author's reluctance in making her an object of male desire. For more often than not, historically, a woman's 'development is subject to definitions coming from an other' (Irigaray, *Speculum*, 163). She 'has no gaze, no discourse for her specific specularization that would allow her to identify with herself' (*Speculum*, 224). In making her heroine repeatedly decline the name of the Father by literally keeping her own, Williams is showing her resistance to what Irigaray suggests is a common practice in Western culture – that of a man using a woman to 'duplicate his own identity' (*Speculum*, 235).

Indeed, Julia's obstinacy in remaining single is hardly surprising in the context of the negative portrait of paternal authority found in the du Fossé narrative in *Letters from France*, and in the context of eighteenth-century society as depicted in Williams's novel. While there is no explicit condemnation of Burkean premises about marriage and patriarchy in *Julia*, neither is there an endorsement of these axioms. Not one happy marriage is portrayed in the novel, a fact which seems to suggest, albeit implicitly, that the Burkean paradigm is an illusive myth. As we have seen, the alliance of Charlotte and Frederick proves fatal to the peace of mind of both, but other examples abound. For instance, the union of Mr Seymour to Miss Melbourne is one motivated by vanity and wealth: '... he had married Miss Melbourne, whose person he did not admire, and whose character he disliked, because she had twenty thousand pounds' (1:53). After their nuptials he continues to pursue 'the gratification of his passions with indefatigable perseverance' (1:169) by having amorous intrigues with other women. Another couple who also wedded for financial and social gain, Mr and Mrs Charles Seymour, is described ironically by Williams as living 'together on the most fashionable terms; too careless to regard decorum, and too indifferent to feel jealousy' (2:244). As in the novels of Wollstonecraft and Hays *Julia* disputes the conservatives' belief in the social and moral efficacy of marriage.

As an alternative to a social order headed by a patriarchal figure of authority, an order which is characterized by competition, ambition, separation, and the desire for domination, Williams presents a communal arrangement motivated by caring, connectedness, and sensibility which, according to Chodorow's and Gilligan's theories, would be associated with the female and the maternal.[16] As we have seen, both Julia's and Charlotte's actions stem from well-intentioned and altruistic motives rather than from a sense of rivalry with each other. Williams also makes a point of showing Julia do charity work around the neighbourhood. In addition, two other incidents in the novel point out that Williams may be, in fact, exploring an alternative female-oriented way of dealing with social issues. One is the digressive tale of Sophia Herbert, and the other is that of Mrs Meynell.

The most obvious function of the love story of Captain F. and Sophia Herbert, inserted in epistolary form at the end of volume 1, is to illustrate the 'dreadful ... effects of war' and how war made 'happiness impossible' (1:263). We know that Williams was a pacifist from her youthful poems 'An Ode to Peace,' 'Peru,' and 'The Slave Trade' published in the 1780s.[17] Through sentimentality and pathos Williams points out that war is falsely glorified, and that no conquest is gained without pain and sorrow. She asserts that 'every form of evil and misery is in [war's] train: the groans of despair are mingled with the song of triumph, and the laurels of victory are nourished with the tears of humanity' (1:263). However, perhaps another consequence of the short tale, with its far-away setting of Virginia during the American War of Independence, is to reveal the thematics of women's writing. For as a daughter Williams is able to see differently than a son, as she is only partially within the symbolic order and does not wholly embrace it as a son does. The result is a questioning of, and a complex attitude towards, the figurative and the symbolic.

That war is a form of murder is a common enough platitude, but because Williams literalizes the statement in the short narrative, it creates a powerful impact. For the young girl, Sophia, as her American father and brothers struggle against the English army, war is not the killing of an abstract and unnamed 'enemy'; rather, it is the execution of someone she loves by one of her own family. In her delirium after the news of the death of her lover, the British captain, she hallucinates and mistakenly accuses her patriotic brother of murdering her lover: '... save him ... have you the cruelty to kill him?' (1:259). As a woman writer, Williams, like Wollstonecraft and Hays, understood that the death of the literal was necessary in order to make the symbolic order possible. For war to become a rational and logical enterprise, one has to conceive of human beings symbolically as representatives of the countries of America or Britain. Sophia's inability to see beyond the literal identities of her brother and her lover makes her unable to accept the consequences of the bloodshed, which is in fact a symbolic act.

As with Wollstonecraft and Hays we see that the symbolic or figurative order, in this case accountable for carnage and violence, is not necessarily preferred or privileged by a woman writer. The female character in this case is shown to be dissociated from the symbolic order by her disregard for its nationalistic demarcations. She can only focus on the literal effects of the battle, which are the deaths of her lover and her younger brother. But along with revealing a woman writer's ambivalent feelings towards the symbolic, this digression also illustrates the danger of identifying too closely with the literal. Sophia's inability to see beyond the literal results in her own demise. Upon learning of the death of Captain F. 'there was a wildness and disorder in her countenance,' and the following night 'her reason entirely forsook her' (1:258–9). Shortly after, she 'sunk into almost total insensibility' and died (1:261). While the story seems to be an indulgent means of satisfying the craving of eighteenth-century female readers for sensibility, for tender scenes of distress,[18] it also, shows Williams's awareness of the perils of the connection to the literal. However problematic it can be, participating in figurative conception affords a distancing that enables one to function within the symbolic and largely male order which dominates society.

The other digression from the main plot, the case of Mrs Meynell, is the closest we come in the novel to a refutation of the Burkean belief in the protection and felicity afforded by patriarchy to women. Mrs Meynell's plight is that of the poor gentlewoman, one that we have already seen in both of Hays's novels. Mrs Meynell, née Forbes, is an orphan girl who grows up in her aunt and uncle's household. However, upon the death of her benefactors she becomes a dependent of her cousin, Mr Seymour, who claims to think of her welfare but 'has the assurance to make downright love to her' even though he is married (2:73). To escape his attentions, she weds a 'captain on half-pay' (2:73) who professes to be wealthy. This marriage, however, affords neither economic security nor physical protection, as Mr Seymour continues his vile machinations against her, and Captain Meynell, who turns out to be penniless, treats her with his customary 'sordid meanness, vulgarity, and ill-humour' (2:91). Without using a polemically charged plot, Williams, like the more outspoken Wollstonecraft and

Hays, also invalidates Burke's ideal of the judicious and benevolent husband through the examples of both Mr. Seymour and Captain Meynell. By means of a digressive tale within the narrative proper, then, Williams undermines the logic of the anti-Jacobins and criticizes the society that allows for the abuse of masculine authority.

In addition to social criticism the Meynell story enables Williams to suggest a female-oriented solution to problems engendered by patriarchal culture. Without confronting Mr Seymour or accusing him of charges of attempted adultery or seduction, Julia is able to resolve Mrs Meynell's difficulties, firstly by helping Captain Meynell find an appointment in India, and secondly by inviting Mrs Meynell to 'take up her residence' and 'find an asylum' in Julia and her uncle's house. The ecstatic Mrs Meynell praises Julia for her 'gentleness' that 'heal[s] every wound of [her] heart' (2:184). The narrator comments: 'Benevolence was the ruling passion of Julia's soul. To sacrifice her own gratifications to those of others, to alleviate distress, and to diffuse happiness, were the most delightful occupations of her mind' (2:189). What the author is advocating, in fact, is an ethos based on charity, caring, connectedness, and community. I am suggesting that, according to Chodorow's and Gilligan's studies, this non-confrontational and non-aggressive method of dealing with an issue is characteristically more feminine than masculine. While Williams lived long before the formulation of these theories, her fiction shows that she was, in fact, attempting to work out an alternative means of effective action based on a woman's sense of relationship. Thus, while sexual politics is kept to a minimum in the novel, the aggressive, selfish deeds of the male characters are displayed against the altruistic, affective endeavours of the females. In this way a questioning of masculine values is suggested, albeit implicitly.

Finally, as Janet Todd observes, the 'triangle' of 'two women loving the same man' in *Julia* ends 'interestingly' as 'it is the man rather than the woman who dies under the strain.'[19] Williams seems to have avoided the easiest and most obvious solution, which is the elimination of one of the women in order to end with the traditional heterosexual couple. She does tease her readers with such a 'happily-ever-after' ending when both Julia's and Charlotte's lives are endangered in the last twenty pages of the novel. Julia has an accident in her sedan chair, sustains a cut on her forehead which 'bled violently' (2:207), grows 'pale and thin,' and loses her appetite (2:213); while Charlotte is 'seized with some degree of fever' after the delivery of her son (2:224). However, that Williams refrains from the conventional form of narrative closure has exciting implications for feminist readers. Rachel Blau Duplessis's comments about twentieth-century authors are applicable to Williams:

> To change the story signals a dissent from social norms as well as narrative forms. This is because people are relatively more comfortable with stories whose elements are 'renewed, recreated, defended and modified'; they are naturally drawn to those events, emotions and endings which are recognizable, apparently corresponding to 'experience.' The poetics of critique of the women authors here, that questioning of the construction of gender in narrative form, is cast in very literary terms ('disobeying the novel') precisely because it must distance the reader from codes of expected narrative and from patterns of response that seemed to command universal or natural status.[20]

To replace the old story with a new ending reveals a dissatisfaction with the ramifications of patriarchy involved in the tidy closure of the marriage of the heroine. Instead, Williams chooses to have her heroine 'refus[e] many honourable offers of marriage' and fulfil her charitable and maternal duties by devoting much time to the 'exercise of benevolence' and to the 'improvement' of Seymour and her cousin's child (2:245). While this solution may not be as radical as those proposed by Wollstonecraft or Hays, it nevertheless represents a challenge to the conservative ideal of the docile, submissive wife who defers to the husband. Among other things, *Julia* proposes that love for a man was not the only possible answer in women's lives.

CHAPTER FIVE

Disruption and Containment
The Mother and Daughter in
A Simple Story

Elizabeth Inchbald's first novel was written over a period of a little more than a decade; the first part was begun around 1778, and the second finished by 1789. It has been described as 'autobiographical' and 'pre-Jacobin,'[1] but I want to argue that this work, especially when considered in its entirety as a combination of two parts, shows interesting affinities with the writing of the revolutionary and outspoken feminists of the 1790s. Like the heroines in Wollstonecraft's *The Wrongs of Woman; or, Maria* (1797) and Hays's *Memoirs of Emma Courtney* (1796) Inchbald's Miss Milner is a woman who refuses to be confined within the boundaries of the 'feminine' in the patriarchal order, who resists the ideals of the docile, domestic woman as described in the conduct books and novels of Jane West and Hannah More. She appears instead to desire 'everything' and, in Luce Irigaray's words, wants 'always something more and something else besides that *one* ... that you give them, attribute to them.'[2] That her desire, as a woman, is 'feared' and interpreted as 'a sort of insatiable hunger'[3] can be seen in the efforts of the figures of authority in the novel to curtail and circumscribe both Miss Milner and, subsequently, her daughter, Matilda.

In her brilliant reading of *A Simple Story* Terry Castle focuses primarily on the episode of the masquerade and the significance of the carnivalesque in the first half of the novel. She accounts for the absence of the masquerade in the second half by arguing that 'Matilda's story represents not a disavowal but an internalization of the carnivalesque.'[4] While Castle asserts that 'the topos is bound up with larger failures of continuity and uniformity' (128), she does not develop this notion fully, contending rather that 'the transformational energy of the masquerade in the second half moves into the private world of the bourgeois household, and on a subjective level, into the realm of individual psychology' (325–6). This explanation does not adequately account for the abrupt shift in tone and vigour in the second part of the novel, and it overlooks the ideological implications of the story of the daughter. Castle's reading suggests an optimistic conclusion to the work, an ending in a utopian 'realm of ideal freedom' (295), which I would like to contest.

I want to argue instead that in terms of the psycho-linguistic theories of Lacan, and the feminist psycho-social theories of Chodorow, *A Simple Story* reveals Inchbald's ambivalent feelings about her relation to language and the world of the Father, demonstrating the anxieties of woman's writing in a predominantly patriarchal world at the close of the eighteenth century. As we have seen, the consequences of the retention of the earliest or pre-Oedipal language has fascinating implications for woman's writing. Texts produced by daughters tend to reveal what Julia Kristeva calls a 'subject in process,' rather than a polished finished product.[5] In her attempts to write as a daughter of the symbolic order, a woman often shows ambivalence between the symbolic within which she is trying to function and the pre-symbolic or the literal to which she is still connected. The first story of Miss Milner, then, can be seen as a girl's refusal to participate in what can be described as a Lacanian symbolic order; while the second story of Matilda 'revises her mother's, by having the girl accept her entry into the father's law.'[6] However, this acceptance by the girl of the second generation, deferred for two decades, comes with a price for woman. For the embracing of the daughter by the father is made possible only with the banishment and literal death of the mother, who represents transgression and female desire. Matilda can be received into her father's arms precisely because she, unlike her mother, is non-threatening and submissive to the paternal order.

The contrast between the mother and the daughter has been re-marked and interpreted in various ways. Because of the two-part structure of the novel and the rather problematic final phrase of 'A Proper Education,'[7] traditional scholars have construed the novel's central theme as the 'proper education' of young girls. For example, Utter and Needham summarize the book as follows:

[Inchbald's] *Simple Story* pointed out in 1791 that the trouble with the old model was her education. The heroine, Miss Milner, is too frivolous for

her high-minded husband to do anything with her. That is the thesis of
Part I. In Part II, her daughter, Matilda, is better educated, and has the
better fortune her author thinks she deserves.[8]

Similarly, in examining the 'Reversals and Parallels' in the novel, Gary
Kelly sees 'the contrast of Miss Milner's education with that of her
daughter' as an important 'structural principle.'[9] According to Kelly,
repetition of incidents shows the difference between the characters of
mother and daughter, and proves the latter to be stronger. Matilda
'has no vanity,' is equipped with 'intellectual resources' which her
mother did not possess, and 'attempts to atone for her mother's error.'[10] In privileging the docile daughter at the expense of the disruptive mother, both these readings imply a valorization of female
restraint, submission, and control, characteristics which are idealized
by conservative upholders of the status quo.

One eighteenth-century reader who disagrees with such a view is
Mary Wollstonecraft, who in the *Analytical Review* laments the weakness
of the daughter's character. Of Matilda she writes:

> Educated in adversity she should have learned (to prove that a cultivated
> mind is a real advantage) how to bear, nay, rise above her misfortunes,
> instead of suffering her health to be undermined by the trials of her
> patience, which ought to have strengthened her understanding. Why do
> all female writers, even when they display their abilities, always give a
> sanction to the libertine reveries of men? Why do they poison the minds
> of their own sex, by strengthening a male prejudice that makes women
> systematically weak? We alluded to the absurd fashion that prevails of
> making the heroine of a novel boast of a delicate constitution; and the
> still more ridiculous and deleterious custom of spinning the most pictur-
> esque scenes out of fevers, swoons, and tears.[11]

In examining the function of the two females in the novel, I find that
I am more inclined to agree with this early critic's assessment of
Matilda's character than with that of more recent critics who exalt the
daughter as a paragon or who see her as an emblem of liberation or
of the domestic carnivalesque. If anything, compared to her energetic
mother, Matilda is a figure of compromise and resignation. She is a
descendant of Horace Walpole's Lady Matilda of *The Castle of Otranto*,
who is erroneously murdered by her own tyrannical father, Manfred,
and prefigures Mary Shelley's heroine in *Mathilda*, which depicts the
pseudo-incestuous love and reunion of a sheltered adolescent girl and

her cold, distant father. Like her namesakes Matilda both benefits and suffers from the temperamental passions and love of her domineering father.

My belief that Matilda represents a concession to the patriarchal order rather than an ideal stems from both biographical and textual evidence. The original version of *A Simple Story*, comprising only the Miss Milner and Dorriforth love story, was rejected by Stockdale in 1779. By 1789 Inchbald was working on a more conventional tale and decided to fuse the two into one novel.[12] The success of her plays up to this point must have made her aware of the sort of things late-eighteenth-century audiences enjoyed. In fact, in her preface to the novel she writes that instead of 'heavenly inspiration' the Muses have sent her 'NECESSITY' as a motivation for creation, calling it her 'all-powerful principle' (2). If the necessity to earn a living was forcing her to write, it may have had some influence in the shaping of the second part, as Inchbald attempted to make her work more acceptable to the reading public.

In her other pieces Inchbald reveals that she was conscious of the fact that acceptance into the symbolic order often entailed a sacrifice of female will and independence. In her play called *Wives As They Were, and Maids As They Are* (1797) the ideal wife is the subject of discussion. Lady Priory, who has been taught by her protective husband to practise 'humble docile obedience' and 'to pay respect to her husband in every shape and every form,'[13] says to a libertine: 'Sir, I speak with humility, I would not wish to give offence, but, to the best of my observation and understanding, your sex, in respect to us, are all tyrants. I was born to be the slave of some of you – I make the choice to obey my husband' (4.2 [p. 51]). Rather than didacticism or triumph, it is this attitude of conscious resignation that characterizes the second half of *A Simple Story*, as Inchbald attempts to negotiate between female desire and female compliance.

In contrast to this attitude of submission Miss Milner's story, which constitutes the first part, is one of disruption and subversion. It is indeed, as Castle puts it, about 'law and its violation ... about the breaking of vows, the crossing of boundaries, the reversal of prohibitions.'[14] In Kristeva's terms Miss Milner could be said to represent the semiotic pulsions which are constantly erupting and disrupting the orderly symbolic structure.[15] For instance, upon meeting her for the first time, the normally controlled priest and father-figure Dorriforth experiences an 'agitation of his heart – the remotest sensations of his soul' (13). In his subsequent dealings with Miss Milner he is unable to rely on his rational, intellectual, and ecclesiastical training as she constantly overturns and disturbs conventions and expectations. Modelled after the author herself, Miss Milner is difficult to categorize systematically because she is full of contradictions and surprises: '... there was but one passion which at present held a place in her heart, and that was vanity' (19); yet we are told in the same paragraph that she had 'a heart inclined, and oftentimes affected by tendencies less unworthy' (19); and given an example of her kindness through the testimonies of Mrs Hillgrave and the young Henry Rushbrook. As Miss Milner says of herself at one point: 'I am weak, I am volatile, I am indiscreet, but I have a heart from whence some impressions can never be erased' (69). Vanity and disinterested generosity, volatility and permanence, these are but some of the inconsistencies which make Miss Milner so attractive and dangerous to the stability of the rather austere Catholic household in which she is placed.

Miss Milner's refusal to participate in the symbolic order can be heard in her speech, in her employment of equivocation and suggestion. She makes use of the enigmatic and the feminine in language, which are characteristics associated with Kristeva's semiotic, as revealed in this conversation with Dorriforth:

'You have a greater resemblance of your father, Miss Milner, than I imagined you had from report: I did not expect to find you so like him.'
'Nor did I, Mr. Dorriforth, expect to find you anything like what you are.'
'No? – pray, madam, what did you expect to find me?'
'I expected to find you an elderly man, and a plain man.'
This was spoken in an artless manner, but in a tone which obviously declared she thought her guardian both young and handsome. (15–16)

Here it is tone and implication, gestures and looks more than words, which convey meaning. More than once the narrator comments on the unreliability of language as a means of expression. Inchbald writes: '... how unimportant, how weak, how ineffectual are *words* in conversation – looks and manners alone express' (17). She also notes that high society often speaks 'in the unmeaning language of the world' (18).

While Inchbald here is not writing in the rhythmic, suggestive, poetic language of modern writers like Joyce or Mallarmé, it does seem as if she is writing from what Kristeva has termed the *chora*, which is associated with the maternal and the feminine, 'the heterogeneous, disruptive dimension of language, that which can never be caught up in the closure of traditional linguistic theory.'[16] According to Kristeva the semiotic, which may be manifested in such ways as 'the voice as rhythm and timbre, the body as movement, gesture, and rhythm,' is always present but 'rarely noticed due to the dominance of the communicative function of language.'[17] The pre-verbal semiotic language of gestures, exclamations, looks, and manners, which would have been particularly familiar to Inchbald, who had dramatic training, constitutes a large part of Miss Milner's means of communication and is an element of her attractiveness and her enigma.

Just as she resists symbolic language, Miss Milner also refuses simply to be what Irigaray calls the 'specularized object' of discourse.[18] She is not willing to follow eighteenth-century courtship rituals, which, for a female, meant being the mirror or object of a man's desire and merely having the power of veto in the selection of a partner; rather, she wishes to have the power of choice. When Dorriforth asks her to decide between the rake Lord Frederick Lawnly and the wealthy but rather blasé Sir Edward Ashton, Miss Milner rejects them both. Instead she violates religious, cultural, and social codes by falling in love with her guardian, a Roman Catholic priest, and the man she 'promised ever to obey ... as her father' (13). She confesses her feelings to the horrified Miss Woodley: 'I love him with all the passion of a mistress, and with all the tenderness of a wife' (72). Not only does she break social taboos by adoring the man who is the father-figure in her life, but she is also disregarding church law by avowing passion for a man who has taken the oath of celibacy. By making Dorriforth at once the father, the legal protector, and the priest, Inchbald unites three representative figures of authority in one character. In winning Dorriforth's love and passion in spite of her rebellious tendencies, Miss Milner overleaps the barriers of three cultural structures or institutions. Her triumph, albeit short-lived, can be viewed as a female victory over familial, legal, and religious patriarchal authority. This success is different from what would have been termed in the eighteenth century the prevalence of passion over reason. In the novel Inchbald does not portray Dorriforth suddenly overcome with sexual lust, but instead shows his gradual yielding to the repressed and pre-symbolic side of himself.

In what I suspect to be an ironic tone Inchbald laments that it is Miss Milner's lack of an education (which 'would have given such a prohibition to her love') that is responsible for the 'passion, which had unhappily taken possession of her whole soul' (74, 73). Yet at the same time as she seems to be condemning her heroine, one cannot help but feel that Inchbald is also celebrating this powerful female impulse which goes against social and religious taboos. Descriptions such as 'Miss Milner loved Dorriforth without one conscious check to tell her she was wrong' (74) and, '[her] emotions, which she laboured to subdue, passed, however, the bounds of her ineffectual resistance' (80) serve only to glorify and heighten the strength and the force of feminine feeling. In fact, the first part of the novel can be read as a story of male education,[19] as Dorriforth learns to trust less in language and the symbolic order, and to have more faith in the pre-verbal, semiotic rhythms – gestures, looks, half-articulated utterances – which are associated with the feminine and the world of emotions.

We can trace a progress in Dorriforth's comprehension of the non-symbolic which parallels his education in love and feeling, also taught by Miss Milner. Initially he is confused by Miss Milner, as can be seen in an interview with her about her gallant Lord Frederick. Dorriforth comments: 'Your words tell me one thing, while your looks declare another – which am I to trust?' (51). At the close of the conversation she 'left her guardian ... as much at a loss to decide upon her real sentiments, as he was before he had thus seriously requested to be informed of them' (52). A little further on in their relationship however, he is more able to communicate without the use of speech, Dorriforth pays Miss Milner a visit after her illness:

'It is impossible my dear Miss Milner,' he gently whispered, 'to say, the joy I feel that your disorder has subsided.'

But though it was impossible to say, it was possible to *look* what he felt, and his looks expressed his feelings. – In the zeal of those sensations, he laid hold of her hand, and held it between his – this he himself did not know – but she did. (98)

Here linguistic expression is beginning to be unnecessary as Dorriforth learns to signify with gestures and looks. Ultimately, during the scene before their climactic union, the verbal becomes totally expendable:

She instantly stifled her tears, and looked at him earnestly, as if to imply, 'What now, my lord?'

He only answered with a bow, which expressed these words alone: 'I beg your pardon.' And immediately withdrew.

Thus each understood the other's language, without either uttering a word. (180–1)

At the risk of simplifying the division between the symbolic and the semiotic, between the verbal, linguistic realm of the Father and the rhythmic pulsions associated with the Mother, I would nevertheless associate Dorriforth with the first term and Miss Milner with the second. It is the multiplicity of meanings, the enigmatic, the unspeakable, and unrepresentable within traditional linguistic theory which characterize Miss Milner and make her enchanting to her sober-minded priest and father, who is representative of symbolic law. Writing as a daughter herself, Inchbald would identify with the subversive tendencies in her heroine, who does not negate the pre-verbal, disruptive language, and who refuses to participate fully in the rational, symbolic system of signification.

While I have been arguing here on behalf of the subversive tendencies of the semiotic, I am also aware that this Kristevan concept has its limitations. As Judith Butler puts it:

> [Kristeva's] theory appears to depend upon the stability and reproduction of precisely the paternal law that she seeks to displace. Although she effectively exposes the limits of Lacan's efforts to universalize the paternal law in language, she nevertheless concedes that the semiotic is invariably subordinate to the Symbolic, that it assumes its specificity within the terms of a hierarchy immune to challenge.[20]

The implicit hierarchy of the Law of the Father is reflected in the novel. The author presents a series of transgressions against the patriarch but cannot envision a world other than that dominated by him. As Hays's Emma Courtney has made clear, in Inchbald's day society did not provide women with many alternatives or means of support. Her novel suggests that she understood and attempted to challenge the social and ideological constraints of middle-class women, but could not or did not want to sustain the resistance throughout the work.

Limitations notwithstanding, a number of scenes reveal Miss Milner's capacity for rebellion and disruption through her deliberate violation of the Law of the Father. For instance, she insists on attending the masquerade, an act which surprises Dorriforth, now Lord Elmwood: '... he never suspected she meant to do so, not even at the time she said it, much less that she would persist, coolly and deliberately in so direct a contradiction to his will' (155). This transgression of the forbidden is accompanied by a breach of the prescriptive conventional sexual codes. Miss Milner chooses a costume which 'was ... the representative of the goddess of Chastity, yet from the buskins, and the petticoat made to festoon far above the ankle, it had, on the first glance, the appearance of a female much less virtuous' (155). This equivocal habit demonstrates her refusal to conform to the most common stereotypes of women: in it she is neither angel nor whore, neither the Virgin Mother nor the temptress witch figure. Miss Milner seems to embody both Eve and Mary at the same time. Her evocation of both chastity and sexuality is indicative of the ambivalent and contradictory position in which women are placed, as their subjectivity is constituted by conflicting forces: the desire to be sexually pure, as well as the desire to allure.

Significantly, not only does the costume suggest two dichotomous female roles, but it also tends towards a confusion of gender. When Lord Elmwood discovers that she has gone to the masquerade, he questions two servants about Miss Milner's attire. The footman claims that 'she was in men's cloaths' (160), while her maid swears that she was in 'a woman's dress' (159). These conflicting reports emphasize the equivocal and multiple tendencies of Miss Milner's character. Her outlook, actions, and attitude are not those of a typical eighteenth-century woman; rather, they verge on the androgynous and sexually ambiguous. Her refusal to be categorized into one gender role or the other can be viewed as a disruption, a blurring, of the rigid boundaries that divide the positions of the two sexes in her contemporary society.

Her power, representative of female revolutionary as well as sexual energy and *jouissance*, can be seen by the number of times Dorriforth breaks down and submits to her. Dorriforth's retraction or annulling of promises, vows, and social codes shows the force of feminine will triumphing over masculine law. For example, early in their relationship, in an effort to curb Miss Milner's late-night attendance of balls, plays, and other amusements, Dorriforth commands her 'to stay at home' that evening (29). Expecting defiance and disobedience, Dorriforth is surprised, softened, and pained at her compliance: 'He feared he had treated her with too much severity – he admired her condescension, accused himself for exacting it – he longed to ask her pardon' (32). The episode ends with Dorriforth demanding her 'submission ... a second time' by keeping her appointment (33). That the second patriarchal injunction in fact negates or contradicts the first one is both ironic and touching. The scene is one of a series wherein Miss Milner causes a disruption and overturning of male command or authority.

Another crucial scene occurs when Dorriforth departs from his 'sacred character' and the 'dignity of [his] profession and sentiments' because of Miss Milner (62). Upon seeing Lord Frederick 'devour' Miss Milner's hand 'with kisses' (61) without her approval, Dorriforth acts impulsively and out of character by striking the rake. Immediately after, Dorriforth feels 'all shame and confusion for what he had done' and asks for forgiveness upon his knees before Miss Milner (61). Even she recognizes 'the indecorum of the posture he had condescended to take,' the 'same impropriety as if she had beheld a parent there' (62). This is an example of how the power of the female can result in reversals and disturbances in hierarchical positions and roles. Inchbald reveals how easily social and religious codes, modes of signification, can be disbanded by impulses, bodily drives, and sensations – qualities Kristeva links with the semiotic and female rather than with the symbolic and male.

Miss Milner does not only fulfil her wish to 'stimulate passion, in the place of propriety' in Dorriforth, now Lord Elmwood (115), but also attempts subsequently to test the limits of her power. Miss Milner explains her decision to challenge Dorriforth's authority: 'As my guardian, I certainly did obey him; and I could obey him as a husband; but as a lover, I will not' (154). This statement reveals the extent and limitations of Miss Milner's resistance. It also hints at the suffering she will endure in the last ten years of her life. While she dares openly to acknowledge her defiance of a 'lover' who has no legal authority, she is aware that, as guardian and husband, Dorriforth does have a socially sanctioned power over her. However, once more, she makes him break a vow, this time that they should separate 'for the future' (163) after the episode of the 'forbidden' masquerade. This last negation of a vow results in their union, which happens swiftly and almost anti-climactically. It is as if Inchbald has been preparing us for this culmination all along with the series of disruptions, and felt that she did not need to dwell on the details of the scene.

Lord Elmwood's acceptance of Miss Milner as wife, despite his earlier promises to leave her, represents the final and most significant victory of the feminine in this section. For he receives her in spite of her many violations and her persistent refusal to conform to the Law of the Father. It may seem rather ironic to insist that a courtship which ends in the social, economic, and legal subordination of the woman in marriage is a triumph of what I have been calling the 'feminine.' But in the context of the novel, in which both Lord Elmwood and the priest, Sanford, heads of different patriarchal institutions, relent and go against their word, it certainly seems to be so. Inchbald is careful to show that it is not lust that finally overcomes Elmwood. It is Sanford, the old counsellor, who causes the marriage to take place when he says: 'I now firmly believe, it is for the welfare of you both, to become man and wife' (191). Miss Milner is more than merely an object of desire; she is the one thing that can make 'this world ... dear to' Elmwood (130), as Sanford now acknowledges. Moreover, much can be made of the fact that it is she, not he, who chooses. One scholar believes that the importance placed on love and choice in courtship and marriage is a sign of 'woman's emergent role as affective individual'[21] towards the end of the eighteenth century.

Inchbald recognizes this rather charged and dangerous situation wherein female desire triumphs unmediated by the Law of the Father, and she revises the scenario in the story of the daughter. *A Simple Story* has been compared to Emily Brontë's *Wuthering Heights* not only because of its double narrative structure, which tells the story of two generations, but also because of its communication of the 'reserves of the most intense feeling.'[22] Another work the novel has affiliations with is Frances Sheridan's *Memoirs of Miss Sidney Bidulph* (1767),[23] which tells the history of not two but three generations of women. Like Inchbald's novel *Sidney Bidulph* (Part 1) culminates with a wedding performed in haste between the hero and the heroine, Faukland and Sidney, then Mrs Arnold, the consequences of which are not worked out until the next generation. This tendency of female authors to postpone closure until the next generation may reflect their hesitancy in committing themselves to the finality of submission to the patriarchal order, which they saw as necessary for their being accepted into the symbolic order.

In addition, in order to be widely received by the reading public, writers like Inchbald who wrote from financial need had to be conscious of, and were constrained by, their audience's taste and ideological preferences. To end with the triumph of a rebellious female figure would have offended traditional readers. In Foucault's terms, avoiding this kind of ending would be an instance of self-policing by a woman novelist who has internalized the social system of power.[24] The contrast between generations, then, can be seen as the manifestation of textual self-censorship. But the two opposite ways of dealing with female will and desire represented in the difference between generations can also show the writer's ambivalent attitudes towards the symbolic order and the Law of the Father. Contrasting the two eras becomes a means of questioning the beliefs and assumptions of the patriarchal order, and a means of revealing the consequences of female constraint in more than one example.

In socio-political terms the woman who refuses to submit with docility and grace to the head of the family could be deprived of all the privileges and security afforded by the bourgeois household.[25] In psycho-linguistic terms the all too powerful Mother, who represents chaos, disruption, and female desire, has to be killed, or removed from textuality, and replaced by 'substitutes that resemble the original but without its threatening power and independence.'[26] 'Educated in the school of adversity' and possessing 'an understanding, a sedateness above her years' (221, 216), Matilda, the daughter, 'negotiates the passage from lawless childhood to adulthood within the symbolic order far more successfully than her mother does.' The 'difference between the mother and daughter's stories,' which can be read as 'stories of female development and daughters' relations to language,' is that while Miss Milner's story demonstrates a girl's 'uncompromising choice to remain ... outside of the father's law,' Matilda's story represents the 'compromise that results when the daughter agrees to be incorporated within the law.'[27] She moves from the heterogeneous semiotic realm associated with the maternal into the world of adulthood governed by paternal authority, while her mother's refusal to do so ultimately leads to her exile from society during her last days. Read together, the two daughters' stories outline not only the normal course of female compliance with the symbolic order, but also the cost and the powerful appeal of women remaining outside the law.

There are several passages to signal to us that in the second part of the novel we have entered a radically different world – one where masculine power and authority allow no opposition. Even Sandford, Lord Elmwood's one-time preceptor and friend, comments to Matilda:

> I believe I am grown afraid of your father. – His temper is a great deal altered from what it once was – he exalts his voice, and uses harsh expressions upon the least provocation – his eyes flash lightning, and his face is distorted with anger on the slightest motives – he turns away his old servants at a moment's warning, and no concession can make their peace.
> (223)

Inchbald shows the dangers of such a tyrannical patriarch, and the threats to the powerless in a world where the Law of the Father rules. Another character remarks that Lord Elmwood 'was no longer the considerate, the forbearing character he formerly was; but haughty, impatient, imperious, and more than ever, implacable' (230). Whereas in the first part, Miss Milner, whom we associated with female force and energy, could resist this figure of authority, the narrator says, '...

the magic which once enchanted away this spirit of immutability was no more – Lady Elmwood was no more, and the charm was broken' (251). Even the tone and attitude of the narrator become more ominous and forbidding.

One might say that in the second half of the novel we have entered a world dominated by the Law of the Father. In the light of the events in France around the time of the composition of this section, it is not improbable to link the depiction of Elmwood's attitude and authority with the tyrannical abuse of power in France, and by association, with every household headed by a domestic monarch. Inchbald was to use this association of despotism and domesticity more fully in her second novel, *Nature and Art*, which has been called her 'thoroughly Jacobin novel.'[28] Here, just as Ann Radcliffe, Wollstonecraft, and others would exploit the connection between the familial and the political,[29] in her Gothic-like delineation of the 'magnificent' Elmwood castle, its foreboding owner, and its unnatural restrictions, Inchbald is implicitly criticizing unrestrained patriarchal power. By exposing the harsh and cruel character of Lord Elmwood, who was once priest and guardian, and is now father, Inchbald may be commenting on the hidden but perhaps real nature of masculine authority. Representative of three different cultural, social, and religious institutions, Elmwood is now an unmasked version of the figure of authority. What Inchbald may be suggesting through him is that all forms of paternal power are arbitrary, oppressive, and menacing.

Writing as a daughter, Inchbald reveals a tendency to literalize metaphors and figurative associations in her work. In this section not only is the mother, Miss Milner, killed off in the text, but the mention of her name is forbidden by the father. Elmwood has given an 'interdiction' to every servant and resident at the castle never to 'mention' the 'subject' of Lady Elmwood to him because of her infidelity and indiscreet behaviour (206). The language of the father becomes 'law' here. The extent and cruelty of this injunction are revealed when an elderly gardener at the house, 'a man of honesty and sobriety, and with a large indigent family of aged parents, children, and other relatives,' is dismissed from his position and loses his 'house by the side of the park, his garden, and his orchard' all because he mentioned to Lord Elmwood unthinkingly that 'her ladyship had many years ago approved' of certain plans for the garden (270–2). This capricious use of power can be read as a critique of the despotic possibilities inherent in male authority. Dorriforth could be and once was an example of what Burke would exalt as a benevolent patriarchal figure, but now disappointed and frustrated, has become a cruel aristocratic tyrant in his own household.

Instead of resistance and rebellion from the female figure, however, we find fear and terror. Indeed, Matilda's reaction to her father is very much like the attitude of Gothic heroines to the villainous father or uncle figure – a mixture of virginal attraction and dread in the face of the powerful, the mysterious, and the demonic.[30] As the Gothic intensifies the apprehensions of the everyday, so too does the second half of *A Simple Story*. Domestic space, which is perhaps the only refuge of the feminine, is transformed to a realm of the forbidden, the unattainable, and the representation of paternal ownership. Fathers are no longer protective, loving, and familiar, but become alien, authoritative, and fearful. The household is altered; no longer home and hearth, it is now a prison.

That we have now entered the realm dominated by the Law of the Father is made apparent by Lord Elmwood's strict injunctions. Matilda is permitted to reside in Elmwood Castle only on the condition that she avoid Elmwood's 'sight, or the giving [him] any remembrance' of her mother (213); that is, Elmwood places Matilda under his protection, but his rules require Matilda to be mute and invisible to him. This relationship becomes paradigmatic of woman's position in eighteenth-century patriarchal society, in which women are tolerated, even protected, by their husbands and fathers, but only on the condition that they remain obedient and obsequious. The difference between Matilda's and her mother's attitude to Dorriforth is striking. At one point Matilda 'burst into tears' at the thought of him and felt 'an apprehension at mentioning his name' (217). Whenever Sandford spoke to her, 'she listened sometimes with tears, sometimes with hope, but always with awe, and terror, to every sentence wherein her father was concerned' (218). Upon looking at the 'full length portrait of Lord Elmwood,' she 'shrunk back with fear, and it was some time before she dared venture to cast her eyes completely upon it,' after which she would 'sigh and weep' to it (220). In the neighbourhood she is not acknowledged or visited because of her father's stipulations: '... and as Lord Elmwood's will was a law all around, such was the consequence, of his will being known or supposed' (221). Her excessive weakness, reticence, and apprehension, which had irritated Wollstonecraft, contrast directly with the defiant and wilful attitude of her mother. She embodies the qualities of submission, docility, and deference to masculine will which were considered by West and More as the traits of an ideal wife. However, rather than being intended as a model, she is more likely meant to be indicative of the compromises, the curtailment of female will and desire, to which a woman was expected to submit in order to be accepted into the world of the Father.

That Matilda inspires love in the sincere, but rather helpless, Henry Rushbrook is significant. Ironically it is through Miss Milner's supplication in the previous generation that Rushbrook is now recognized as a relation of the family, and consequently, Elmwood's heir. Rushbrook himself speculates whether his love for Matilda had sprung from 'gratitude and pity' (250) only. As in Brontë's *Wuthering Heights* the romance of the second generation is a paler and more insipid version of that of the first. It does not quiver with the ardour and the passion of the tempestuous Miss Milner's and the stern Dorriforth's relationship. The most courageous thing Rushbrook ever attempts is to mention Matilda's name before Lord Elmwood, an action which nearly costs him his uncle's protection and his inheritance. As a dependent of the figure of authority he is circumscribed by his obligations, gratitude, and loyalty to Dorriforth. His inclination to rebel is checked, and opposition remains indirect. At one point, when he has been advised not to meddle with Matilda's situation, Rushbrook 'bowed ... apparently submissive' but 'took a resolution of paying [her] a visit' (307). Unlike Miss Milner he does not confront the patriarchal lawgiver first-hand, but is ultimately rewarded for his diligence and patience.

What is suggested from this alliance of two relatively delicate and submissive characters is rather fascinating. Certainly, by creating a subdued and gentle male figure as a match for the acquiescent Matilda, Inchbald is depicting a much more moderate, even repressed world. The ending directs us to focus most of our attention on the filial relationship. It is the union of father and daughter, and not the heterosexual union, that is the central concern of the second part of the novel. Indeed, when Dorriforth and Matilda are finally united, Inchbald writes: 'These were the happiest moments she had ever known – perhaps the happiest *he* had ever known' (329). How can Rushbrook ever hope to better the superlative that is already used to describe this connection? While there are hints of the Oedipal complex present in the novel, on the whole the second part suggests more than just a study of a specific psychoanalytically based disturbance.

The short climactic section of Part 2 seems to show Dorriforth relenting, however slightly. Dorriforth 'felt his mind ... too much softened for ... harshness' and is said to be 'milder now in his temper than he had been for years before' (333, 334). Yet I would hesitate to read these developments in the celebratory way Castle does. Dorriforth withdraws some of the rules and laws he has decreed. But Matilda's and Rushbrook's excessive submissiveness and fear of him make the rules unnecessary. In fact, Matilda and Rushbrook have so thoroughly internalized the Law of the Father that they will police themselves. Foucault suggests that it is this 'disciplinary individual' who by the eighteenth century has superseded the 'old accusatory justice' system.[31] That the young people who represent the future will only cower before Elmwood is an indication of the potentially dangerous strength of the patriarchal institutions he represents. Certainly, there is no one in the second generation who matches Miss Milner's energy and obstinacy. The Law of the Father may no longer be as harsh as before, but its power has already made its mark on those dependent upon it.

The overall effect of the depiction of the domineering male figure is to leave readers with an uncomfortable awareness of the inadequacy of the ideal of the benevolent patriarch. Rather than inspiring respect or love, Elmwood's austere authority creates weak and fearful subjects out of those for whom he is supposed to care. His benevolence and protection are revealed to be arbitrary and fickle, dependent upon his mood, sense of propriety, and temper. The first demonstration of his affection for Matilda, the act that finally proves him 'a father' to his daughter, occurs only when violence is about to be perpetrated upon her (324). We are left wondering whether the deed is motivated by love or by a sense of injury to his property. In any case, his temperament offers those who are under him little security. Viewed in this light, the second part of *A Simple Story*, like the feminist novels of Wollstonecraft and Hays of the same decade, also offers a serious critique of the Burkean paradigm of the domestic monarch.

Ultimately the contrast between the stories of the mother and daughter shows the limited subject-positions open to eighteenth-century women. For however liberating and attractive the female energy that is associated with Miss Milner's was, it is disruptive to the patriarchal and symbolic order. Inchbald recognized its power and enchantment but also knew that the death of the maternal, of the heterogeneous impulses connected with the female, was necessary for acceptance into the symbolic order, or the world dominated by the Law of the Father. In *A Simple Story* we see how one writer identifies with the potentiality of female force but then kills off and represses this power in her text because of its dangers. In this way the novel is both a celebration of and an elegy on the energetic possibilities of woman.

CHAPTER SIX

Resisting the Symbolic
Exile and Exclusion in
Nature and Art

Elizabeth Inchbald's second novel, *Nature and Art*, which Gary Kelly says 'was written at the height of liberal ferment in England' and is the author's 'thoroughly Jacobin novel,'[1] is one of the few works of this study with male rather than female protagonists. This use of the masculine perspective may have resulted from the novel's being inspired, according to Kelly, 'not by [Inchbald's] personal experience as a woman, wife, and daughter, but by her experiences amongst the liberals and men of letters of London in the 1790s.'[2] Inchbald may also have felt the need for distancing in this work, which was initially called a 'satire upon the times.'[3] Though she has changed the gender of the main characters, Inchbald does not alter her penchant for stories of two generations – this time she features a pair of fathers and sons who, predictably enough from the title, are representative figures of the opposition between nature and art.

While the two fathers are brothers, they are noticeably different, and I would argue that through them Inchbald is still working out her ambivalent feelings about the patriarchal world or what Lacan calls the symbolic order. For the story of William and his son represents the course of the usual male's entry and integration into the world of the Father, while the story of Henry and his son demonstrates a resistance to this world. Significantly, the Henrys are identified with exile and exclusion, and often associated with the literal, which I have argued is closer to the maternal or the pre-symbolic. On the other hand, the Williams are representative figures of authority, holding both legalistic and religious power. Furthermore, in *Nature and Art*, Inchbald, like the other revolutionary authors we have discussed, turns around the Burkean paradigm of the benevolent patriarch and reveals how domestic chaos can be a reflection of the larger confusion and corruption of a society dominated by the Law of the Father.

As its title suggests, the novel achieves its didactic purpose through the contrasting perspectives of the Henrys and the Williams. Shortly after obtaining a deanship for his brother William through his fiddle playing, Henry becomes disenchanted with English society and sets sail for Africa with his young son. Young Henry, educated among the 'savages,' not taught 'to know habits of English society – nor faults of savages, but only to love his neighbour ... to hold in contempt all frivolous vanity,' and having 'read no books,'[4] is representative of 'nature' – he is very much like Swift's sometimes naïve and gullible hero in *Gulliver's Travels*. Conversely, young William is 'taught to walk, to ride, to talk, to think like a man – a foolish man, instead of a wise child, as nature designed him to be' (1:45). Because Henry is brought up in exile, excluded from culture and society as we know it, his relationship to language and the symbolic order is comparable to that of a woman who, though brought up within society, is often marginalized or excluded from certain social practices and means of self-representation. One could say that unlike William, Henry has not been severed from the earliest, pre-verbal language and has not fully entered into the world of the Father. In psycho-linguistic terms he is still learning to negotiate between the language of the literal and the symbolic, and in the course of this mediation, like a daughter, does not always prefer the non-literal or the Father's world.

Through the young Henry's naïvety and simplicity, Inchbald satirizes the eighteenth-century upper class and their customs. When he first arrives in England, he has trouble with contemporary fashions and is confused by the difference between what one might call the signifier and the signified. Upon entering his uncle's room, for instance, he does not know whether to bow first to his uncle or his uncle's wig, as his uncle seemed to put so much importance on the 'great white thing which grows upon [his] head' (1:63). When the dean explains that wigs are worn 'as a distinction between us and inferior people ... worn to give an importance to the wearer,' Henry replies: 'That is just as the savages do; they stick brass nails, wire, buttons, and entrails of beasts all over them to give them importance' (1:64–5). In Henry's mind there is no distinction between the practices of savages and those of Englishmen, as he has not yet understood the symbolic importance of wigs in contemporary culture. His association of the dean's hairpiece with the ornaments of the Africans enables Inchbald to make a telling statement about the 'savagery' of certain English practices.

Similarly, on another occasion, Henry's adherence to the literal function of language inadvertently becomes a sombre comment on aristocratic customs. The dean tells him that 'in this country, polite children do not call their parents father and mother' (1:68). Henry asks: 'Then don't they sometimes forget to love them as such?' (1:68). To Henry calling one's parents 'father' and 'mother' is equated literally with treating them with the love, devotion, and affection due to them, while other common eighteenth-century appellations such as 'Honoured Sir' or 'Madam' may have seemed unnecessarily affected or formal to him.[5] In the novel Inchbald condemns the tendency towards artificiality and affectation, or 'art,' which to her was often a mask for insincere or duplicitous behaviour.

Young Henry's persistent 'misconception and misapplication of many words' (1:80) result from his connection with literal rather than the symbolic language. Like that of Swift's Houyhnhnms, Henry's vocabulary does not allow for euphemisms or equivocation, which Inchbald saw as the means by which gentility allowed for various forms of unacceptable behaviour. Henry would 'call compliments, lies – Reserve, he would call pride – Stateliness, affectation – and for the monosyllable war, he constantly substituted the word massacre' (1:81). By substituting a more accurate term for the more polite one, Inchbald attempts to get closer to the 'true' meaning of the action, one which is not veiled by figurative language. As I have argued concerning Williams's *Julia*, a connection with the literal often made women writers advocates of peace. Here, for example, Henry cannot distinguish between war and massacre because both occur 'when human beings are slain, who have it not in their power to defend themselves' (1:83). Viewed in this literal manner, war loses its symbolic purpose and hence its justification.

Identification with the literal gives Henry the distance from the symbolic world of the Father, which is the system Inchbald wished to criticize. Difference, which is so necessary to human signification, is revealed to be oppressive to those without power or privilege. Figuration frequently entails ignoring the needs or rights of a section or group of people of a particular race, gender, or class – in this case, it happens to be the poor. For instance, the dean writes a pamphlet praising England's 'salubrious air, fertile fields, wood, water, corn, grass, sheep, oxen, fish, fowl, fruit and vegetables' (1:99). Yet at the same time he informs Henry that there are 'poor creatures who have not a morsel, or a drop of anything to subsist upon, except bread and water' (1:100). When Henry asks why the poor cannot partake of the earth's luxuries, he is told that 'they must not,' and that nothing the earth produces belongs to the poor (1:101). At another point the dean justifies his social position by saying that 'the poor are born to serve the rich,' and when they do so, 'they will be rewarded in a better world than this' (1:77–8) because 'God has ordained it' to be so (1:79). That this passage is strikingly similar to the 'Evangelical defence of the *status quo*,' which was commonly couched in precisely these terms, has been noted by one critic.[6] The dean, like other upholders of the status quo, can maintain his position and his conception of the beauties of nature only by disregarding literal concerns – the needs of the poor, their limited access to the enjoyment of the 'salubrious air, fertile fields, wood, water, corn, grass' (1:99) which he celebrated. Even the belief that the poor will be rewarded in heaven is an abstraction that requires distancing from the literal, which Henry, and Inchbald, who herself as a daughter has close ties to the literal, find difficult. For them the immediacy and the practical concerns of the indigent prevent their total participation in either a figurative appreciation of the country that excludes the destitute or the symbolic elevation of the afterlife.

In fact, what Inchbald demonstrates is that abstraction or figuration, neglecting the literal, can be cruel and heartless. The dean's practice of 'rigid attention to the morals of people in poverty, and total neglect of their bodily wants' (1:53) is hardly an adequate means of alleviating the conditions of the needy. Unlike the dean, who 'forced [the poor] to attend church on every sabbath,' but cared not 'whether they had a dinner on their return' (1:153), Inchbald, like the other revolutionary writers, was very aware of social realities, of the day-to-day and pragmatic requirements of the needy. For all his preaching, someone tells Henry at the death of his uncle, Dean William 'was above speaking to poor folks'; he 'did ... nothing at all for the poor' and used to send them 'to the workhouse. His dogs ... fared better than we poor' (2:176–7).

Those who are most fully entrenched in the symbolic order, those who possess the power in the patriarchal society, are the ones who seem to be most guilty of ignoring the literal or the quotidian. The aristocratic couple, Lord and Lady Bendham, for example, are wholly indifferent to the practical and everyday needs of the indigent. While they themselves are constantly in debt, living beyond their means, they wonder 'how the poor might live most comfortably with a little better management' (1:125). Lady Bendham believes that the needy should feel 'much obliged' to the rich for their charity. Henry, on the other hand, who represents the critical attitude of the author, sees it as 'the greatest hardship of all' that 'what the poor receive to keep them from perishing, should pass under the name of gifts and bounty' (1:128). He thinks that 'Health, strength and the will to earn a moderate subsistence, ought to be every man's security from obligation' (1:128). The opportunity to work, to subsist independently, gives human beings a far greater sense of dignity than being the recipient of charity, which Inchbald sees as only loading 'the poor with obligations, and the rich with praise' (2:145).

In plays such as *Such Things Are* (1787), *Next Door Neighbours* (1791), and *Lovers' Vows* (1798) Inchbald also points out the insensitivity of the rich to the plight of the impoverished and the oppressed. While in these dramatic pieces there is a good-humoured, if somewhat fortuitous, resolution to the problems presented, in *Nature and Art* the abuse of power and the neglect of the needy by the wealthy are shown to have serious and detrimental consequences. For the affluent are also frequently those with political and religious power, as the novel shows. Their corruption becomes an indication of the extent of the degeneration of the nation, if one subscribed to Burke's notion that a family unit was in fact a microcosm of the state. By revealing how there is strife, discord, dissolution, and immorality in the very homes which are supposed to be models of ideal households, Inchbald is able to demonstrate the weaknesses inherent in the Burkean paradigm.

The dean, for instance, who like Dorriforth of *A Simple Story* is important because he is a figure of authority in more ways than one, is shown to be somewhat of a failure in his own home. As a husband and father, as well as a clergyman, he should be able to govern his family or little 'monarchy' with respect and influence. However, his small state seems in disarray as his wife the socialite runs 'from house to house, from public amusement to public amusement, but much less for the pleasure of seeing than for that of being seen' (1:89). As the wife of a man of religion, Lady Clementina, with her vanity and love of earthly pleasure, sets a bad example for the rest of the community. At one point she even becomes the subject of scandal sheets, as she notes: 'My reputation is destroyed – a public print has accused me of playing deep at my own house, and winning all the money' (1:92). That she should be so concerned for the defamation of her character in public without any qualms about the morality of the situation is an indication of her corruption and the unsuitability of her household as a model.

Before the writing of her second novel, Inchbald had already used aristocrats as an object of ridicule. In *I'll Tell You What* (1785), *Appearance Is against Them* (1785), *Everyone Has His Fault* (1793), and *The Wedding Day* (1794), for instance, she makes fun of the amorous intrigues of the upper class. While one may be tempted to excuse their folly, plotting, and sexual perversity on stage as part and parcel of the entertainment typical of Restoration and eighteenth-century theatre, the same kind of indulgence is not extended to them in the novel. The sharp contrast between the attitudes of the two young men – one characterized by self-interest and callousness, the other by love and generosity, – and the telling of the story from the perspective of the wretched, especially towards the end, prevent the light-hearted apolitical attitude which the plays allow. If anything, Inchbald resorts to the appeal of the sentimental, the fiction of sensibility, as a means of enabling her readers to see the materialism and self-centredness of contemporary patriarchal society.

The difference between young William and young Henry – the one who has been brought up within the symbolic order, and the other who for most of his life has been excluded from 'civilized' society as we know it – is most startling in their treatment of the women they meet: 'William the gallant, was amorous and indulged his inclination to the libertine society of women, but Henry it was who loved them' (1:117). In the novel William objectifies and categories women, while Henry feels sincere affection for them. Representative of the artful society of the late eighteenth century, William divides his women into two kinds: those whom he would marry because of family influence and wealth, and those with whom he indulges his sensual pleasures. I want to argue that this distinction is possible only because William participates in the symbolic and the figurative, as it is only by ignoring the literal aspect of the girl or woman whom he seduces that he is able to debauch her, and not feel guilty about his act. Henry neither wishes nor is able to betray the girl of his choice because he identifies intimately with her, rather than seeing her as a symbol of pleasure or an object of male desire.

The second volume of *Nature and Art* could in fact be subtitled 'the wrongs of woman' or even the 'victim of prejudice' because it is here that Inchbald comes ideologically closest to outspoken radicals like Wollstonecraft and Hays. The target of William's passion is a figure oppressed in more than one way: she is female, economically poor, from a lower-class family, and, being uneducated, is described as 'ignorant and illiterate' (1:180). In betraying her trust, William is abusing his power as benevolent patriarch and squire of the country estate. He becomes the antithesis of the Burkean ideal of paternalism when he takes advantage of his position, wealth, class, and education to seduce, abandon, and subsequently condemn Hannah Primrose.[7] Like Dorriforth in *A Simple Story* and his father the dean, young William is vested with more than one symbol of male authority: not only is he the squire, but he becomes a magistrate and therefore a representative of the justice system. His callous treatment of Hannah becomes indicative of the values of the social structures and systems he exemplifies.

Inchbald's awareness that this part of her novel had political implications is demonstrated by the warning she gives her readers just prior to Hannah's narrative:

> Reader of superior rank, if the passions which rage in the bosom of the inferior class of human kind are beneath your sympathy, throw aside this little history ... But you, unprejudiced reader, whose liberal observations are not confined to stations, but who consider all mankind alike deserving your investigation, you will, perhaps venture to read on ... (1:138–9)

This authorial intervention in the narrative suggests that Inchbald was aware of class and social differences not only between her characters, but also between her largely middle-class readers and her subject. The ideological ramifications of the Hannah story are central to the text as is revealed by Inchbald's manipulation of reader response through her association here of the 'unprejudiced' and 'liberal' reader with those with egalitarian sympathies, those who 'consider all mankind alike deserving ... investigation.' The result of this narrative intrusion is that the readers become psychologically prepared to suspend, albeit momentarily, class and social preferences and prejudices for Inchbald's 'liberal' or revolutionary ideas.

The story of Hannah's tragedy is indeed powerful and disturbing. As Mona Scheuermann points out, 'William's carefully detailed destruction of Hannah becomes a symbol of the callousness, cruelty, and stupidity with which the upper class acts in relation to those less powerful than themselves.'[8] William claims to love Hannah to 'distraction' but, as Henry notes, not enough to marry her (1:147). He rationalizes the seduction by saying that the sacrifice of her chastity 'must be her own free choice,' as he has made 'use of no unwarrantable methods ... made her no false promises – offered no pretended settlement – vowed no eternal constancy' (1:148). Yet through Henry's naïvety and identification with the literal, or the immediate, Inchbald makes

William's guilt clear. With full cognizance of the fatal consequences, William systematically courts and woos the innocent Hannah until her love for him encourages her to believe 'she could easily forego ... so precious a sacrifice to him' (1:144). He deliberately obtains 'her heart, her whole soul entire – so that loss of innocence would be less terrifying [to her] than separation from him' (1:145). Subsequently, when his father informs him of the plans to unite him to a Miss Sedgeley, the niece of Lord and Lady Bendham, William then heartlessly orders Hannah never to see or speak to him again.

Hannah's tale may seem overly sentimental or exaggerated, but is, in fact, a dramatic version of the difficulties women encounter as marginalized and often silenced figures in society. Unlike Henry's friend, Rebecca Rymer, who reads and was taught 'to think' (1:133), the cottage girl Hannah is described only in terms of her emotions or sensibility: 'Unhappily, Hannah was endowed with a mind so sensibly alive to every joy, and every sorrow, to marks of kindness ... so liable to excess in passion that once perverted, there was no degree of error from which it would with firmness revolt' (1:132). She is rendered vulnerable to William primarily because of her lower-class roots, but her problems are compounded by her illiteracy, which renders her even more powerless in the symbolic world. In 'The Power of Discourse and the Subordination of the Feminine' Irigaray points out that 'women are "products" used and exchanged by men. Their status is that of merchandise, "commodities".'[9] Irigaray says that 'women's social inferiority is reinforced and complicated by the fact that woman does not have access to language, except through recourse to "masculine" systems of representation' (*This Sex*, 85). In *Nature and Art* Hannah's plight can be read as a manifestation of this crisis of woman's self-expression. Left by William in the village of Anfield, Hannah cannot inform him of her pregnancy because she cannot write. When she receives a short note from him, she treasures the sheet of paper but is unable to decipher its meaning. Through Hannah, Inchbald gives us a perfect example of how women are 'literally' excluded from the symbolic order and have no access to language or 'masculine systems of representation.'

William, on the other hand, can conceive of woman only as a product or commodity, as Irigaray suggests. For him, Hannah was a means of achieving sexual satisfaction, while the woman destined to be his wife is similarly not valued for herself as a subject, but for the 'connections, interest, honours' which would be a result of the alliance. Reflecting on his forthcoming marriage, William 'thought nothing but places, pensions, titles, retinues' (1:170). That he values the public or symbolic over the personal is evident: '... his private happiness William deemed trivial, compared to public opinion' (1:168). Inchbald demonstrates that this attitude is not unique to William but pervades late-eighteenth-century upper-class society. Both William and his wife enter into matrimony for public or material reasons rather than for private, emotional, or spiritual fulfilment. They are contrasted with Henry, who asserts, '... when I wish to ascertain the real felicity of any rational man, I always enquire whom he has to love. If I find he has nobody – or does not love those he has – even in the midst of all his profusion of finery and grandeur, I pronounce him a being in deep adversity' (2:84). That Inchbald values the emotional and the private world may be attributed, according to the theories of Kristeva and Chodorow, to her writing as a daughter who has not completely severed her attachments to the semiotic or the maternal. She would appreciate and valorize connection and emotional ties more than a son, who has had to turn away from the mother.

In addition, Inchbald's insistence through Henry on the importance of familial 'love' and domestic happiness is consistent with Lawrence Stone's observations about the 'rise of the companionate marriage' towards the end of the eighteenth century.[10] Stone argues that among the 'lesser nobility, the squirarchy and gentry, and the professional and upper middle classes ... the choice of a spouse was increasingly left in the hands of the children themselves and was based mainly on temperamental compatibility with the aim of lasting companionship.'[11] Katherine Green argues that this change is part of a 'general shift in consciousness in eighteenth-century England' in which courtship novels played a major role.[12] Green says that 'courtship novelists quietly championed women's rights to choose marriage partners for personal, relational reasons rather than for familial, economic ones.'[13] This gradual alteration in attitude would account for the emphasis placed on the two Henrys' devotion to their wives. Through her association with William Godwin and Thomas Holcroft, Inchbald would also have been influenced by the tenets of the English Jacobins, who, according to Gary Kelly, saw 'the necessity for romance at the mundane level,' and took love to the 'heart of their philosophy.'[14] Kelly notes that these writers meant love in the 'widest sense,' including the 'necessity of philanthropy.'[15] In the case of *Nature and Art* the couple who exemplifies 'nature,' Henry and Rebecca, not only love each other but are charitable to those who are in need, while those who embody 'art,' William and his wife, marry mainly for financial gain and social distinction, and are avaricious and self-indulgent.

The differential valuation of the personal and the public, the semiotic and the symbolic, held by the two young men is further demonstrated in their treatment of Hannah and her illegitimate baby. Henry, who accidentally finds the baby abandoned on the road, pities the infant and brings it home to care for it. Without realizing that he was the father, William self-righteously pronounces: 'Its mother ... ought to have been immediately pursued, apprehended and committed to prison' (2:27). Lord and Lady Bendham, concerned more with appearances than morality, proclaim the seducer 'a vicious youth, without one accomplishment to endear vice ... The youth sinned without elegance, without one particle of wit, or one atom of good breeding' (2:36). The only one who defends the mother is Henry, who observes: '... the father was most deserving a prison, the poor woman had abandoned only one – the man, in all likelihood, had forsaken two' (2:27). Notice here that it is Henry, himself brought up excluded from the world of the Father, who speaks for the mother. The others are not concerned with the literal difficulties experienced by the mother, but condemn a symbolic representation, a whore or harlot stereotypical figure. They can adopt this attitude only by distancing themselves from the real woman, the destitute and suffering mother, and her plight.

Inchbald emphasizes, then, that these people from the upper classes and the aristocracy who, according to Burke, are supposed to be the ideal rulers of their households and, hence, the country do not, in fact, deserve their roles as figures of authority. The author shows how they manipulate power for their own ends and do not come close to the model of the benevolent patriarch. For instance, once Hannah confesses to the dean that the father of the child is William, the incident is hushed up and the name of the father is left unscathed. The dean dismisses the case as an 'affair of some little gallantry' (2:70) on the part of his son, and Hannah is soon exiled from her own family and community, becoming what Hays would call a 'victim of prejudice' in her vulnerable position as a single woman with a tarnished reputation.

What is innovative about Inchbald's story of seduction is not the actual events, because Hannah's life then follows the predictable stages that William Hogarth depicted in his *Harlot's Progress*,[16] but the detailed delineation of her day-to-day or literal concerns and activities. Just as Hays was to rewrite Richardson's Clarissa narrative, Inchbald, too, retells the conventional story of a woman's 'fall' by emphasizing her exclusion from the world of the Father linguistically, economically, and socially. Again I would argue that although the narrative here seems sentimental and excessive, it is a powerful illustration of the lack of social, cultural, and professional alternatives available to single women in late-eighteenth-century England. Poor, uneducated, and illiterate, Hannah becomes an easy prey to the intimidation of those with power and wealth:

> Awed by the rigid and pious character of the new bishop, the rising honours and growing reputation of his son, she ... felt her own unworthiness even to become the supplicant of those great men ...

> ... at length self-defence, the fear of ridicule, and the hope of favour, induced her to adopt that very conduct from which her heart revolted. (2:108–9, 111)

Hannah becomes a prostitute in order to save her own life and that of her son's: '... her feelings of rectitude submitted to those of hunger – Her principles of virtue ... received a shock when she engaged to be the abettor of vice ... but ... was she then to perish?' (2:107). In Inchbald's novel, as in other Jacobin writings such as Godwin's *Caleb Williams*, society, the justice system, and even the church are clearly to blame for the individual's predicament. What is significantly different about Inchbald is that she makes gender as well as class an ideological issue. Here Hannah is forced to adopt a subject-position which she abhors, that of becoming wholly the object of masculine specularization and desire, because all other positions are closed to her.

Implicitly, Hannah's oppression is potentially a version of every woman's in her society as it is was historically structured. Hannah sees herself connected to William through emotional attachments, even without external, public rituals such as a marriage ceremony. To her the semiotic ties, the early affection they shared, and the child they conceived are enough to bind them together. Furthermore, she possesses nothing, neither goods nor shelter – a situation which was not uncommon even for a married woman under eighteenth-century property laws, as Wollstonecraft's *Maria* demonstrated.[17] Conversely, in Hannah's mind, William, the male, has everything. Journeying towards London she reflects:

> William! In your luxurious dwelling! Possessed of coffers filled with gold! Relations, friends, clients, joyful around you! Delicious viands and rich wines upon your sumptuous board! Voluptuousness displayed in every

apartment of your habitation! – Contemplate, for a moment, Hannah, your first love, with her son, your first, and only child, walking through frost and snow. (2:101)

While the juxtaposition of the woman with nothing and the man with everything may seem exaggerated, it can be read as an accurate critique of the patriarchal system that privileges males and places women in total dependence upon their husbands. In the passage above the imagery of the gold, delicious viands, rich wines, and other luxuries is used to highlight the difference between the upper-class, professional male and the lower-class, unemployed female.

A politically effective instance of the literalization of gender and class injustice and inequality occurs near the end of the novel. Inchbald has William destroy Hannah not once, but twice, the second time in a literal way. As a magistrate William is the judge who is presiding at the court where Hannah is brought before the bench and charged with stealing. He sentences her to death for her crime without recognizing her, and she is executed before her letter of appeal reaches him. Thus, as Scheuermann says, 'William's seduction of Hannah is not, as he and his family would have it, merely a youthful indiscretion; it is murder.'[18] This literal destruction is indicative of the extent of the crime Inchbald believed was perpetrated by male figures of authority upon females and the less privileged. These wielders of social and judicial power are revealed to be self-interested and callous, whether intentionally or unintentionally, and very unlike the model of the benevolent patriarch depicted in Burke's paradigm.

Inchbald's strong indictment of patriarchy disintegrates by the conclusion of *Nature and Art*, as she terminates the novel with a rather idyllic, romantic end. The younger Henry returns with his father from the savage lands following an absence of nineteen years. He marries his childhood sweetheart, Rebecca Rymer, who remains the same: as 'it was her mind which had gained her Henry's affection; that mind had undergone no change, and she was the self-same woman he had left her' (2:190). Together they withdraw from society and form a self-sufficient, paradisal community of their own. Settling in a 'hut, placed on the borders of the sea' (2:196), they fish, raise poultry, and tend a garden.

This retreat into nature seems to provide a facile solution to the problems presented in the earlier sections of the novel. Scheuermann says that Inchbald's 'social vision collapses' and that the book 'simply comes up short in its own failed vision,' and dismisses the ending as 'simplistic' and 'absurd.'[19] In contrast, Gary Kelly sees the end of *Nature and Art* not as a failure, but as part of the English Jacobin novelists' tendency to transform 'ideas of general reform' into 'the romance of sympathy.' The 'literary Jacobins' were 'reluctant to engage in direct political action' because of the events of 1794, 'the Treason trials and the nation-wide conservative reaction,' as well as the excesses of the French Revolution.[20] Kelly also argues that sympathy was a 'characteristic response of women,' and adds, 'it is a fair assessment of *Nature and Art* to see it as deliberately offering a woman's solution to the ills of the age, the "condition of England."'[21]

While there is something to be said for both Scheuermann's criticism and Kelly's explanation, I believe that the psycho-linguistic theories we have been using can further illuminate the problematic ending. The retreat into nature is Inchbald's attempt to dissociate herself from the symbolic world, or the Law of the Father, since this world has been shown to be dominated by vicious and corrupt authority figures. While the rustic society established by the two Henrys and Rebecca can be read as an unrealistic withdrawal from society, or a further marginalization of already outcast figures, it can also be read positively as an endeavour to establish an alternative society, one that takes into account one's emotional, or pre-symbolic, desires and needs. The two Henrys, who have both lived outside civilization or the patriarchal world dominated by the Father, can now create a social order in which external or public appurtenances, such as wealth, titles, and social position, are not important. Instead personal, emotive ties and bonds, the concerns of the literal and the quotidian which are usually associated with the maternal, are valorized.

In many ways the conclusion of *Nature and Art* is similar to the end of Voltaire's *Candide,* another eighteenth-century text exposing corruption and evil in the world. One critic has noted connections between Inchbald's second novel and *Candide*[22] but has not related the two endings. In Voltaire's philosophical tale, after Candide undergoes his many adventures and misadventures, he finally settles down with his little group of friends and together they cultivate their garden. A Turkish philosopher advises them that work is the answer to their problems, for work removes the three great evils of life – boredom, vice, and need. In Inchbald's novel work is likewise praised, in a passage which almost paraphrases Voltaire: 'Labour gives a value to rest, which the idle can never taste; and reflection gives to the mind content, which the unthinking never can know' (2:198). Inchbald does not merely echo Voltaire's sentiments; she literalizes then through Henry, who concludes:

> I once ... considered poverty a curse – but after my thoughts became enlarged, and I had associated for years with the rich, and now mix with the poor, my opinion has undergone a total change – for I have seen, and have enjoyed, more real pleasure at work with my fellow labourers, and in this cottage, than ever I beheld, or experienced, during my abode at my uncle's; during all my intercourse with the fashionable, and the powerful of this world. (2:198–9)

This energetic pronouncement valuing a practical solution to the world's problems is slightly undercut, however, by Christian platitudes and the belief in the afterlife. The narrator reassures us that

> we should consider, that it is not upon earth we are to look for a state of perfection – it is only in heaven – and there, we may rest assured, that no practitioner in the professions I have named (physician, soldier, lawyer, king) will ever be admitted to disturb our eternal felicity. (2:202–3)

That *Nature and Art* ends on such an ambiguous note is not surprising in the light of what we have discussed about women's writing. Just as I have demonstrated is the case in Wollstonecraft's fiction, for example, Inchbald's novel shows how a female author vacillates between the literal and the symbolic, between maternal and paternal values. While, for the most part, the novel tends to condemn the Law of the Father, it also reveals a hesitancy with respect to total commitment to the world without the Father, or the pre-symbolic. *Nature and Art* still stands as a powerful critique of eighteenth-century patriarchy, but it also demonstrates the ideological polarities, the historically and socially specific discourses, that were available to a woman at that time.

CHAPTER SEVEN

Contradictory Narratives
Feminine Ideals in
Emmeline

Like Wollstonecraft's *Mary, a Fiction* and Inchbald's *A Simple Story*
Charlotte Smith's first novel, *Emmeline; or, The Orphan of the Castle,* may
be considered a pre-revolutionary novel because of its composition and
publication date of 1788. Yet in this early work Smith already demonstrates a strong feminist sensibility because she, like Wollstonecraft,
Hays, and Inchbald, does not hesitate to criticize patriarchy and its
ideals, especially the belief in the male figure of authority. Unlike the
other more radical and outspoken writers we have examined, Smith
often takes an oblique approach in her critique. The reasons for this
caution or indirectness are financial and practical: the subsistence of
Smith's family depended on the popularity of her work, and so her
novels were written to please and entertain a general public, rather
than to offend. Smith's experience with the translation of *Manon
Lescaut,* for example, taught her that English morals were not as liberal
as French, and therefore not all topics were acceptable to the English
public.[1] Because of her pecuniary straits, she had to be careful of the
subject matter and tone of her compositions.

What I want to demonstrate, however, is that *Emmeline* is by no
means merely a light, delightful, and, by implication, rather innocuous
piece of fiction, as some contemporary readers seemed to believe. Sir
Walter Scott had praised it as a 'tale of love and passion, happily
conceived, and told in a most interesting manner.'[2] Sir Egerton
Brydges called it an 'enchanting fiction with a new kind of delight'
and wondered about the author: 'How a mind oppressed with sorrows
and injuries of the deepest dye, and loaded with hourly anxieties of

the most pressing sort, could be endowed with strength and elasticity to combine and throw forth such visions with a pen dipped in all the glowing hues of a most playful and creative fancy, fills me with astonishment and admiration.'[3] However, its criticism of patriarchy, of the customs of marriage and domestic life, is as vehement as those levelled by more forthright and radical feminists such as Wollstonecraft and Hays. In fact, the novel is a rich blend of romance, sexual politics, and social critique. While I agree with Jane Spencer, who notes in *A Dictionary of British and American Women Writers 1600–1800* that Smith's 'feminist interests are evident in her attempt, particularly in the later novels, to portray strong heroines whose fortitude and intelligence show them to be the equals of men,'[4] I would argue that Smith's feminism is not limited to just the portrayal of role models or 'strong heroines'; rather, it consists of a questioning of the basis of patriarchal ideology. In *Emmeline, Desmond,* and *The Young Philosopher* Smith examines and deconstructs the traditional definitions of domestic felicity and the ideal wife, as they would be presented in the mid-1790s by conservative writers such as Jane West and Hannah More. Mary Anne Schofield says that Smith 'displays her tendency toward unmasking and realism,' and 'uncovers several romantic conventions in *Emmeline*.'[5] It is this rejection and yet, at the same time, conscious employment of romantic convention that create much of the tension in Smith's fiction. She challenges accepted eighteenth-century notions of the importance of woman's sexuality in male/female relationships but seems as if she is perpetuating existing ideologies. Through textual strategies such as multiple plots and double discourses Smith rewrites these concepts, revealing the weaknesses of the ideal, and the constraints on female subjectivity and desire.

Read in the light of Mikhail Bakhtin's notion of heteroglossia, or double-voiced discourse,[6] *Emmeline* becomes a complex narrative containing both a 'dominant' story and other 'muted' stories, what Sandra Gilbert and Susan Gubar identify as a 'palimpsest.'[7] The dominant story, that of the sweet, helpless orphan Emmeline, conforms to the conventions of the romance: the young heroine, relying on her beauty and goodness, survives the trials and tribulations of her entrance into the world and finally marries a worthy and wealthy suitor.[8] But behind this dominant story are two muted ones which do not fit into the fairy-tale-like, happily-ever-after mould. Mrs Stafford's history shows the plight of an intelligent woman of the eighteenth century who is united to an insensitive brute whom she has to respect as husband and authority figure, while Lady Adelina's case examines adultery from the point of view of the so-called 'fallen' woman. Both tales demonstrate the need for reform in the existing social and marital customs. As well they serve to balance or undercut the romance of the dominant narrative.

The female protagonist, Emmeline, is very close to a paragon of virtue, and as Egerton Brydges noted, she is very much like Smith's other heroines. Brydges comments on Smith:

> What are the traits which characterize every heroine delineated by her pen? An elevated simplicity, an unaffected purity of heart, of ardent and sublime affections, delighting in the scenery of nature, and flying from the sophisticated and vicious commerce of the world; but capable, when necessity calls it forth, of displaying a vigorous sagacity and lofty fortitude, which appals vice, and dignifies adversity.[9]

This description of Smith's female characters suggests a valorization of a number of qualities which have also been praised by the other women novelists of this study: simplicity, closeness to nature, personal rather than public or social values, morality, and strength of character. As I have argued in the case of Inchbald's dichotomy of nature and art, the tendency to prefer the natural, the affective, or the unsophisticated reveals an affinity for the traditionally feminine, and in the light of Burkean politics of the 1790s, may also suggest a non-conformist attitude towards the male-dominated world ruled by the Law of the Father. Like Wollstonecraft, Hays, and Inchbald, Smith demonstrates a hesitancy to endorse fully the symbolic or the public sphere, particularly as that world is depicted as greedy, shallow, and artificial.

Like Inchbald's two Henry figures, Emmeline grows up in virtual exile, away from the corrupting influences of society. Up to the age of sixteen Emmeline is brought up by a housekeeper 'in a remote part of the county of Pembroke,' in 'an old building' which belonged to 'the ancient family of Mowbray' (1). This isolation from the materialistic and self-seeking society, combined with her intelligence and 'intuitive knowledge' (2), makes her into a heroine who is capable of thinking and acting independently of conventional societal values. We admire Emmeline from the outset because of her spirited nature. In the all-important question of marriage, for example, she unfailingly makes the right decisions. At the beginning of the novel, though believing herself penniless and friendless, Emmeline nevertheless rejects young Frederic Delamere's professions of love for her even though he is the only son and heir of Lord Montreville. Her thoughts of becoming Delamere's wife show her sound understanding and judgment:

> Splendid as his fortune was, and high as his rank would raise her above her present lot of life, she thought that neither would reconcile her to the painful circumstance of carrying uneasiness and contention into his family; of being thrown from them with contempt, as the disgrace of their rank and ruin of their hopes; and of living in perpetual apprehension lest the subsiding fondness of her husband should render her the object of his repentance and regret.
>
> The regard she was sensible of for Delamere did not make her blind to his faults; and she saw, with pain, that the ungovernable violence of his temper frequently obscured all his good qualities. (73)

Notice that neither rank nor fortune, the values of conventional society, entices Emmeline into 'carrying uneasiness and contention into [Delamere's] family.' She does not wish to let worldly ambition affect familial ties and at the same time is level-headed enough not to be blinded by youthful passion.

In contrast to Emmeline are a number of silly girls in the novel, such as Miss Ashwood, who

> had learned all the cant of sentiment from novels; and her mama's lovers had extremely edified her in teaching her to express it. She talked perpetually of delicate embarrassments and exquisite sensibilities, and had probably a lover, as she extremely wanted a *confident* ... Of the 'sweet novels' she had read, she just understood as much as made her long to become the heroine of such a history herself. (229)

This passage shows that Smith understood the conventions of romance and was not entirely unaware of the ideological implications of art, of the fact that literature can 'interpellate' the reader, offering the reader the position which is most obvious, that of the 'subject in ideology.'[10] In *Emmeline* Smith attempted to create a heroine who, although constrained by her position as a female with no family or fortune, is able to act according to her sense of honour and self-esteem rather than according to the values of the bourgeois or aristocratic world.

One reader who felt that Smith's heroine was a bit too faultless and perfect was Jane Austen, whose character Catherine Morland is a deliberate inversion of Emmeline.[11] Emmeline, with no formal education, only with her 'uncommon understanding, and unwearied application,' 'acquired a taste for poetry, and the more ornamental parts of literature' (2, 4). At sixteen 'her understanding was of the first rank' (6). Later she even teaches herself to draw miniature portraits and to sing, with her voice 'soft and sweet' (41). In *Northanger Abbey* Austen makes fun of Emmeline's flawlessness by making her heroine unable to learn anything before she was taught, unable to play any instrument, and deficient with the pencil.[12] This deliberate parodic treatment, however, does not mean a total condemnation of Smith's works. Parody can often reveal a grudging admiration for the master text.[13] Indeed several scholars have shown how Austen was in fact indebted to Smith and other lesser-known female authors of the 1790s.[14] Nevertheless, Austen's criticism does raise an interesting question of authorial awareness on Smith's part.

Because of the details of Smith's own marriage and other life experiences, we know that the author herself could not have endorsed wholeheartedly the model of docility, submission, and self-sacrifice represented by a heroine such as Emmeline. For in her characterization of Emmeline, Smith adheres to almost all the accepted notions of the ideal woman, one that West and More would have approved of. One could read the character of Emmeline almost as a deliberate exaggeration of the conventional notions of the feminine since she is frequently referred to in epithets of perfection, from the discourse of romance novels, which verge on the ludicrous. For instance, she is an 'angelic friend' (445), one possessing the 'lovely purity' of character (388); Godolphin, her suitor, in ecstatic happiness, pronounces her to be 'adorable, angelic goodness ... best, as well as the loveliest of human creatures' (446); he is enchanted by her 'softness,' thrilled that he is dear to her 'angelic bosom' (488). In her infallibility, her purity, and her self-sacrificing attitude towards both Delamere and Adelina, Emmeline comes close to the incarnation or all the qualities that Virginia Woolf would later term the 'angel in the house' figure:

> She was intensely sympathetic. She was immensely charming. She was utterly unselfish. She excelled in the difficult arts of family life. She sacrificed herself daily ... in short she was so constituted that she never had a mind or a wish of her own, but preferred to sympathize always with the minds and wishes of others. Above all – I need not say it – she was pure.[15]

Woolf explains that it was this figure who haunted her when she came to write, and speaks of the necessity of murdering this angel or phantom: 'Had I not killed her she would have killed me ... For ... you cannot review even a novel without having a mind of your own, without expressing what you think to be the truth about human relations, morality, sex.' According to Woolf, if women are to be this 'angel in the house' figure, they cannot write because they 'must conciliate, they must ... tell lies if they are to succeed.'[16]

I suggest that the dilemma Woolf articulates is precisely the problem which faced Smith as she wrote her many novels. As a woman living in a predominantly patriarchal society, Smith was aware of the subject-position expected of her; she was conscious of the need to sympathize and sacrifice, to 'conciliate' and 'tell lies.' Yet her experiences as wife and mother, as sole supporter of her large family, taught her how difficult it was to sustain this role and even perhaps made it necessary for her to act otherwise in order to survive. In *Emmeline* we see how she works out this predicament by presenting us with multiple versions of the feminine. Consistent with the model of female psychological maturation proposed by such a feminist as Nancy Chodorow, Smith does not confront or 'murder' the 'angel in the house' figure; instead, she attempts a compromise and an accommodation.[17] In her first novel she portrays the 'angelic' figure as well as two other non-stereotypical ones which are more in keeping with her own experiences as a woman and wife in a male-dominated society.

The heroine of the dominant story, Emmeline, embodies all the traditional, proper 'feminine' virtues. In the area where she grew up, for example, the 'ignorant rustics' saw Emmeline as possessing 'the beauty of an angel, administering to their necessities and alleviating their misfortunes, looked upon her as a superior being, and throughout the country she was almost adored' (5). Emmeline's friend Mrs Stafford asserts that Delamere will nowhere meet with 'a more lovely person, a better heart, a more pure and elegant mind' than Emmeline's (62). The narrator comments that unlike others who are 'attentive to pecuniary or selfish motives' Emmeline 'was liable to err only from the softness of her heart' (97). In many instances we are shown her generosity and her sympathy: with Mrs Stafford, who is in difficult financial straits; with Lady Adelina, who needs a nurse and a friend; even with the infatuated Delamere. It is almost as if Smith consciously tried to depict her heroine after a paragon for public approval.

Just as Richardson's *Pamela* uses elements of the Cinderella fairy tale, so Smith's *Emmeline* employs this story of a poor girl turning princess in her novel. Indeed the dominant story can be read as a theme of 'virtue rewarded.' Like Fielding's Tom Jones, Emmeline is a fortunate 'foundling' in many ways. In the beginning she is believed to be an illegitimate, penniless orphan, the 'natural daughter' of Mr Mowbray (1); but by the end, through some papers discovered in ancient caskets, she is recognized as the legitimate 'heiress to a large fortune' (472), the rightful 'princess' and owner of Mowbray Castle. Her aunt, Lady Montreville, who seems always ready to call Emmeline by 'harsh and injurious appellations' (55), and who is full of 'pride and malignity' (133), is a fairly close recreation of the wicked stepmother. Though Emmeline does not attend a ball, like Cinderella, she is swept off her feet by a dashing young prince from the Isle of Wight, Captain Godolphin. Godolphin, noble, generous, and patient, acts as Emmeline's knight in shining armour and escorts her through her difficult period of trials and adjustment. His unselfish nature is demonstrated early on in his friendship with Emmeline: upon discovering that 'his heart was irrecoverably gone,' he avoids her in order 'not to embitter *her* life with the painful conviction that their acquaintance had destroyed the happiness of *his*' (304). He also successfully wards off Emmeline's inappropriate suitors, the gallant Chevalier Bellozane and the impetuous Delamere.

This charming romance, which affirms the belief in moral goodness, the belief that passive female suffering will be ultimately rewarded, is doubtless the aspect of the novel that so delighted contemporary readers like Hayley[18] and Brydges. However, this fairy-tale-like narrative is not the only story in *Emmeline*. Without destroying the appeal of the sentimental tale, Smith nevertheless undercuts it or renders it ironic with the more realistic or 'literal' stories of two unhappily married women. In essence, the 'muted' stories of Mrs Stafford and Lady Adelina deconstruct the myth of the princess as exemplified by Emmeline. Their presence in the novel calls into question the very feminine ideals that Emmeline seems to represent for those around her. For example, female 'purity,' so highly extolled as a virtue in Emmeline, does not become an issue in Lady Adelina's case. Lady Adelina has violated the codes of what Mary Poovey terms the 'proper lady' by not conforming to the ideal of the tractable female, and by flaunting her sexual desire in her adulterous relationship with George Fitz-Edward.[19] But in Smith's novel the detection and the punishment of the sexual transgression are not the key issues. Rather, through the disinterested concern of Emmeline for the so-called 'fallen' woman, readers are given an example of the positive effects of female generosity, benevolence, and charity. Smith outlines the social and psychological reasons behind Adelina's infidelity and, in so doing, makes her readers sympathetic allies rather than judges of her case.

Smith is careful to suggest that it is the circumstances surrounding Adelina's matrimony and domestic life which are responsible for her subsequent action, and not an inherent 'weakness' or susceptibility to depravity in woman that causes the adultery. At fifteen, Adelina, 'just out of the nursery, where [she] had never been told it was necessary to think at all' (211), consents to wed the first gentleman who dances with her at the request of her father. Note that the age of Adelina and the motives of marriage closely parallel the details of Smith's own life. The gentleman's love for her is compared to his fondness for a 'favourite hunter or a famous pointer' (213). 'Neither a friend or a companion ... not even a protector,' Trelawny 'was hardly ever at home' (216). The 'young men of fashion, who call themselves his friends ... make love to [her], with as little scruple as they borrowed money of *him*' (214). Adelina complains that his conversation 'consisted either in tiresome details of adventures among jockies, pedigrees of horses, or scandalous and silly anecdotes about persons of whom nobody wished to hear' (217). Like the author's husband, Benjamin Smith, he gambles away their fortune, goes abroad to flee his creditors, and leaves Adelina to fend for herself.

This situation, somewhat similar to what Smith herself experienced in marriage, sets the stage for Adelina's extra-marital relationship. In her despair Adelina turns to George Fitz-Edward, who tenderly alleviates Adelina's physical, emotional, and, eventually, sexual needs. His appearance at a moment of vulnerability, when she feels abandoned and disillusioned with her husband, makes his actions seem more heroic than usual in Adelina's eyes. Her 'partiality' for him increases until she feels that 'it was no longer in [her] power to live without him' (219, 222). The liaison results in Adelina's pregnancy, and her attempt to hide from Fitz-Edward, from her own 'family, and from all the world' (224). That Smith did not want her readers to think she condoned Adelina's actions is shown in her careful attempt not to be lenient towards Adelina. When Emmeline meets Adelina, she has become a sincere, almost 'extravagant,' penitent,[20] wishing only 'to remain, and to die ... unknown' in seclusion (224). Throughout the novel Smith does not have Adelina see Fitz-Edward again, and only in the last pages of the novel, after the death of Adelina's husband, does she suggest a possible reunion between them.

However, Smith's sympathetic treatment of Adelina, the fact that she allows the heroine to befriend her,[21] as well as the similarities in the depiction of the 'pure' and the 'fallen' woman suggest a challenging of conventional dichotomies. One example of Smith's subversion of

Puritanical values may be the perhaps unintentional lexical confusion of descriptions of Emmeline and Adelina. Both characters are described in practically the same terms, suggesting affinity rather than obvious or distinct differences. For instance, Emmeline is alluded to as the 'lovely orphan' (250); while Adelina has a 'lovely figure' (227). Adelina is full of 'sorrow' and 'regret,' and possesses a 'great sensibility of heart' (227), while Emmeline, too, has a 'tender and susceptible mind' (73), and is frequently depicted as 'melancholy and repining' (72). One could argue that these repetitive passages are clichés from sentimental fiction, but Smith may be using these analogous portraits to question the stereotypical binary opposition of the traditionally 'good' and 'bad' woman, or of the angel and whore figures.[22] Despite her infidelity to Trelawny, for Smith, Adelina is as 'pure' as the virginal Emmeline.

Another subversive strategy is in the conclusion of the Adelina subplot. By not dooming Adelina to a tragic death or to a life of prostitution, the conventional endings for the unfaithful wife who dares defy patriarchal rules of propriety,[23] Smith is implicitly giving a critique of the society and of the literary conventions which support the belief that a woman who expresses admiration, and subsequently, sexual preference for a man to whom she was not legally bound, is in fact a depraved 'monster.' For Lady Adelina, while not 'virtuous' in the traditional sense, is not 'corrupt' either. Her example shows that the distinction between good and evil, purity and iniquity, madonna and temptress, is in fact a more complex issue than the question of mere sexual chastity.

In addition, her affection for Fitz-Edward asserts the presence and validity of female desire, which is a notion contradictory to the ideas espoused by conduct books and by writers such as Gisborne, More, and West. These and other traditional thinkers believed that a wife should have no desires of her own, but should be 'like a Mirrour which hath no image of its own, but receives its stamp from the face that looks into it.' A woman must not only obey her husband, but must bring 'unto him the very Desires of the Heart to be regulated by him so far, that it should not be lawful for her to will or desire what she liked, but only what her husband should approve and allow.'[24] In depicting Adelina's love for a man who is not her husband, Smith is defying these beliefs in female subservience and submission to the male authority figure in her home. Implicitly, she is also opposing the belief in the necessity of the effacement of female desire in matrimony.

Similarly, the history of Mrs Stafford challenges the plausibility of a woman's achieving happiness or domestic felicity solely through marriage and the traditional family. Specifically, her case examines and rejects what Burke would later defend as the notion of the benevolent patriarch as the best ruler of the household. Like the author herself Mrs Stafford is married to one who is not her intellectual equal. In fact, the story so strongly resembles the experiences of Charlotte and Benjamin Smith that biographical studies of the author's life have tended to quote directly from *Emmeline* for illustrations of Smith's own life.[25] One contemporary critic censured Charlotte Smith for mixing life with art. The poet Anna Seward wrote the following after reading the first novel of her rival literary lady: 'Whatever may be Mr. Smith's faults, surely it was as wrong as indelicate to hold up the man, whose name she bears, the father of her children, to public contempt in a novel.'[26] Seward's charge of Smith's 'indelicacy' may be true, but it is precisely the exposition of the unpleasant 'truth' of many domestic arrangements that Smith desired. The Stafford sub-plot not only illustrates the inadequacy of the patriarchal ideal, but also illustrates a woman's economic and social helplessness, and her total dependence on the whims of her husband once she embarks on the marital state.

Like the other revolutionary writers discussed in this book Smith was aware of the illusory pleasure of marriage and was wary of idealizing it as the ultimate goal for every woman. Though many of her own novels have the conventional ending of matrimony, this closure must be read in the context of her own life, as well as the digressive tales or sub-plots of the other female characters in the novels. The inclusion of Mrs Stafford's unhappy conjugality in *Emmeline* makes visible women's frustrations and disappointments. Trapped as a writer as her characters are trapped as women, Smith may not have invented a new ending for her heroine, as Williams did, for example, but she does articulate her dissatisfaction with the social, economic, and psychological reality of marriage. Through Mrs Stafford, Smith demonstrates some of the difficulties encountered in the construction of female subjectivity. Mrs Stafford's subject-position as wife is antithetical to her subject-position as an adult capable of reason and judgment. For as wife in the social order of the eighteenth century she has to submit to the caprices of her husband, even while recognizing their foolishness. Like Geraldine Verney's situation in Smith's most radical novel, *Desmond*, Mrs Stafford's narrative demonstrates that by social and legal definition, a wife was virtually a piece of property to be disposed of as the husband wished.

Mrs Stafford's tale can be read as a 'double-voiced discourse' because of a potentially radical critique behind its seemingly conservative façade, sentimental discourse, and moralistic lesson. While seeming to extol traditional female virtues of compliance, self-sacrifice, and acceptance of woman's lot, the story actually decries the injustice of the power relations structured in matrimony. Mrs Stafford's problem is as follows: despite possessing a 'very superior understanding,' a mind 'originally elegant and refined ... highly cultivated, and embellished with all the knowledge that could be acquired from the best authors in the modern languages' (43), Mrs Stafford is forced to submit to the caprice of her husband, who, 'ever in pursuit of some wild scheme,' was 'fond of improvements and alterations' which never amounted to anything but expense and disappointments for his family (44, 190). Though he is married 'to a woman who was the delight of her friends and the admiration of her acquaintance,' Mr Stafford grew 'irritable in proportion as his difficulties encreased' and 'sometimes treated his wife with great harshness; and did not seem to think it necessary ... to excuse or soften to her his general ill conduct' (177). At one point Mrs Stafford, like the author herself, is reduced to either following 'her husband to a prison, or prevail[ing] on him to go to the Continent while she attempted anew to settle his affairs' (301). Like Wollstonecraft in *The Wrongs of Woman* Smith lets her heroine speak at length about her afflictions, demonstrating that the woman is affected not only by the degradations of her physical conditions – her clothing, food, and shelter – but that she has to undergo mental and spiritual agony as well.

Perhaps the greatest disappointment in Mrs Stafford's marriage is the descent from an upper-middle-class society to that of her husband's lower-middle-class or commercial circle. Mrs Stafford explains:

> ... born with a right to affluence and educated in its expectation, with feelings keen from nature ... to be compelled ... to solicit favours, pecuniary favours, from persons who have no feeling at all ... I have endured the brutal unkindness of hardened avarice, the dirty chicane of law ... I have been forced to attempt softening the tradesman and the mechanic, and to suffer every degree of humiliation ... Actual poverty, I think, I could have better borne. (458)

While Smith makes an impassioned plea on behalf of herself and her heroine, this appeal is limited in its scope to a specifically middle-class sensibility. Here Smith is not advocating a total system of reform which would benefit all who are oppressed, but targets her criticism to a specific social and cultural phenomenon which often circumscribed middle-class women.

Reviewing *Emmeline* in the *Analytical Review,* Mary Wollstonecraft called Adelina 'a character as absurd as dangerous' because of her adultery and her subsequent melodramatic repentance, and contrasted her with the admirable Mrs Stafford and her 'rational resignation.' At this time, relatively young and inexperienced herself, Wollstonecraft praised Mrs Stafford for turning 'to her children instead of to romance' when disappointed in her husband.[27] While Mrs Stafford does seem to be a model of 'resignation,' as Wollstonecraft suggests, the fact that Smith embeds her disagreeable experiences in the midst of a conventional romance draws the reader's attention to the short-comings of both the literary practice of ending with a matrimonial celebration, and the socio-cultural custom of viewing marriage as the answer to every single woman's search for fulfilment. That both Adel-ina's and Mrs Stafford's experiences, which are in the background, influence Emmeline's story, which is in the foreground, is revealed by the heroine herself. At one point when Delamere tries passionately to persuade her to meet and marry him secretly, she refuses as 'she had lately seen in her friends, Mrs Stafford and Lady Adelina, two melan-choly instances of the frequent unhappiness of very early marriages; and she had no inclination to hazard her own happiness in hopes of proving an exception' (230). This comment is an ironic reminder of quotidian reality and hard truth amidst the easy flow of fantasy which seems to characterize the rest of the novel.

Finally, one other aspect of the novel which has often been regarded as Smith's specialty is the use of Gothic elements. In *Emmeline* the Gothic castle with its dark and mysterious passages, the secret papers in ancient caskets, and the tyrannical uncle suggest a similarity to perhaps the most highly developed romance of the 1790s, Ann Rad-cliffe's *The Mysteries of Udolpho,* which was written a few years later. Indeed Smith has been regarded as a forerunner of the genre of Gothic romance.[28] However, the use of the Gothic in *Emmeline* is rather scant and is different in many ways from how it is used by Radcliffe and her followers. Whereas Emily St. Aubert is transported from a pastoral, idyllic landscape to the terror of the castle in Udolpho, Emmeline begins in Mowbray Castle and is restored to it as its rightful owner by the end. For Emmeline, unlike other abducted maidens in unfamiliar surroundings, the castle represents a place of comfort and familiarity: 'There she had passed her earliest infancy, and had known, in that period of unconscious happiness, many delightful hours which would return no more' (36). When she leaves the castle, which was 'still frowning in gothic magnificence' with 'its venerable towers ... the ruins of the monastery ... the citadel ... covered with ivy,' (37), it is with sadness and melancholy. For Emmeline the castle is not a prison; rather, it is a haven or, as one critic says, 'a refuge from ... power.'[29]

It is only with the intrusion of males from the public or symbolic world of the Father that the castle poses any danger to the heroine. Kate Ellis suggests that 'Terror appears in *Emmeline* when she is confronted with sexuality, and thus with a need to assert herself,'[30] but I think terror stems from male invasion and not from female sexuality itself. When besieged, Emmeline eludes those who would assault her virtue by deliberately running into dark, bewildering passages which are known to her. In Smith's novel it is the men who are frightened of the dark. For example, Lord Montreville's French valet, Millefleur, missing a turn, blunders 'about till the encreasing gloom, which approaching night threw over the arched and obscure apartments, through windows dim with painted glass, filled him with apprehension and dismay' (14). When he encounters Emmeline, he attempts to molest her, but she flies 'hastily back through those passages which all his courage did not suffice to make him attempt exploring again' (15). With Delamere, Emmeline similarly escapes from his attention by running 'lightly thro' the passage, which was very long and dark' (33). Emmeline deliberately lets her candle 'fall after her' to confuse Delamere and leave him in 'total darkness' (33). This ability to negotiate the dark long passages of the castle, which are often associated with the feminine, the female body, the mysterious, and the chaotic, suggests an affinity to what Kristeva calls the 'semiotic' or the pre-symbolic world. This capability to function in dark and mysterious passages may also imply a knowledge of or, at least, a certain connection with female sexuality and the body. Implicitly Smith may be pointing out Emmeline's latent female desires or sexuality while depicting her as a seemingly 'pure' and 'angelic' heroine. Appropriately, the castle is where Emmeline experienced youthful 'unconscious happiness' (36) with her care-giver and substitute mother, Mrs Carey. With the death of this mother figure Emmeline is displaced from the cosiness of the feminine Gothic castle, and thrown into the male-dominated world of power and greed.

In psycho-linguistic terms we can read the castle as the place without the Father, where male power, male desire, and even male logic cannot penetrate. The long, darkened corridors where Emmeline moves without a light, 'feeling her way' (31) until she reaches what she believes to be safety is analogous to the area Irigaray describes in 'La Mystérique,' the 'place where consciousness is no longer master, where, to its extreme confusion, it sinks into a dark night that is also fire and flames.'[31] By making her heroine agile at escaping from male predators in a landscape they are unfamiliar with and terrified of, Smith suggests a realm of 'other' which is not dependent upon the symbolic authority of the Father. Emmeline triumphs over her would-be assailants, but the victory is short-lived and rather limited because soon after these incidents she is expelled from the familiar world of Mowbray Castle. The dark passages offer a temporary refuge, but one cannot stay there forever. In a sense, Emmeline has to be educated and exposed to the world outside with its symbolic representation and masculine values before she returns to the castle as its legitimate owner.

In her use of the Gothic, Smith, like Radcliffe, Wollstonecraft, and Inchbald, makes connections between politics and terror, the incompatibility of human reason and a society based on fear and tyranny.[32] In *Emmeline* she hints effects of male domination, arbitrary authority, and the misuse of power as her heroine is forced to flee from one threatening man to another. Paradoxically it is mostly outside of the maternal, dark, and mysterious castle that Emmeline is at risk. Without parental protection, Emmeline is persecuted by the unwanted attentions of the steward, Maloney; young Delamere; the rich old banker Mr Rochely; the handsome but presumptuous Bellozane; and a host of other suitors. She is kidnapped by Delamere at one point but escapes injury because of high fever and her determination not to yield to his impetuosity. However, unlike the novels written after the French Revolution, *Emmeline* does not offer a consistent parallel between castles and tyrants, between domesticity and monarchy. The authority figure in the novel, Emmeline's uncle, is not a complete tyrant or villain like Radcliffe's Montoni. Lord Montreville does show compassion for Emmeline on several occasions, even to the point of defending her against the snobbery of his wife (183), but Smith depicts him as avaricious, self-centred, and, if not cruel, certainly an inadequate patriarch. He claims to possess Mowbray Castle and embezzles the sum of 'four thousand five hundred a year' (433) from the orphan heroine, though almost inadvertently. His legal and financial adviser, Sir Richard Crofts, conceals the truth of Emmeline's birthright from him, thus leading to believe she has no legitimate claim to the estate. However, the fact that Montreville cared so little about his affairs as to trust everything to the cunning Crofts may suggest a subconscious wish to believe in, and a willingness to comply with, the lucrative propositions of his lawyer.

On the whole, the novel is not as radical or forthright as those written by Wollstonecraft, Hays, or even Inchbald. Feminism in *Emmeline* is often manifested in more subversive ways, as we have seen. Through narratives that seem to contradict each other, through the conflation of seemingly 'pure' and corrupt characters, or the depiction of apparently kind-hearted figures who turn out to be not so benevolent, Smith questions the moral and social values of her contemporary society. The explicit challenge to patriarchy was to culminate in a work written four years later, *Desmond, a Novel.*

CHAPTER EIGHT

Revolutionary Politics
Domesticity and Monarchy in *Desmond*

The criticism of patriarchy which was only implied in *Emmeline* becomes explicit in *Desmond*. Published in 1792 during the reactionary period following the French Revolution, *Desmond* is perhaps the most overtly political of Smith's many novels. That the author was aware of the ideological implications of her book is revealed in the Preface, where she states: 'I feel some degree of that apprehension which an Author is sensible of on a first publication ... in sending into the world a work so unlike those of my former writings.'[1] Smith's hesitation can be attributed to several reasons. Firstly, as Diana Bowstead observes, *Desmond* is 'the only epistolary novel among the ten Smith published between 1788–1798,'[2] and Smith was doubtful whether she would succeed 'so well in letters as in narrative' (1:i). Secondly, the novel is feminist in spirit, both because Smith defies the common belief that women 'have no business with politics' (1:iii) and because she makes connections between domestic and political oppression by male figures of authority. In addition, instead of the conventional romance of a single man courting a single woman, as in *Emmeline*, this novel is about 'a young man, nourishing an ardent but concealed passion for a married woman' (1:ii). Lastly, *Desmond*, on the whole, is in favour of republicanism in France, a view which Smith felt 'may be displeasing' (1:i) to some of her readers in that volatile era of the 1790s.

One reader the novel did not please was Sir Walter Scott, who had earlier expressed admiration for Smith's *Emmeline*. He thought *Desmond* a poor work and wrote on 16 March 1826, 'In the evening, after dinner, read Mrs. Charlotte Smith's novel of *Desmond* – decidedly the worst of her compositions.'[3] Nevertheless, it had some influence on him. He borrowed from it, according to Leigh Hunt, 'the foundation of his character of Waverley, and the name besides.'[4] The reason for Scott's dislike of the novel, and its general unpopularity, is its tendentious nature combined with the awkwardness of the epistolary form. In *Desmond* there are long passages which are journalistic-like reports from France narrated sometimes by the hero, but not necessarily experienced by him. These reports are often second-hand accounts of examples either of tyranny under the old system or a new-found freedom under the new. While Samuel Richardson had developed and perfected the epistolary 'writing to the moment' particularly in *Pamela* and *Clarissa*,[5] by the middle of the century, in Smith's *Desmond*, until the third and last volume, there is little sense of the same kind of immediacy or urgency in the letters. One scholar of epistolary form, Janet Gurkin Altman, suggests that letters can be used as 'distance breakers instead of distance makers.'[6] However, in Smith's case, I would argue that the form is used to create distance, not between characters, but between the author and the political beliefs she is expounding. For, as I have suggested with the case of *Emmeline*, because of pecuniary reasons Smith had continually to think of her audience and the selling potential of her novels. Letting her characters hold republican sentiments or morally dubious beliefs was less risky than having them expressed by an omniscient narrator, whom the public might identify with her. Hence, though the epistolary form seems rather contrived, the fact that it allowed for divergent voices and perspectives made it almost ideal.

While in her first novel Smith was careful to make the main plot conform to the conventions of the romance, in *Desmond* she dares to place her own difficulties as wife, the 'muted' story in *Emmeline*, in the foreground. Rousseau's *La Nouvelle Héloïse* comes to mind as the most popular and influential eighteenth-century epistolary novel about adulterous love. Altman suggests that the epistolary form seems 'tailored' for the 'love plot,' particularly the 'novel of seduction,' with its emphasis on 'separation and reunion,' and the 'interrelation of presence and absence.'[7] Smith could have written an epistolary 'best seller' if she had concentrated on the elements of forbidden love and scandal. But in *Desmond* she seems deliberately to have played down the adulterous angle in order to focus the readers' interest on politics. In the early part of *Desmond*, for instance, the love interest plays only a minor role because, as Geraldine is already married with children, Desmond can but worship her from a distance. Compared to other eighteenth-century epistolary novels of seduction, for example, Richardson's *Clarissa* or Laclos's *Les Liaisons dangereuses*, where the love plots are the central focus from beginning to end, Smith's novel discusses a wider range of topics and moves slowly towards the union of the main characters. Desmond reveals that he has 'cherished' his love for Geraldine in secret for 'above two years' before deciding to go abroad for a year (3:48). Then it takes another year and a half before Desmond finally proposes to her. Clearly, for Smith, the passion and progress of the illicit romance are not the only items of interest in *Desmond*.

To illustrate how competing ideologies can shape our conception of actuality in both the public and the personal world, Smith often has a number of characters express their opinions on one incident or subject. At the beginning of the novel, for instance, Desmond confides in Bethel, his former guardian, about his 'dangerous indulgence' (1:1), which is his love for Geraldine Verney. The older and more experienced man serves mainly as a confidant, or a reader within the text, with whom we can identify. As a rather cynical man, he gives us a rational and critical perspective of the hero's infatuation, which he calls a 'wild and romantic passion' (1:14). However, when he confesses that he, too, finds Geraldine attractive, Desmond's folly may not seem so extraordinary to the readers of the novel. At one point he wonders whether 'in endeavouring to cure' Desmond of his infatuation, he has himself 'caught the infection' (2:97). Towards the end he is as much in love with her as Desmond is: 'I never saw a face that gave me so much pleasure in the contemplation of it, as hers does ... her form, too, is, in my opinion, the very perfection of feminine loveliness; yet it seems to owe all its charms to her mind' (3:35). Bethel's conversion to Geraldine's allure is meant to support Desmond's statements about her as a 'model of perfection' (1:53). In making a sceptical intradiegetic reader describe her charms, Smith hopes to then convince us, her extra-textual readers, of the worthiness, rather than the silliness and impropriety, of Desmond's adoration. Bethel's support of· Desmond's love for a married woman becomes a political statement about the integrity of that love, and may help influence readers in their thinking about the validity of the relationship.

One epistolary device which Smith uses in the novel and which has political implications is the withholding of information. Writing from France, Desmond very tantalizingly tells Bethel, without giving an explanation, that he has 'already become unworthy' (2:22) of Geraldine. Only much later do we find out that Desmond was referring to his affair with the unhappily married Josephine de Boisbelle. Furthermore, that Smith was keenly aware of the actual experience of reading and writing[8] is made evident several times in the novel. For instance, the sheer manual necessity of writing is emphasized when Desmond has to have someone else write for him as he is 'wounded by a pistol shot in the right arm' (2:10). In another instance, Smith keeps Bethel and her readers guessing as to the whereabouts of Desmond when Geraldine's life is in peril. Bethel complains to Desmond that his letter is 'not dated, either as to place or time' (3:167), so that he can only surmise that Desmond 'is at a great distance' since he 'receives ... letters, which are sent to the care of his bankers in London, very long after they are written' (3:197). These technical details about the correspondence demonstrate Smith's ability to manipulate the conventions of time and setting afforded by the genre of letters. She did not straightforwardly transfer a narrative into epistolary form without understanding some of its effective uses. As well, the concealment of vital information as a means of subterfuge questions the objectivity of reporting and writing. By omission, Desmond hopes to divert Bethel's attention and conceal the fact that he has been acting as a knight escorting Geraldine in France. This suppression of information becomes vital when it is linked to the politics of the 1790s. In a novel that raises issues about the factual or historical 'truth' of the revolution, Smith shows her awareness of the influence of gaps, omissions, and silences on one's assessment of an event.

According to Smith's novel, one man guilty of erroneously assessing or distorting events is Edmund Burke. In *Desmond* Burke is ridiculed a number of times by the hero and his correspondents. According to Desmond, many facts about the revolution have been misrepresented and 'industriously propagated' by the English (2:60). He contends that 'all the transient mischief has been exaggerated; and we have ... lost sight of the great and permanent evils that have been removed' (2:60). The book 'lately published by Mr. Burke' is not mentioned by title, but called 'an elaborate treatise in favour of despotism written by an Englishman' (2:62). Like Wollstonecraft in her *Vindication of the Rights of Men* Smith criticizes Burke for his rhetorical flourishes: 'Abusive declamation can influence only superficial or prepossessed understanding – Those who cannot, or who will not see, that fine sounding periods are not arguments – that poetical imagery is not matter of fact' (2:62–3). Some of the key issues which Smith's hero takes up are: man's 'right to chuse in what way he would be governed;' the use of 'common sense' rather than 'precedent' and fashion in courts; and the right to speak about or question government without being regarded with 'impudence and madness' and loaded with 'every other crime' Mr Burke can imagine (2:64–5). Smith recognizes one of the weaknesses in Burke's assertion about the divinity of kings when she points out the contradiction implicit in this belief after the ascension of William, who was given the crown by the 'self-elected Parliament' in 1688 (2:67) rather than inheriting the kingship. Smith questions whether the man-made compact of 1688 should be regarded as binding forever if in future there should be another inept or profligate king.

Through her hero's supposedly 'first-hand' view of France, Smith contradicts other statements made by Burke about the revolution. Desmond writes about the 'calmness and magnanimity shewn by the French people, on the re-entrance of the King into Paris' to deny Burke's description of the country's 'bloody democracy' (3:89). At another point Desmond depicts a festive and 'well dressed' group of people in Rouen and mockingly comments: 'this is a specimen of universal national misery – of the fierce and sanguinary democracy so pathetically lamented by Mr. Burke' (3:139). In retrospect, of course, Smith's wholehearted support of the revolutionary government becomes ironic in the light of the execution of Louis XVI the next year, in January of 1793, and of Robespierre's subsequent Reign of Terror. We have to acknowledge Burke's perceptive foresight here. But her enthusiasm for what the republican government represented should not be judged too harshly by our hindsight. Like Williams, Smith was writing as the events occurred and could not predict that the cause which promised liberty and equality to so many would become another form of oppression.

In addition to refuting Burke, the novel also attempts to show the extravagant abuse of power by aristocrats and the otherwise empowered, or the ruling-class hegemony both in England and in France. Once Smith establishes the injustice of despotism in the first part of the novel, she then draws parallels between the situation in governments and the situation at home. A striking example of aristocratic irresponsibility is Lord Newminster, who is lazy and obnoxious, and though a member of the House of Lords, cares not 'a curse for their damned politics' (2:41). As he feeds his favourite dog some chocolate, he states that he would rather 'all the old women in the country should fast for a month,' than that his dog should not have its belly full (1:58). It is not surprising that Smith depicts him as sympathetic towards the equally unrestrained king and lords of France, whose titles have been abolished by what one of his friends calls 'low wretches, this collection of dirty fellows' (1:60). Another vignette of immoderation is that of the two prosperous gentlemen whom Desmond encounters at Dover. While professing to criticize the French for their notion of liberty and for their treatment of the clergy, they callously refuse alms to a starving widow and her children. Their political debate eventually regresses to a discussion of game and fish, at home and abroad, and when they part, the squire invites the clergyman to partake of a feast of turtle soup, 'fat ducks and pigeons,' all ably prepared by the squire's 'negro fellow' (1:90, 91). The ironic implications of the conversation are heightened when Smith calls them 'these two worthy companions of British faith and British liberty' (1:90). While ignoring other people's needs, these heads of religion and the community gourmandise and indulge their bodily appetites, exploiting, if necessary, the freedom and labour of a different class or different race of human beings.

Smith links these insensitive Englishmen to the nobles of France through their shared attitudes as well as through friendships between some of these characters. For instance, the patriotic British squire who professes to 'detest a Frenchman' (1:84) laments one effect of the revolution:

> I understand, that one of the things these fellows have done since they have got the notion of liberty into their heads, has been, to let loose all the taylors and tinkers and frisseurs in their country, to destroy as much game as they please. Now, Sir, what a pity it is, that a country where there is so much, is not ours, and our game-laws in force there. (1:86)

That this country gentleman cares only for shooting rather than the larger consequences of the revolution is ironic. But his support of English game and penal laws, which had been excessively repressive and harsh since the early part of the century, reveals a further streak of inhumanity in this patriarchal figure.[9] The obsession with hunting and the right to hunt is parallel to the attitude of the French Baron de Kermanfroi, who claims to be the 'absolute and only proprietor' (1:261) of all fish that swim in the river that happens to run partly through his property, all 'the rushes, reeds, and willows' that grow near it, and 'all the birds of whatsoever nature or species' that fly across or upon the property (1:261–2). The poor farmer with a property nearby who unluckily injures a pigeon is fined heavily and threatened with the death penalty. Eventually he loses his land and a beloved oak tree because the autocratic baron fancied making a pond on his part of the estate. Such injustices occur in France, but through the association of hunting and game Smith reminds her readers of the dangers of abuse by both the English and French ruling class. At one point Desmond cites the penal laws as one of the 'defects in the structure of the English constitution' (2:130). He points out the horror of the penal laws, 'by which murder, or a robbery to the amount of forty shillings, are offenses equally punished with death' (2:131). Implicitiy Smith is warning the ruling class in her country to beware of becoming as oppressive as its French counterpart.

For the most part, the French aristocrats linked with the *ancien régime* are depicted as tyrannical and dictatorial. For example, in order that their daughters might 'not be an incumberance' on their estate, the family of Desmond's friend Montfleuri 'compelled the second and the youngest of them to become nuns; and married the eldest and the third, who were remarkably beautiful, to the first men who offered' (1:117). In contrast to his parents the '*ci-devant* Marquis de Montfleuri' (1:107), who is held up as a paragon of an enlightened and liberated courtier, attempts to rectify the situation of his sisters by withdrawing them from the monasteries and sheltering one of his unhappily married siblings. His acceptance of his change of status is contrasted with that of his uncle, the Comte d'Hauteville, who refuses to yield his aristocratic title or the privileges of his position. Their attitudes to the revolution and to change are mirrored in the management of their estates. Montfleuri's château is 'an old building, but it is neither large nor magnificent – for having no predilection for the gothic gloom in which his ancestors concealed their greatness, he has pulled down every part of the original strure, but what has actually useful to himself' (1:169). He has endeavoured to bring his estate 'to those plans of comfort and convenience' (1:174) and has made his 'vassals and dependents content, by giving them all the advantages their condition will allow' (1:176). He is indeed an ideal governor, and is much beloved by his dependents, whom he calls 'neighbours' (1:179). The limitations of Smith's radicalism and her conception of liberty can be seen in this instance. By praising Montfleuri, who is depicted as an ideal benevolent patriarch, Smith is not challenging the essentially feudal and patriarchal structure of his estate; she merely decries its abuses.

In contrast to Montfleuri is the Comte d'Hauteville, whose dismal and neglected estates reveal his careless and irresponsible attitude towards his tenants and his property. The château and its surroundings are described in terms of absences, lacks, and negatives. Desmond notes, for example, that in the vineyards, 'people were at work; but we no longer heard the chearful songs, or saw the gay faces that we had been accustomed to hear and see in the Lyonois' (1:203). The grounds are uncultivated, covered with 'grass, where it was not mole-hills' (1:203). What used to be 'an avenue of beech trees' is now 'the ruins of trees' from 'the frequent application of the ax' (1:203). Whereas Montfleuri's tenants were comfortably housed and fed, here 'not a cottage arose to break the monotony of this long line of disfigured vegetation. – Nothing like a lodge, animated by the chearful residence of a peasant's family, marked its termination' (1:204). Smith constantly provides us with an ideal and its unsatisfactory realization by stressing what should be there but is not. Hauteville's estate, like Montfleuri's, has the potential to be a useful and congenial community, but the count's adherence to the old ways – signified by the strong connection of the house with the Gothic, the 'damp, musty smell' and the 'deep gloom' of the rooms (1:212) – prevents it from becoming one. Significantly, it is in this house that Desmond has his one and only nightmare – a vision of Geraldine 'cold as marble' and dying on a bed (1:217). Death and 'dreary horrors' (1:212) are associated with the count, who is against the revolution and change.

Though Geraldine's husband, Verney, is himself not an aristocrat, he is friendly with the titled of both England and France. Depicted always among them, he joins them in their decadence and luxury. The significance of this association is clear: the men who irresponsibly govern the country, who wield power and control the money, are the same who rule thoughtlessly and rashly at home. Like the character of Mr Stafford in *Emmeline* Verney is wild and shiftless, and has squandered the family fortune on hunting, lavish parties, and gambling. Writing from France, Desmond comments, 'In every English newspaper that I have seen since I left London, there is some account of Verney's exploits upon the turf – and of his winnings or his losings' (1:161–2). Perhaps because of her own difficult experiences with an indolent husband, Smith is at her strongest and most vehement in the portrait of Verney. His rare visits home, for instance, cause his wife more pain than pleasure. Of her husband Geraldine says: '... for of the understandings of all women he has the most contemptible opinion; and says, "that we are good for nothing but to make a shew while we are young, and to become nurses when we are old."' (2:32). Geraldine believes that for Verney as well as for 'half the men in the world,' a 'woman even of talents is only considered by man with that sort of pleasure with which they contemplate a bird who speaks a few words plainly' (2:33). This anti-feminist stance of her husband reveals itself frequently. At one point Verney comes home and instead of greeting his family, sends them away, crying: '... away with ye all, there get ye along to the nursery, that's the proper place for women and children' (2:36). This insensitivity towards his wife and children reveals his unsuitability as decision-maker, while his tyrannical attitude is an indication of the kind of 'government' to be expected from him as head of the household.

In *Desmond* Smith does more than merely exploit the contemporary fever of interest in the French Revolution by using it as a topical and interesting background: she uses the revolution to draw a disconcerting parallel between political and domestic tyranny. She refutes Edmund Burke, who had supported the continuation of the monarchical system, made explicit links between the head of the household and the head of the state, and argued for the necessity of obeying both. By likening the despotic and oppressive rule of France's absolute monarchy over its people to Verney's authority over the heroine, Geraldine, Smith shows the inadequacy of the Burkean paradigm of the benevolent patriarch. Using the example of France, Smith points out that just as power is misused in the state, so it could similarly be abused in the family. Geraldine serves as a prime illustration of how the life of a woman of superior understanding and sensibility becomes wasted. For she is perpetually treated as 'object' rather than as 'subject,' first by her father, and later by her husband. Geraldine recalls: 'My father, indeed, would not condescend to suppose that our sentiments were worth forming or consulting ... he was a very Turk in principle, and hardly allowed women any pretensions to souls, or thought them worth more care than he bestowed on his horses, which were to look sleek, and do their paces well' (3:133). Perhaps not coincidentally, the unfavourable association of women with horses is repeated indirectly by Verney. After dismissing his wife to the nursery, Verney changes the subject and asks Bethel if he could buy Bethel's 'hellish clever trotting mare' (2:37). Implicitly, Smith is revealing Verney's presumption that he can exchange women as objects between men just as he does with horses.

Smith literalizes the horrors of eighteenth-century laws which make women virtual commodities or properties of their husbands. Verney commands and uses Geraldine as one would an object, a slave, or an animal. Her case illustrates Hays's and Wollstonecraft's complaints about female dependence. Geraldine herself acknowledges her position when she refers to Verney as 'the unfortunate man whose property I am' (3:148). Irigaray's belief that 'the exchanges upon which patriarchal societies are based take place exclusively among men. Women, signs, commodities, and currency always pass from one man to another'[10] is illustrated in Smith's *Desmond* as Verney attempts to pay off his gambling debts to the Duc de Romagnecourt by actually selling his wife to him (2:289). Here the exchange is not spiritual or symbolic but becomes a physical and real threat to the woman and her body. As Desmond points out, the 'foreigner had considered the sums he lost to Verney, as a sort of passport to her favour' (3:3). As we have seen in the cases of Wollstonecraft, Hays, and Inchbald, writing as a daughter, rather than as a son who tends to embrace the symbolic order more fully, Smith reveals an affinity for the literal or the pre-symbolic. The novel demonstrates how women with or without their knowledge, are used in a literal manner, as counters in the predominantly male society. Verney's selling of his wife's sexual favours realizes the abuse possible in such a paternalistic structure.

In addition, Smith undercuts the validity of the lessons of conservatives such as Hannah More and Jane West by revealing how female submission leads only to further exploitation, rather than to reform in the male figure of authority. Geraldine Verney has learned her lessons from her conduct books well: she obeys her husband without question and without complaint. In the midst of his many acts of folly, she attempts to act as if nothing is wrong. Conscious of her husband's inadequacies and her own unhappiness, Geraldine nevertheless checks her own desire to 'yield too easily to a sensibility of evils' which she feels she should 'bear with equality of mind' (2:79). To her sister she writes: my heart is 'but too apt to feel all the miseries of its destiny – but my children and my duty must and shall teach me to submit unrepiningly to fulfil the latter, for the sake of the former' (2:79). Later, knowing that her husband's demands are unreasonable, Geraldine endeavours to follow his wishes because of what she calls 'duty and obedience' (3:64). Smith demonstrates, however, that this docility only prompts more exorbitant requests from the husband and causes more sorrow for Geraldine. Desmond, and even the rational Bethel, point out the folly of adhering to her husband's commands. Unlike the novels of West and More, Smith's *Desmond* challenges the beliefs of the conservatives, which included suffering in silence, submission without question, and forgiveness at all costs.

As in *Emmeline* Smith uses multiple or parallel plots to illustrate the difficulties created by conflicting notions of woman in the construction of female subjectivity. Geraldine Verney and her French counterpart, Josephine de Boisbelle, are both caught in the struggle to reconcile their conceptions of the dutiful daughter, the faithful and obedient wife, with their own psychic and emotional self-realization. That these subject-positions demand contradictory responses becomes evident when the women become dejected and confused while trying to fulfil the social and cultural expectations demanded of them. Their difficulties can be seen, not as the effect of individual, personal failings, because Smith shows the same thing happening to two women from different countries, but as the result of socially and historically produced structures which maintain power relations that subordinate women, regardless of their skill or intelligence, to men.

Another consequence of the parallel plots is to bring out the notion of female desire. Josephine de Boisbelle, whose plight is very similar to that of the heroine, dramatizes the story of the 'other' as she expresses what the heroine cannot or will not do. Smith uses her as a double, as the woman who enacts the unspeakable and repressed desires of the eighteenth-century proper lady. Safely tucked away in France, she is Gilbert and Gubar's 'madwoman in the attic' figure for Smith.[11] Her similarity to Geraldine is emphasized several times. When Desmond first meets her, he describes her as a 'very lovely and interesting woman' who has a husband who is 'one of the most worthless characters in France' (1:118–19). Like Geraldine, she is 'beautiful and very unhappy' (1:164) and so excites the sympathy of Desmond. Often Desmond tries 'to fancy her' as Geraldine when he is with her (1:187), and Geraldine at one point expresses some 'envy' of 'the opportunity she has had to soothe [Desmond's] hours of pain and confinement' (2:84). Their analogous domestic situations emphasize yet again the connection between England and France as their lives seem to mirror one another.

Both Geraldine and Josephine have been victims of parental tyranny. They have similarly been manipulated by their greedy bourgeois parents, who use their daughters as a means of economic exchange or as a means of social aggrandizement. Geraldine explains: '... riches and high birth were ever the most certain recommendations to the favour of my mother – Merit unattended by these advantages, we were always taught to shun' (3:134). Like the English Jacobin novelists such as Godwin, Holcroft, and Bage, Smith was advocating a 'progressive' rather than a 'fixed' society wherein people were to be judged by individual merit rather than ranked by birth or class.[12] She attacks the upper-class and aristocratic practices of matchmaking and matrimony based solely on wealth and rank. Geraldine elaborates:

... for every single man of large fortune, though decrepid with age, or distorted by the hand of Nature, though half an ideot from his birth, or rendered worse than an ideot by debauchery, we were taught to throw our encouragement; and, I really believe, if the wandering Jew, or the yellow dwarf, or any other fabled being of hideous description, could have been sent on earth to have personified men of eight or ten thousand a year, we should have found it difficult to have escaped being married to them, if they had offered good settlements. (3:133–4)

This description, verging on the satiric and the ludicrous, nevertheless illustrates the contemporary custom of using women as counters, using them as commodities to be bartered on the market. In a corresponding way, Josephine de Boisbelle's parents have given very little thought to their daughters as human beings, as subjects rather than objects of economic exchange. Josephine complains that she, too, has been 'betrayed ... into marriage with a man, for whom it was impossible she ever could either feel love or esteem' and that as a consequence she suffers from 'all the miseries of such a connection' and feels that 'her life is irrecoverably dashed' (1:274).

However, the similarities between the two women end here. The 'other' woman, Josephine, whose dilemma is comparable to that of the pure and suffering heroine, does not remain passive, obedient, and dedicated to her husband. For through her adulterous relationship with Desmond, Josephine de Boisbelle rebels against the conservative prescriptions of wife and proper woman, who was by definition supposed to mould all her desires to suit her husband's will. While Geraldine had only rather wistfully expressed an abstract regard for Desmond, Josephine acts upon it. Geraldine comments at one point: 'But why should it be wrong to admire and esteem an excellent and amiable man, from whom I have received more than brotherly kindness?' (2:255). She wonders whether being married can 'prevent our seeing and loving excellence wherever found?' (2:256). But despite her inclinations she remains submissive, faithful, and obedient to her husband and their marriage vows. Josephine, however, actually indulges her passion and love for Desmond, giving him her 'gay and unguarded heart' (3:338) and body. Through the breaking of her promises made at matrimony, Josephine reveals her own suppressed desires and those of other similarly unhappily married women. Her attempts to break out of her forced marriage, which is for her a form of prison just as the convent was for her sisters, reveal how being a wife and mother does not necessarily mean felicity for the woman, contrary to the lessons of the conservative novelists.

Placed side by side, Geraldine's and Josephine's responses to the same situation can be viewed as Smith's desire to accommodate rather than to confront patriarchal authorities. In this sense, which is in keeping with the model of female psychological maturation proposed by feminists such as Nancy Chodorow, the creation of the angel and the 'madwoman' or 'other' figure can be understood as the 'articulation of simultaneous, if contradictory, self-images.'[13] For while Geraldine, like Emmeline and to a certain extent Mrs Stafford, is a model of feminine virtue, at the same time the presence of the French woman, Josephine, or Lady Adelina in the first novel, who dares to follow her inclination, illustrates the difficulties, if not the impossibility, of attaining the paradigmatic ideals. Smith's artistry is manifested in her ability to appear to conform with, rather than to confront, conventional beliefs about female subservience in her main plot. Without antagonizing her readers, and thus jeopardizing her 'professional' career, she nevertheless challenges notions of wifely submission and the belief that women possessed or should possess little or no sexual desire.

In *Desmond* as in *Emmeline* Smith resists the straightforward simplicity of a one-heroine story. Instead she opts for the richness of multiplicity, for doubling and echoing, for the mingling of the political and the personal, giving her readers the actual details of domestic difficulties without seeming to subvert the patriarchal structure, without directly confronting the assumptions of male authority and female submission. For the most part, the background or 'other' voices disrupt the sanctity and the acceptability of the foregrounded story, whether it be of the exemplary woman or of exemplary England. These marginal tales suggest the possibility of a breakdown of order, a revolution of ideas, and show how completely at the mercy of paternal power every woman is, a suggestion that may well work to undermine any redemptive value in the romantic notion of the perfect marriage or, by analogy, the perfect Burkean household. Thus the politics in *Desmond*, at once national and sexual, are as crucial as its romantic narrative.

CHAPTER NINE

Celebrating the Ex-Centric
Maternal Influence in
The Young Philosopher

Though one early critic has categorized Charlotte Smith's *The Young Philosopher* (1798) as marking the third stage of English revolutionism – from initial sympathy with the French reformers, to reaction against the excesses of Robespierre, and finally to a reflective overview of the revolution as a whole, by which time Smith, having 'lost faith in reform,' is now a 'philosophic Revolutionist'[1] – the novel is still very much a tribute to radicalism, to revolution or change, though no longer linked specifically to France, and to what I have termed the 'ex-centric,' the out of the ordinary as well as the de-centred or marginalized. In spirit *The Young Philosopher* is like Inchbald's *Nature and Art*, where in a contest between a type of Rousseauistic primitivism and civilized artificiality, the former clearly wins. But more than merely a struggle between city and country, nature and art, or eighteenth-century London and America, the novel celebrates female energy and the feminine powers of connection, sympathy, and faith. *The Young Philosopher*, like a number of novels written by women, such as Sheridan's *Memoirs of Miss Sidney Bidulph*, Hays's *Victim of Prejudice*, Inchbald's *A Simple Story*, or Brontë's *Wuthering Heights*, is a two-generational narrative featuring the experiences of a mother and her daughter. While in most of these twice-told tales of female exploits the mother's life functions as a negative example or warning, in Smith's work the first heroine serves rather as a paradigm for the second one. The repetition of events thus provides a system of sustenance and emphasizes endurance, rather than reversal or transformation.

Like many of Smith's other novels *The Young Philosopher* attacks two social groups whom Smith felt held unjustifiable control over individuals, especially young, dependent women. These are tyrannical parents and manipulating legal advisers. It is evident that Smith drew from her own experiences in her satiric portraits of these people, for she says in her Preface: 'If a Writer can best describe who has suffered, I believe that all the evils arising from oppression, from fraud and chicane, I am above almost any person qualified to delineate.'[2] Like the other writers of this study, she is also writing against 'oppression' and prejudice of various kinds – sexual, economic, and intellectual. It is perhaps not coincidental that she anticipates the charge of 'plagiarism' from critics for some scenes depicted in her novel which are similar to *The Wrongs of Woman*, because she describes Wollstonecraft as 'a Writer whose talents I greatly honoured, and whose untimely death I deeply regret' (1:v). Given the historically charged climate of the 1790s, it is not surprising that the events of the times elicited in novelists comparable responses, as well as creative manifestations of these reactions, as they were often influenced by the same ideas and currents of feeling of the period.

As in Inchbald's *Nature and Art*, while the hero of Smith's *Young Philosopher* is a male character, he is depicted as an outcast, a man outside the symbolic world of the Father. The 'young philosopher' of the title, George Delmont, 'though he had seen as much of the world as any man of his age, had, since he became his own master, lived very much out of it, and according to the dictates of his own reason rather than according to its fashions' (1:28). Being the second son of the family, he is not expected to inherit the fortune or the ancient title of his uncle, Lord Castledanes. When he was a child, his mother kept him out of 'grammar school,' and 'took it into her head to keep him at home and instruct him herself' (1: 33). As a result of the maternal influence and his exclusion from patrimony, he has decided at 'twenty-one' not to 'make his fortune by following a profession' such as in law, medicine, or the church, but to be a farmer and a philosopher (1:34). Thus, although he is a man, he is in many ways marginalized like a woman, placed literally and figuratively outside the world of the Father.

Because of his unusual upbringing as an outsider, George Delmont is able to look at the patriarchal society with a critical eye. Smith stresses original thinking as one of the strengths of his character, which is contrasted with the ways of the established men of the community such as Dr Winslow:

Delmont had acquired, whether from hereditary prescription or not, a way of looking at whatever proposition was presented to him, not as Dr. Winslow had been used to do, exactly as it was shewn, but in every light it would bear. The Doctor had never thought of any object but exactly as his predecessors, his masters, had told him to think. (1:155)

It is stressed that his mother is largely responsible for this untraditional behaviour: she 'made him a Philosopher,' with 'a set of opinions of his own' (1:34). Her influence on him is great, as she 'seemed to have in her hands the heart of her son, to be able to mould it as she pleased, and the use she made of her power was to teach him to reason on every thing he learned instead of seeing all objects, as they are represented, through the dazzling and false medium of prejudice, communicated from one generation to another' (1:86–7). Smith associates reason here, not with masculine logic, but with independent and 'excentric' thinking, as it is placed in opposition to the traditions and customs of society. One cantankerous character laments that 'in having a mother who desired to accustom him to an early use of his reason, instead of compelling him always to act from custom, or according to the humour of others, and never suffering him to reason at all,' George is corrupted and rendered wicked (1:213). Actually, as the novel progresses, the teachings of his mother save George from fully participating in the world of the Father, which is revealed to be self-seeking, materialistic, and morally debased.

For instance, a foil to George is his elder brother, Adolphus, a favourite of his father and his uncle, who 'had never felt a wish that he did not imagine he had a right to gratify' (1:46). Brought up as the heir to a noble house, he is used to being courted and praised by his relations, his tutor, his servants, and his dependants. Upon the death of his parents, he receives ten thousand pounds, and his brother merely three, but he still 'thought it scandalous that in any country, the younger branches of a family should be suffered to diminish the property of the elder' (1:135). After gambling away his possessions, he does not hesitate to call upon George to pay his debts. Adolphus becomes a soldier in the army like his father, while George learns to abhor war from his mother: she hoped 'that her youngest son might be one day something better than either a general or an admiral – the benefactor instead of the successful destroyer of his fellow men' (1:87). This refusal to follow in the footsteps of his brother, his father, and his uncle, his refusal to participate in the world of the Father, can be read as a critique of patriarchy and its customs. Delmont, like his friends

Armitage and Glenmorris, chooses exile and 'ex-centricity' rather than involvement with beliefs he cannot sanction.

George Delmont's 'ex-centricity' is demonstrated to be a positive and redeeming quality in many instances. While his brother Adolphus is so full of 'ideas of his own consequence ... that he lost sight of every other consequence' (3:8), George's mother 'taught him that the feelings of others were to be consulted as well as his own' (1:48). He is very liberal with his pocket money, and in the neighbourhood it was known that George 'could never refuse a request' for charity from the hungry, the poor, or the infirm (1:52). In contrast to his brother, he is sensitive to the plight of the unfortunate, for he says while travelling in Ireland: 'I should be miserable where I must daily witness, without having the power materially to alleviate, the miseries of the lower classes of people' (3:138). After the death of his mother George takes up the duty of being the 'protector' of his sisters (1:64), but he also vows to be their 'guardian' rather than their 'governor' (1:266). Unlike his brother, he has distanced himself from society, so that he does not share its values, especially its love of money. George is 'philosopher enough' (1:240) to ignore the charms of Miss Goldthorpe and her fifty thousand pounds, while Adolphus has no scruples about marrying her just for her fortune. These qualities – delicacy, sympathy, and sensibility – which are often associated with the feminine, and which have been inculcated by the mother, set George apart from the rest of the men around him, making him an outsider in the calculating, self-serving systems and institutions of the patriarchal world.

In London, which is the centre of commerce and industry, the hub of high society, and the seat of Chancery and other courts, George Delmont feels isolated and alienated: 'He felt himself no longer an inhabitant of the world he saw about him, yet had no ambition to renew his existence in it' (3:3). It is in London that we meet the most vicious characters of the novel, attorneys and lawyers who 'prey ... on the unfortunate' (3:109). Smith's satiric portraits of lawyers verge on the grotesque. In an earlier novel, *Marchmont,* she says that the system of justice is such that 'the best of all possible laws are abused, to the very worst of all possible purposes.'[3] It is significant that the target of Smith's invective is legal advisers, who have a role as manipulators and interpreters not only of law but of language. Women's feelings of exclusion from the symbolic order are made even more acute when they deal with this profession, which was entirely masculine in the eighteenth century and which rendered them silent by the use of technical terms and jargon. Like Smith herself, Laura Glenmorris, the mother of the heroine, experiences many frustrations as she attempts to recover what she believes is rightfully hers. Mr Petrify, the solicitor whom she goes to see for temporary financial assistance, is one 'whose heart seemed callous to every impression but those made by his own, pursuit of money' (3:96). 'Cold and repulsive,' he tells her that 'these were times when a man might well be justified in refusing pecuniary help even to his own father' (3:97). Delmont, paraphrasing another attorney's legal jargon as 'according to their said several claims, liens, demands, and rights ... manors or reputed manors, or any other property or properties, wheresoever and whatsoever,' says that this 'unintelligible jargon' is the 'style by which Sir Appulby hopes to drive people away, whom he has no inclination to satisfy' (3:57). The jargon mystifies law and prevents those who are not in the profession, and in the novel these are often women, from participating in any kind of meaningful exchange. The articulation of their desires is thus doubly prevented, first because of the restraints imposed upon them by culture, and secondly, by their inability to speak the language of the profession.

A host of other legal advisers, many with names appropriate to their natures, such as Cancer and Loadsworth, are similarly motivated by avarice and devoid of humanitarian feeling, which is most frequently associated with the maternal or the feminine in the novel. One lawyer, Brownjohn, is described in this way:

> Not supported by the regular practice of his profession, but living by shifts, he contrived by impudence, and a flourishing way of talking, to pass himself off as a man of fortune ... Destitute of every principle, and totally without feeling, he made no scruple of taking money from two adverse parties. (3:108–9)

Another attorney, now a consequential politician, Sir Appulby Gorges, had been in the habit 'of taking advantage of every body who by any chance fell in his power; and had for the most part done it with impunity ... He had robbed, and helped to rob his own relations, and since had as successfully robbed the public' (3:276–7). These portraits, which reveal the dishonest practices of men who have powerful judicial and governmental authority, implicitly question the nature of this power and its liability to be abusive. While the novel as a whole does not champion the rights of women and men in the same way that *Desmond* had, it is concerned with many of the same political and philosophical issues raised by the French Revolution, particularly as these related to women. By the end of the 1790s, despite the failed promises of the revolution, it became increasingly hard to extol and idealize the wielders of patriarchal authority, as these men were shown to be untrustworthy and cunning rather than benevolent and generous as Burke had described.

While in *The Young Philosopher* both women and men become victims of the ruling-class hegemony, it is the two female characters whose experiences literalize or physically embody social, economic, and sexual oppression. Together the narratives of Laura Glenmorris and her daughter Medora illustrate the plight of the weak and the dependent female, and offer a criticism of a society that over two generations has continued to tolerate and encourage a type of Gothic barbarity. Of the four volumes which make up the novel, more than two are devoted to accounts of abduction, extortion, attempted rape, and confinement. The cumulative effect of all these injustices is a picture of a chaotic, violent, and rapacious contemporary Britain. Through the parallels between the stories of the mother and the daughter, which take place some twenty years apart and in different locations, Smith shows how society remains unenlightened and unprogressive, continuing a system based on violence, greed, and brutality. The transposition of the Gothic-like horrors experienced by the mother in the primitive Scottish Highlands to the civilized location of London serves to emphasize the incongruity and anachronism of the actions. Both mother and daughter survive their ordeals through sheer will and quick thinking, but the implications of their experience are somewhat problematic and ironic.

In Laura Glenmorris's narrative, which occupies most of the second volume, we have a compendium of those abuses women suffer which emphasize their dependent state. First of all, as the younger daughter of the house, Laura is ignored as a subject by her ambitious parents, who want to marry off the eldest daughter with a great dowry to a baronet. While the sister is to inherit the family's worldly possessions, Laura is to be 'sacrificed to some old man, who, in consideration of [her] youth and beauty, will take [her] without a fortune' (2:22). Here Smith criticizes the way desire for grandeur and power can sever close familial relationships, breaking the natural bond between parent and child, sister and sister. Escaping the sacrifice by eloping with Glenmorris, Laura is then besieged by his old, domineering, witchlike great-aunt, Lady Kilbrodie, whose 'pride and ... poverty had made her avaricious, not for herself ... but in the hope of aggrandizing her two sons' (2:97). The fact that Laura escapes one scheming family only to be placed in the hands of another is ironic, but it also reveals what Smith saw as the pervasiveness of greed and self-interest in eighteenth-century aristocratic and upper-middle-class circles.

Deprived of the protection of her husband, Laura Glenmorris experiences a series of adventures which have Gothic affinities. Pregnant with the possible heir to the Glenmorris estate, Laura is forced to quit their home and taken to the 'abbey of Kilbrodie,' with its 'masses of ruins ... a single tower,' its 'large, cold, and dreary' rooms and 'dark horrors' (2:100, 101). The surrounding countryside matches the 'horrors of the cell,' as it is 'mountainous and barren' with 'chaotic and misshapen masses of rock,' inhabited only by a 'pair of eagles' (2:102, 103). Laura asserts that 'no dreary description, drawn from imagination of tombs and caverns haunted by evil spirits, could equal the gloomy horrors of the place' (2:113). Her gaoler resembles a 'female warlock': a 'shrivelled and distorted countenance, disfigured ... by evil passions ... a long and sharp nose ... little fierce grey eyes ... two withered lips' (2:103–4). Here in this Gothic-like castle Lady Kilbrodie menaces Laura with threats and with superstitious portents of death. As in the case of other Gothic heroines, imagined fears are mingled with real horrors in Laura: 'The horror which seized on my mind is not to be described. Sometimes I so yielded to the influence of this dread, as hardly to have any other consciousness of my existence than that which fear impressed' (2:110). While in many Gothic novels the prison or the 'locked-room' is the 'forbidden, dangerous place,' often attractive because it is 'closed, obscure, exotic, and alluring,'[4] in Laura's case the Highland castle represents the 'locked-room' of her subconscious: here we find the enactment of her deepest fears and her repressed anger. For as a prisoner of Lady Kilbrodie, Laura can safely channel her fury against greedy parents onto this witchlike shrew while not seeming to rage against her own mother, who had similarly confined her as a subject by not giving her freedom to choose, or at least, veto the choice of a husband. The episode in Scotland then functions as a physical and more literal manifestation of the deprivations Laura experienced as the younger daughter in her own family. In addition, it reveals some common female fears about sexuality and maternity. As the time of her lying-in approaches, Laura is full of apprehension because she believes that Lady Kilbrodie's 'inhuman purpose' (2:107) is to murder her unborn baby and perhaps herself. This concern for her body in her vulnerable state mirrors the virginal Gothic heroine's anxieties about violation and assault. Both stem from what Kristeva would classify as one's earliest pre-verbal or semiotic fears of death and pain as a result of the destruction of the body.

Not only does the mother's narrative challenge parental prerogative and judgment, it also serves to reveal the dangers of paternal power. Soon after the premature birth of her infant, Laura Glenmorris is subjected to the unwanted attention of the laird of Kilbrodie, who feels that she should be 'honoured by his preference' and makes her understand through his 'ferocious' and brutal nature that she was 'wholly in his power; that it was impossible ... to escape him' (2:131). That women are frequently the targets of unwelcome masculine desire and will is illustrated when Laura escapes from Kilbrodie with the help of Lord Macarden, only to be confronted with a similar situation in the home of her rescuer. Although in this house Laura is treated with gentleness and kindness by Lord Macarden, she is also subjected to the malevolence and jealousy of Mrs Mackirk, Lord Macarden's older half-sister who lives with him, and subsequently to the amorous declaration of Lord Macarden himself. There is, of course, a difference between the gentle courtship of Macarden and the more brutal one of Kilbrodie, but the corresponding circumstances only prove the vulnerability of women and the difficulties of becoming anything other than the specularized object of male desire.

Set back in time, placed in the Highlands of Scotland, and self-contained as a flashback in the second volume, the narrative of the unpleasant experiences of Laura Glenmorris, the mother, seems at first to be non-threatening and extraneous to the main plot, which deals with the growing friendship between George Delmont, the young philosopher, and the Glenmorris women. However, the relevance of the despotic treatment of daughters, of kidnappings, and threats of rape soon becomes apparent as these very experiences are then lived through again by the daughter, Medora. The repetition of the wrongs the mother had suffered not only emphasizes the self-perpetuating and unprogressive nature of the social order, but also draws parallels between the cultural practices of the more 'primitive' and superstitious Scottish clans and those of the more 'civilized' and advanced society of London. That there is essentially no difference in the two cultures' treatment of women becomes a telling and deprecating comment on eighteenth-century English society.

Medora's experiences present a 'literal' version of the abuses and harassment the mother is subjected to by her attorneys. For while the mother is rendered metaphorically 'helpless' by the constant procrastination and inaction of the lawyers, the daughter is made a physical captive of their greed. Tricked by a forged letter – an example of the male manipulation of language – Medora is kidnapped by the attorney

Brownjohn and his brother, Darnell, who hope to make her marry Darnell and thereby to secure her fortune. She is taken to a house in Yorkshire, where she is confined and menaced by the 'ignorant and vulgar' mother of Darnell (4:254). This scene is reminiscent of the way her mother was threatened by Lady Kilbrodie. In fact, in her 'prison' she recollects her 'mother's singular story, and particularly the time when she was a prisoner, a sick and suffering prisoner, in the Abbey of Kilbrodie' (4:157). Significantly both Medora and her mother are imprisoned, not for themselves as subjects, but for the commodities or objects they will produce: a fortune in Medora's case; an heir in Laura's case.

Perhaps not intentionally so, Smith depicts the kidnapping and subsequent escape of Medora from the ridiculous and 'half a fool' (4:222) Darnell as almost a parody of Gothic abductions, because instead of inspiring fear and awe, he only arouses her contempt and scorn. In addition, despite the fact that Medora had been praised by George Delmont earlier as an innocent 'child of nature,' very pretty, and with 'no mind' of her own (1:244), she manages to flee from the clutches of her abductors as a result of some quick-witted thinking and action. For instance, she escapes her prison by forcing her way through the 'iron bars' of her window and agilely climbing down a vine which covers the side of the house (4:264). Later, she exchanges her clothes with a chambermaid, trading her 'fine laced cloak for a common handkerchief shawl ... her hat, and her beautiful sprigged muslim gown for a common cotton gown, an oldish black bonnet' (4:120). She then finds her way to London, concealing herself in wheat fields and getting rides in farmers' wagons. As if self-conscious of the tradition of abducted maidens from Richardson to Radcliffe, Smith has Medora wonder if her rashness was in part a result of 'novels and romances' where men are 'represented as carrying off damsels, and involving them in very disagreeable adventures' (4:290).

That Smith was torn by contradictory subject-positions of woman is revealed by her somewhat inconsistent depiction of Medora. Sometimes Medora seems to be unlike the helpless damsels of 'novels and romances' because of her 'courage and propriety of conduct' (4:203). In fact, in the midst of her distress, she recollects the lesson on 'firmness' of character given by her mother: '... the mind which has acquired a certain degree of reliance on itself, which has learned to look on the good and evil of life, and to appreciate each, is alone capable of true gentleness and calmness' (4:227). Yet, in the safety of her home, Medora's docility and submission to authority are extolled. Her mother had also taught her 'never to appear inquisitive, never to seek to know more than she thought proper to tell [her]' (4:210). While Medora fends off her attackers very well herself, in the presence of Delmont she appears rather faint-hearted: she lets him take charge of the situation and represses her 'uneasiness and suspicion' (4:351). Smith attempts to correct the portrait of the conventional defenceless virginal heroine, such as that of Radcliffe's Emily St Aubert or Inchbald's Matilda in A Simple Story, but she betrays a lack of conviction and somewhat ambivalent feelings towards these feminine ideals by not fully rejecting the cultural stereotype of the gentle female in her novel.

As well as illustrating conflicting ideologies of woman, Medora's narrative contains a strong indictment of patriarchy and the Burkean paradigm of the benevolent patriarch. For while her abductor may be a comic version of Lovelace, Sir Harry Richmond, whom Medora encounters on the way back to London, certainly is not. In fact, he is a very physical and real embodiment of a romance heroine's worst nightmare. Sir Harry, who is described as a 'tyrant both from nature and habit,' (4:140), has a large fortune, and an equally large reputation for philandering. Delmont hears the story of a 'poor country girl of seventeen' whom Sir Harry had seduced. After having two children by him, she was forced to marry one of his huntsmen, a man of 'a fierce and brutal disposition' who frequently 'beat her during the five miserable years she lived with him' (4:165). After hearing this tale, and realizing that Sir Harry fancies Medora, Delmont thinks 'whether there were not too many ways by which such a man as Sir Harry Richmond might take advantage of the simplicity of a girl hardly seventeen, and so new to the world as was Medora' (4:185). The prevalence of this type of abuse leads Delmont to comment: '... these are indeed among the wrongs of woman' (4:166). The reference to Wollstonecraft's The Wrongs of Woman; or, Maria, which was published the same year as The Young Philosopher, makes the connection between the two works clear. While Smith's novel does not explicitly advocate women's rights in the same way as Wollstonecraft's, it shares a similar concern with the injustices or 'wrongs' suffered by women and other marginalized or 'ex-centric' figures.

Indeed the narrative form of The Young Philosopher, with its frequent digressions and repetitions, is analogous to the echoing structure of Wollstonecraft's Maria. For the cumulative effect of the stories of the mother, the daughter, and the unnamed victims of Sir Harry is one of claustrophobic discomfort and awareness of the oppression of the social system. Compared to Wollstonecraft, Smith is perhaps less consistent in her critique of patriarchy in the strictest definition of the word, because mothers are often shown to be just as guilty of tyranny and abuses as fathers are. Nevertheless, the disapproval of the social customs and the legal institutions that perpetuate the system remains deliberate and forceful.

Another similarity between *The Young Philosopher* and *Maria* is the one that Smith herself notes in the Preface, namely, the 'incident of the confinements in a mad house' of Laura Glenmorris (1:v) by the lawyers and advisers of her elderly mother, Lady Mary. As we have seen in Wollstonecraft's novel, this incarceration is a literal manifestation of the social, economic, and moral imprisonment experienced by a woman of the late eighteenth century. Laura Glenmorris is 'conveyed, as privately as possible, to one of the most remote houses, within twenty miles of London, where lunatics are received' (3:230) to prevent her from pursuing the litigation for her daughter's inheritance. Not only is she restrained there, but her abductors register her 'under the name of Mrs. Tichfield' (3:232) in order to complicate any attempts to rescue her. This change of name becomes representative of the difficulties in identity and subjectivity of women. Laura Glenmorris's subjectivity is rendered more complex by the roles she is forced to assume: the madwoman, the pliant Mrs Tichfield, the dutiful daughter, the constant wife, the Gothic-like maiden imprisoned in Scotland, and so on. Like Wollstonecraft, Smith literalizes female constraints by depicting her heroine in a real prison which confines the woman both mentally and physically.

In the asylum the woman's problems of speech and language in the symbolic world become a nightmare of inarticulation and misconstrued discourse. Laura Glenmorris's excessive concern for her missing daughter are interpreted as 'raving delirium,' while her passive silence and resignation are viewed as a stage of 'melancholy madness' (4:90). Her assertions against those who have imprisoned her are not believed by the apothecary who attends her because he fears that she is only temporarily lucid. Delmont recognizes how this treatment can render even a sane person mad: 'Confined, ill treated, driven perhaps by despair to the very state' of madness (4:321). The whole episode is yet another instance of injustice or 'wrongs' suffered by woman, and reinforces Smith's diatribe against tyranny in general.

As I have argued previously in my discussion of Williams, I want to suggest that in coming up with a fictional remedy for the legal problem in *The Young Philosopher* Smith was in part influenced by what I have called a feminine ethos, which, according to such feminist theorists as Nancy Chodorow and Carol Gilligan, values relationships and connection rather than competition and separation.[5] While the lawyers and attorneys are at an impasse about Medora's right to half of the De Verdun fortune, the sympathetic and generous Mary Cardonnel devises a 'female' solution to the case. Instead of waiting for the legal authorities to justify Medora's claim, she volunteers to share half of her ninety thousand pounds worth of inheritance with her cousin when she comes of age. This action, which may seem overly altruistic and sentimental to cynical readers in our own age, nevertheless suggests an attempt at circumventing the patriarchal and masculinist convention of lawsuits and confrontation, which Smith herself found impossible to deal with. Mary Cardonnel's deed may seem eccentric in the world of the Father, but it seems in keeping with the lessons of caring and generosity given by the mothers in the novel.

Finally, the conclusion of *The Young Philosopher* has some affinities with Inchbald's *Nature and Art* in that the solution proposed is a withdrawal from the world of the Father. Because there have been so many examples of inequality shown through the course of the novel, not only to the female characters but also to Glenmorris, who was himself abducted by pirates and later imprisoned for debt, the morally 'good' characters seem to have no recourse but self-exile. The philosphers, thinkers, and all the characters who do not share the materialistic and corrupt values of civilized society are outcasts. The old man Armitage is a hermit, and by the end of the novel George Delmont decides to leave his estate at Upwood and join the Glenmorris family in America. Glenmorris justifies his intention of returning to America: 'I do not love to be in a country where I am made to pay very dear for advantages which exist not but in idea. I do not love to live where I see frightful contrast between luxury and wretchedness; where I must daily witness injustice I cannot repress, and misery I cannot relieve' (4:391). This answer to the many ills of eighteenth-century society may be naïve and rather idealistic, and may also reflect Smith's own disillusionment by 1798. Whereas at the dawn of the French Revolution her novels seemed to hold a strong belief in the possibilities of social change, here a break with the patriarchal civilization of England seems to be the only solution. To be ex-centric or set apart from society, then, becomes a virtue and the only feasible recourse in Smith's last novel.

Conclusion

This book has been an effort to study how five women novelists of the 1790s attempted to challenge and reform what they perceived to be a male-dominated and androcentric society. In particular, reacting to the liberating ideals of the French Revolution of 1789, and the Burkean conservative response to this event, these writers drew parallels between the domestic and the political, between the private and the public, in their fiction. In doing so, they showed that the problem of female subjectivity, the construction of 'woman' in eighteenth-century culture was not one of limited interest, but one that could involve the whole basis and moral fabric of society. For in undermining the authority of the patriarch, or in refusing to comply with the Law of the Father, these female authors were rejecting the hierarchical structure on which much of Western civilization is based.

While these women were not consistent in their aims and while their works often betrayed their sense of ambiguity and contradiction, they nevertheless explored and contested the notion of the submissive or docile woman as described by Jane West and Hannah More. I have tried to show how they wrote differently because they were daughters rather than sons of the symbolic order, how they would waver between 'semiotic' and rational discourse, and how they frequently employed literalization rather than figurative representation to illustrate their plight. At times, they resorted to exaggeration, to the sentimental, or to the Gothic to demonstrate better the terms of their oppression. And while their novels might seem to be only entertaining and to conform to the genre of the romance, in reality, they present seriously held doctrines, which espouse what are now called feminist arguments and which point out the shortcomings of traditional institutions such as marriage, primogeniture, and patriarchy.

If these novels have not been as easily accepted into our English literary canon as works by others of the same period, it is perhaps because they incessantly question social and narrative conventions, and necessitate a different way of reading and interpretation. In Roland Barthes's terms they are 'writerly' rather than 'readerly' texts. In contrast to the readerly or 'classic' text, which strives for homogeneity, is organized according to the principles of non-contradiction, and purports to be a transcript of reality, the writerly text draws attention to the cultural voices or codes responsible for its enunciation, reveals multiplicity instead of consistency, and signifies flux instead of stable meaning.[1] Often, instead of the aesthetic closure of narrative, the novels by these women use double discourse, a story contained within another which subverts it; employ multiple narratives, accounts which echo each other; or a tale of two generations which becomes a kind of self-criticism. Through these devices they are able to accommodate their desire to satisfy their reading public, their own sense of propriety, and their need to articulate their discomfort and disappointment with the constrictions imposed upon them by society. Refusing to accept the dominant ideology, these writers integrated their intelligence and their specific historical 'experience,' their reason and suffering, their scepticism and their vision, to challenge that ideology, and to assert the need for change.

Notes

1 For a recent survey of novels of the 1790s and after sec Gary Kelly's *English Fiction of the Romantic Period 1789–1830* (London: Longman 1989).

2 Ellen Pollak, *The Poetics of Sexual Myth: Gender and Ideology in the Verse of Swift and Pope* (Chicago: University of Chicago Press 1985), 3

3 See Jane Spencer, *The Rise of the Woman Novelist: From Aphra Behn to Jane Austen* (Oxford: Basil Blackwell 1986); Janet Todd, *The Sign of Angellica: Women, Writing and Fiction, 1660–1800* (New York: Columbia University Press 1989); Dale Spender, *Mothers of the Novel: One Hundred Good Women Writers before Jane Austen* (London: Pandora 1986); Mary Poovey, *The Proper Lady and the Woman Writer: Ideology as Style in the Works of Mary Wollstonecraft, Mary Shelley, and Jane Austen* (Chicago: University of Chicago Press 1984); Ann H. Jones, *Ideas and Innovations: Best Sellers of Jane Austen's Age* (New York: AMS Press 1986); Mary Anne Schofield and Cecilia Macheski, eds., *Fetter'd or Free? British Women Novelists, 1670–1815* (Athens: Ohio University Press 1986); and Katherine Sobba Green, *The Courtship Novel, 1740–1820: A Feminized Genre* (Lexington: University Press of Kentucky 1991).

4 Nancy K. Miller, *The Heroine's Text: Readings in the French and English Novel 1722–1782* (New York: Columbia University Press 1980), xi

5 Eva Figes, *Sex and Subterfuge: Women Novelists to 1850* (London: Macmillan 1982), 18

6 Samuel Richardson, *Clarissa; or, The History of a Young Lady*, 4 vols, introd. John Butt (London: Dent Everyman 1976), 4:157

7 Diana Fuss, *Essentially Speaking: Feminism, Nature and Difference* (New York: Routledge 1989), 2, xii

8 Rosi Braidotti, 'The Politics of Ontological Difference,' in *Between Feminism and Psychoanalysis*, ed. Teresa Brennan (New York: Routledge 1989), 101

9 For example, one early essay which introduced French feminism to American scholars is Ann Rosalind Jones's 'Writing the Body: Toward an Understanding of l'Ecriture féminine,' in *The New Feminist Criticism: Essays on Women, Literature, Theory*, ed. Elaine Showalter (New York: Pantheon 1985), 361–78.

10 Jean Wyatt, *Reconstructing Desire: The Role of the Unconscious in Women's Reading and Writing* (Chapel Hill: University of North Carolina Press 1990), 5

11 Luce Irigaray, *Speculum of the Other Woman*, trans. Gillian C. Gill (Ithaca, NY: Cornell University Press 1985), 166

12 Margaret Whitford, *Luce Irigaray: Philosophy in the Feminine* (New York: Routledge 1991), 45

13 Ibid.

14 Wyatt, *Reconstructing Desire*, 4

15 Margaret Homans, *Bearing the Word: Language and Female Experience in Nineteenth-Century Women's Writing* (Chicago: University Press 1986), xiii. Homans was actually referring to the nineteenth century in this statement, but I believe that her assertion holds true for the novelists of this study, who preceded some of the writers in Homans's text only by a few years.

16 See Homans, *Bearing the Word*, especially chapter 1.

17 Toril Moi, in *Sexual/Textual Politics: Feminist Literary Theory* (London: Methuen 1985), is an example of a critic who tends to divide American and French feminists distinctively into two camps.

18 Mary Wollstonecraft, *Letters Written during a Short Residence in Sweden, Norway, and Denmark* (1796), ed. Carol H. Poston (Lincoln: University of Nebraska Press 1976), 105

INTRODUCTION

1 Richard Polwhele, *The Unsex'd Females: A Poem* (1798), introd. Gina Luria (New York: Garland 1974), 7

2 See, for example, Mitzi Myers, 'Reform or Ruin: A Revolution in Female Manners,' *Studies in Eighteenth-Century Culture* 11 (1982), 199–216,

which studies the shared objectives of Wollstonecraft and More regarding female education; Gary Kelly, 'Jane Austen and the English Novel of the 1790s,' in *Fetter'd or Free? British Women Novelists, 1670–1815,* ed. Mary Anne Schofield and Cecilia Macheski (Athens: Ohio University Press 1986), 285–307, which discusses similar techniques used by Jacobin and anti-Jacobin novelists; and more recently the introductory chapters of Claudia Johnson's *Jane Austen: Women, Politics, and the Novel* (Chicago: University of Chicago Press 1988), especially the Introduction and chapter 1, which explain why some female authors, like Burney, Edgeworth, Hamilton, and Opie, had to disguise their feminist sympathies. Marilyn Butler's *Jane Austen and the War of Ideas* (Oxford: Clarendon Press 1975) was one of the first works to examine the partisan question.

3 Jane Rendall, in *The Origins of Modern Feminism: Women in Britain, France and the United States 1780–1860* (London: Macmillan 1985), reminds us that to use 'feminist' or 'feminism' in reference to works or women before the nineteenth century is anachronistic as the word was not used until 1894 in England from the French *féminism* coined by the utopian socialist Charles Fourier (1).

4 See Ruth Perry, *The Celebrated Mary Astell: An Early English Feminist* (Chicago: University of Chicago Press 1986), especially chapter 4.

5 For a study of these three women, see Jane Spencer, *The Rise of the Woman Novelist: From Aphra Behn to Jane Austen* (Oxford: Basil Blackwell 1986), chapters 1–2; and also Janet Todd, *The Sign of Angellica: Women, Writing and Fiction, 1660–1800* (New York: Columbia University Press 1989), especially chapters 4–5.

6 Edmund Burke, *Reflections on the Revolution in France,* ed. and introd. J.G.A. Pocock (Indianapolis and Cambridge: Hackett Publishing Co. 1987), 70

7 Ibid., 62

8 Johnson, *Jane Austen,* 4, 5. I am influenced by Ronald Paulson's *Representations of Revolution (1789–1820)* (New Haven: Yale University Press 1983) as well as Claudia Johnson's views of Burke's *Reflections* as a tract that verges on the sentimental and even Gothic. See Paulson, chapters 1–3, and 7; and Johnson, chapter 1, especially pages 4–6.

9 J.G.A. Pocock, 'Introduction,' *Reflections on the Revolution in France,* xxxviii–xxxix

10 Edmund Burke, *A Letter to a Member of the National Assembly,* in *Works* (London 1893), 541, as quoted by Paulson, *Representations of Revolution,* 62

11 An account of this incident is given in Claire Tomalin, *The Life and*

Death of Mary Wollstonecraft (London: Weidenfeld and Nicolson 1974), 111.

12 Ibid., 195; and Ralph M. Wardle, *Mary Wollstonecraft: A Critical Biography* (Lawrence: University of Kansas Press 1951), 258–9

13 See Ralph M. Wardle, 'Mary Wollstonecraft, Analytical Reviewer,' *PMLA* 62 (Dec. 1947), 1000–9. These and other reviews are collected in *A Wollstonecraft Anthology*, ed. and introd. Janet M. Todd (Bloomington: Indiana University Press 1977).

14 Charlotte Smith, *The Young Philosopher*, introd. Gina Luria (New York: Garland 1974)

15 Burke, *Reflections on the Revolution*, 70

16 See Paulson, *Representations of Revolution*, 49–52.

17 William Blake, *The Poems of William Blake*, ed. W.H. Stevenson, text by David V. Erdman (New York: Longman Norton 1971). All the poems cited are from this text.

18 Extract reprinted in Marilyn Butler, ed., *Burke, Paine, Godwin, and the Revolution Controversy* (Cambridge: Cambridge University Press 1984), 28

19 Burke, *Reflections on the Revolution*, 11

20 Ibid., 10–11

21 Reprinted in Butler, ed., *Burke, Paine, Godwin*, Letters 6, 14

22 Ibid., Letter 14

23 Ibid.

24 See Jacques Lacan, *Ecrits: A Selection*, trans. Alan Sheridan (New York: W.W. Norton 1977); and Julia Kristeva, *Revolution in Poetic Language*, trans. Margaret Waller, introd. Leon S. Roudiez (New York: Columbia University Press 1984). My interest in Lacan is not so much for himself, but in the response to and use of his theories by feminists in both Europe and North America.

25 Mary Poovey discusses Wollstonecraft's divided attitudes towards emotion and feeling in chapter 2 of *The Proper Lady and the Woman Writer: Ideology as Style in the Works of Mary Wollstonecraft, Mary Shelley, and Jane Austen* (Chicago: University of Chicago Press 1984), especially 56–68. Wollstonecraft's attack on Burke's rhetoric has been studied by Kelly in 'Mary Wollstonecraft as *Vir Bonus*,' *English Studies in Canada* 5, no. 3 (Fall 1979), 275–91; and by James Boulton in *The Language of Politics in the Age of Wilkes and Burke* (London: Routledge; Toronto: University of Toronto Press 1963), 168–76.

26 Mary Wollstonecraft, *A Vindication of the Rights of Men*, extract reprinted in Todd, ed., *A Wollstonecraft Anthology*, 67

27 Ibid., 71

28 Ibid., 82
29 Reprinted in Butler, ed., *Burke, Paine, Godwin*, 110
30 Ibid.
31 Boulton, *The Language of Politics*, 134–5
32 Quoted in Boulton, 147
33 Quoted in Boulton, 138
34 Quoted in Boulton, 144–5
35 See Boulton, chapter 8.
36 Butler, ed., *Burke, Paine, Godwin*, 206
37 Reprinted in Butler, ed., *Burke, Paine, Godwin*, 209
38 Ibid., 211–12
39 Books 9–11 of Wordsworth's *Prelude* are considered his 'revolutionary' books and have been studied in this way by Ronald Paulson (see *Representations of Revolution*, chapter 8). Another critic, Marilyn Butler, in *Romantics, Rebels, and Reactionaries: English Literature and Its Background 1760–1830* (Oxford: Oxford University Press 1981), 58–63, views Wordsworth as a product of the neoclassical revolution. Butler points out that Wordsworth carried out through language 'one interpretation of Neoclassicism's fundamental spirit ... that the artist should imitate Nature – not sophisticated life' (59).
40 Butler, *Romantics, Rebels, and Reactionaries*, 62
41 On the definition of 'Jacobin' see Gary Kelly, *The English Jacobin Novel 1780–1805* (Oxford: Oxford University Press 1976), which emphasizes that the English Jacobin movement was not a 'monolithic party' (2), but was made up of individuals or groups who had a faith in reason, a belief in parliamentary reform, and who 'saw the French Revolution ... as a stimulus to extend the battle for liberties,' but were not revolutionaries themselves (4).
42 Kelly, *English Jacobin Novel*, 8
43 William Godwin, *Things As They Are; or, The Adventures of Caleb Williams*, ed. David McCrachen (London: Oxford University Press 1970)
44 See Kelly, *English Jacobin Novel*, 179; and Harvey Gross, 'The Pursuer and the Pursued: A Study of *Caleb Williams*,' *Texas Studies in Literature and Language* 1 (1959), 401–11.
45 William Godwin, *Enquiry Concerning Political Justice*, ed. and abridged K. Codell Carter (Oxford: Clarendon Press 1971), 27
46 Ibid., 28
47 Thomas Holcroft, *Anna St. Ives*, ed. and introd. Peter Faulkner (London: Oxford University Press 1970). Subsequent page references are to this edition. Holcroft's characters are not simply divided into good and evil according to class, however, as one of the low-born men,

Abimelech Henley, the steward, is capable of duplicity and embezzlement.

48 Quoted in Peter Faulkner's introduction to *Anna St. Ives,* xiii

49 For example, Anna says, 'You think no doubt that the lover ought to yield, and the husband to command; both of which I deny. Husband, wife, or lover, should all be under the command of reason; other commands are tyranny' (264). Another passage on marriage is comparable to or even more radical than Wollstonecraft's ideas: marriage 'ought not to be a civil institution. It is the concern of the individuals who consent to this mutual association, and they ought not to be prevented from beginning, suspending or terminating it as they please' (280).

50 Gary Kelly notes that in the later part of the novel characterization becomes 'so abstract that it is difficult to tell whether the conflict is between Frank and Clifton or Virtue and Vice' (*English Jacobin Novel,* 137); and that 'the neo-Platonic allegory only contributes to the impression of philosophical abstraction as the novel moves to its close' (142). Similarly Marilyn Butler notices that the optimistic end gives the novel a 'didactic and unlifelike air' (*War of Ideas,* 48).

51 See Butler, *War of Ideas,* 76; Kelly, *English Jacobin Novel,* 27; and Peter Faulkner, *Robert Bage* (Boston: Twayne Publishers 1979), 55.

52 J.H. Sutherland, 'Robert Bage: Novelist of Ideas,' *Philological Quarterly* 36 (1957), 211, as quoted by Faulkner, *Robert Bage,* 154. Faulkner's view that Bage's novel maintains a 'well-balanced, and good-humoured' spirit (1955) is in contrast with Gary Kelly's, who argues in *The English Jacobin Novel* that Bage's 'humour is almost too disarming; it conceals the real radicalism of his underlying views' (27).

53 Robert Bage, *Hermsprong; or, Man As He Is Not,* ed. Vaughan Wilkins (London: Turnstile Press 1951). Subsequent page references are to this edition.

54 Polwhele, *The Unsex'd Females,* 32

55 Ibid., 18

56 Johnson, *Jane Austen,* 2

57 See Elaine Showalter, 'Towards a Feminist Poetics,' and 'Feminist Criticism in the Wilderness,' which are reprinted in *Feminist Criticism: Essays on Women, Literature, and Theory* (New York: Pantheon 1985), 125–43, 243–70. Despite the fact that Showalter associates these three phases with distinct periods in the nineteenth and twentieth centuries, her terminology is useful here.

58 See, for example, Toril Moi's dismissive discussion of Showalter in *Sexual/Textual Politics: Feminist Literary Theory* (London: Methuen 1985) 76ff.

59 Chris Weedon, *Feminist Practice and Poststructuralist Theory* (Oxford: Basil Blackwell 1987), 157

60 Jane West, *A Tale of the Times,* 3 vols, introd. Gina Luria (New York: Garland 1974), 2:24. Subsequent page references are to this edition.

61 Jane Gallop, *Reading Lacan* (Ithaca, NY: Cornell University Press 1985), 141

62 See Jacques Lacan, 'The Signification of the Phallus,' in his *Ecrits,* 281–91.

63 Josette Féral, 'Antigone or *The Irony of the Tribe,*' *Diacritics* 8 (Sept. 1978), 14

64 Jane West, *The Advantages of Education; or, The History of Maria Williams,* 2 vols (New York: Garland 1974), 2:234

65 Jane West, *Letters to a Young Lady in Which the Duties and Character of Women Are Considered,* 3 vols, introd. Gina Luria (New York: Garland 1974), 1:37

66 See Poovey, *Proper Lady,* chapter 1.

67 Luce Irigaray, *Speculum of the Other Woman,* trans. Gillian C. Gill (Ithaca NY: Cornell University Press 1985), 133–4

68 Hannah More, *Coelebs in Search of a Wife, Comprehending Observations on Domestic Habits and Manners, Religion and Morals,* 7th ed., 2 vols (London: T. Cadell and W. Davies 1809), 1:2. Subsequent page references are to this edition.

69 In contrast to More and West other more 'innovative' female authors tend to isolate their heroines from their families in order to make them think and learn the right mode of conduct for themselves. For example, most of the heroines of the five writers in this study are orphans of some sort. Similarly in the works of Jane Austen, Fanny Burney, and Maria Edgeworth, the focus is on the heroine's ability to judge and make the correct choices away from parental guidance. In More, however, the actions of daughters mirror or are a result of those of their mothers as the emphasis is on the proper education of female children.

70 Hannah More, *Strictures on the Modern System of Female Education, with a View to the Principles and Conduct Prevalent among Women of Rank and Fortune,* 2 vols. (London: T. Cadell Jun. and W. Davies 1799), 1:152

71 Johnson, *Jane Austen,* 18

72 Luce Irigaray, *This Sex Which Is Not One,* trans. Catherine Porter and Carolyn Burke (Ithaca, NY: Cornell University Press 1985), 84

73 It is not my intention to discuss or summarize the current debate about the 'place' of Austen or Burney in the 'war of ideas' as there has been much work devoted to these writers, particularly Austen. I

have referred already to Claudia Johnson, *Jane Austen;* Marilyn Butler, *Jane Austen and the War of Ideas;* and Gary Kelly's 'Jane Austen and the English Novel of the 1790s,' in Schofield and Macheski, eds., *Fetter'd or Free?* Earlier useful studies on the topic include Mary Lascelles, *Jane Austen and Her Art* (Oxford: Oxford University Press 1939); and Kenneth L. Moler, *Jane Austen's Art of Allusion* (Lincoln: University of Nebraska Press 1968).

For Burney, see Margaret Anne Doody, *Frances Burney: The Life in the Works* (New Brunswick, NJ: Rutgers University Press 1988); Martha G. Brown, 'Fanny Burney's "Feminism": Gender or Genre,' in *Fetter'd or Free?*, 29–39; Joyce Hemlow, *The History of Fanny Burney* (Oxford: Oxford University Press 1958); Mary Poovey, 'Fathers and Daughters: The Trauma of Growing Up Female,' *Women and Literature* n.s. 2 (1982), 39–58; Rose Marie Cutting, 'Defiant Women: The Growth of Feminism in Fanny Burney's Novels,' *Studies in English Literature* 17 (1977), 519–30; and Susan Staves, '*Evelina,* or Female Difficulties,' *Modern Philology* 72 (1974), 368–81.

74 Fanny Burney, *Fanny Burney: Journals and Letters,* vol. 3, ed. Joyce Hemlow (Oxford: Oxford University Press 1973)

75 Irigaray, *This Sex,* 136–7

76 Johnson, *Jane Austen,* 11

77 For a different view of *Belinda* see Beth Kowaleski-Wallace, 'Home Economics: Domestic Ideology in Maria Edgeworth's *Belinda,*' *The Eighteenth Century: Theory and Interpretation,* 29, no. 3 (Fall 1988), 242–62. Kowaleski-Wallace argues that Belinda's high moral standard 'precludes real moral growth or instruction for the heroine ... In short, *Belinda* is not about Belinda' but about 'the implementation of a particular mode of domesticity necessary to ... new style patriarchy' (242). While I find Kowaleski-Wallace's ideas about Lady Delacour and home economics very convincing, I do not think that they necessarily preclude Belinda's development. Belinda does learn through the course of the novel; but what she apprehends is the inverse of what other young ladies learn – she becomes less prudent and learns to trust her heart.

78 Maria Edgeworth, *Belinda,* introd. Eva Figes (London: Pandora 1986), 57. Subsequent page references are to this edition.

79 Lawrence Stone argues that what he calls 'companionate marriage,' a form of marriage based on love and affection rather than on economic or social considerations, developed between the mid and late eighteenth century. See *The Family, Sex and Marriage in England 1500–1800* (New York: Harper and Row 1977), chapter 8.

80 Godwin had consulted with 'Perdita' Robinson over several of her
   novels. See Kelly, *English Jacobin Novel,* 258. In the February 1800 issue
   of the *Anti-Jacobin Review and Magazine* Bage's *Man As He Is* and *Hermsprong* were classed 'with vicious novels such as *Desmond, Nature and
   Art,* and the "trash of Mrs. Robinson,"' (quoted by Kelly, 28).
81 Mary Darby Robinson, *Vancenza; or, The Dangers of Credulity,* 2 vols, 3d
   ed. (London: Bell British Library 1792), vi
82 Nancy Chodorow, in *The Reproduction of Mothering: Psychoanalysis and the
   Sociology of Gender* (Berkeley and Los Angeles: University of California
   Press 1978), contends that the psychic maturation of a young girl neither repeats nor simply reverses the Oedipal configuration that Freud
   identified in young boys. Because mothers are the same gender as
   their daughters, they 'tend not to experience these infant daughters as
   separate from them in the same way as do mothers of infant sons.'
   Primary identification and symbiosis with daughters tend to be
   stronger and to be based on 'experiencing a daughter as an extension
   or double of a mother herself' (109). The girl develops 'important
   oedipal attachments to her mother *as well as* to her father' (127).
83 Margaret Homans, *Bearing the Word: Language and Female Experience in
   Nineteenth-Century Women's Writing* (Chicago: University of Chicago
   Press 1986), 13
84 Mary Darby Robinson, *Walsingham; or, The Pupil of Nature,* 4 vols,
   introd. Gina Luria (New York: Garland 1974). See, for example, 2:283
   and 3:229. Subsequent page references are to this edition.
85 See Gary Kelly's 'Mary Robinson' entry in 'Notes on Individual Authors,' in *English Fiction of the Romantic Period 1798–1830* (New York:
   Longman 1989), 313–14.
86 Paulson, *Representations of Revolution,* 221
87 I am influenced by the studies on the Gothic in *The Female Gothic,* ed.
   Juliann E. Fleenor (Montreal: Eden Press 1983), especially the essays
   by Ann Ronald and Cynthia Griffin Wolff. See also Robert Kiely, '*The
   Mysteries of Udolpho,* an Explication,' in *The English Gothic Novel: A Mis-
   cellany in Four Volumes,* ed. James Hogg (Salzburg: Institut für Anglistik
   und Amerikanistik, Universität Salzburg 1986), 178–91. For a different
   opinion see Elizabeth R. Napier, *The Failure of Gothic: Problems of Disjunction in an Eighteenth Century Literary Form* (Oxford: Clarendon
   1987): 'The genre's preoccupation with subterranean settings does not
   ... necessarily point to a concern with human psychology, female physi-
   ology or the unconscious. The genre, indeed, repeatedly fails to engage these deeper issues ...' (39).
88 Julia Kristeva, *Revolution in Poetic Language,* trans. Margaret Waller,

introd. Leon S. Roudiez (New York: Columbia University Press 1984), 24

89 Féral, 'Antigone or *The Irony*,' 10

90 Paul Smith, *Discerning the Subject* (Minneapolis: University of Minnesota Press 1988), 119–20

91 As Rosalind Coward and John Ellis point out, 'it is necessary to stress that the phallus is not the penis. The term "phallus" is used throughout Lacan's writing, in the way it was used in classical antiquity, as the figurative representation of the male organ: a simulacrum' (*Language and Materialism: Developments in Semiology and the Theory of the Subject* [London: Routledge and Kegan Paul 1977], 116).

92 Ann Radcliffe, *The Mysteries of Udolpho*, ed. Bonamy Dobrée (Oxford: Oxford University Press 1966), 235

93 Elizabeth Hamilton, *Memoirs of Modern Philosophers*, 3d ed., 3 vols (London: G.G. and J. Robinson 1801), Advertisement, xiv. Subsequent page references are to this edition.

94 Linda Hutcheon, *A Theory of Parody: The Teachings of Twentieth-Century Art Forms* (New York: Methuen 1985), 6

95 Mikhail Bakhtin, *The Dialogic Imagination: Four Essays*, ed. Michael Holquist, trans. Caryl Emerson and Michael Holquist (Austin: University of Texas Press 1981), 324

96 Kenneth Neill Cameron, *Shelley and His Circle 1773–1822*, as quoted by Gina Luria, 'Introduction,' *Adeline Mowbray; or, The Mother and Daughter*, 3 vols (New York: Garland 1974), 8. Subsequent page references are to this edition.

97 Felicity A. Nussbaum, 'Eighteenth Century Women's Autobiographical Commonplaces,' in *The Private Self: Theory and Practice of Women's Autobiographical Writings*, ed. Shari Benstock (Chapel Hill: University of North Carolina Press 1988), 148

CHAPTER 1 Female Confinement Literalized

1 I have studied Wollstonecraft's *Letters Written ... in Sweden ...* and its generic origins as a manifestation of Wollstonecraft's divided subjectivity in 'Writing as a Daughter: Autobiography in Wollstonecraft's Travelogue,' in *Essays on Life Writing*, ed. Marlene Kadar (Toronto: University of Toronto Press 1992), 61–77.

2 Sara D. Harasym, 'Ideology and Self: A Theoretical Discussion of the "Self" in Mary Wollstonecraft's Fiction,' *English Studies in Canada* 12, no. 2 (June 1986), 164

3 Mary Poovey, *The Proper Lady and the Woman Writer* (Chicago: University of Chicago Press 1984), 104–5

4   Janet Todd, *Feminist Literary History* (New York: Routledge 1988), 107
5   Julia Kristeva, *The Kristeva Reader*, ed. Toril Moi (New York: Columbia University Press 1986), 95
6   For more on the subject see Janet Todd, *Sensibility: An Introduction* (New York: Methuen 1986).
7   Nancy Chodorow, *The Reproduction of Mothering* (Berkeley: University of California Press 1978), 177
8   Virginia Woolf, 'Mary Wollstonecraft,' in *Women and Writing*, ed. Michèle Barrett (London: Women's Press 1979), 97
9   Mary Wollstonecraft, *Mary and the Wrongs of Woman*, ed. Gary Kelly (Oxford: World's Classics 1976), 72. Subsequent page references are to this edition.
10 Though primarily about nineteenth-century fiction, Gilbert and Gubar's observations about madness and imprisonment could equally apply to Wollstonecraft. In *The Madwoman in the Attic: The Woman Writer and the Nineteenth-Century Literary Imagination* (New Haven: Yale University Press 1979) the authors argue that 'dramatizations of imprisonment and escape ... represent a uniquely female tradition in this period' (85). They believe that though nineteenth-century male writers also 'used imagery of enclosure and escape,' women authors 'reflect the literal reality of their own confinement in the constraints they depict ... women seem forced to live more intimately with the metaphors they have created' (86–7). This notion is in keeping with the idea of 'literalization' I am suggesting in Wollstonecraft.
11 'The novel opens ... precisely at the moment when Maria is about to fall into romantic love for the second time' (Poovey, *The Proper Lady*, 98).
12 Marilyn Butler, 'The Woman at the Window: Ann Radcliffe in the Novels of Mary Wollstonecraft and Jane Austen,' *Women and Literature* ns 1 (1979), 134
13 Elizabeth R. Napier, in *The Failure of Gothic: Problems of Disjunction in an Eighteenth Century Literary Form* (Oxford: Clarendon 1987), says that Gothicism is 'less about evil than a formulaic system of creating a certain kind of atmosphere in which the reader's sensibility toward fear and horror is exercised in predictable ways' (29).
14 Elizabeth MacAndrew, *The Gothic Tradition in Fiction* (New York: Columbia University Press 1979), 49
15 Mary Wollstonecraft, *A Vindication of the Rights of Woman*, 2d ed., ed. Carol H. Poston (New York: Norton Critical Edition 1988), 11, 10
16 As quoted by Lawrence Stone, *The Family, Sex and Marriage in England 1500–1800* (New York: Harper and Row 1977), 331

17   Ibid., 332

18   Eliza Haywood, *The History of Miss Betsy Thoughtless*, introd. Dale
     Spender (London: Pandora 1986), 470

19   Hannah More, *Coelebs in Search of a Wife*, 7th ed., 2 vols (London: T.
     Cadell and W. Davies 1809), 2:170

20   Poovey, *The Proper Lady*, 103

21   Luce Irigaray, *This Sex Which Is Not One*, trans. Catherine Porter
     (Ithaca, NY: Cornell University Press 1985), 32

22   The influence of the story of Jemima on Mary Shelley has been point-
     ed out by Janet Todd in 'Frankenstein's Daughter: Mary Shelley and
     Mary Wollstonecraft,' *Women and Literature* 4, no. 2 (Fall 1976), 21.

23   Luce Irigaray, *Speculum of the Other Woman*, trans. Gillian C. Gill (Itha-
     ca, NY: Cornell University Press 1985), 165

24   Ralph M. Wardle, *Mary Wollstonecraft: A Critical Biography* (Lawrence:
     University of Kansas Press 1951), 25, 26

25   See Kelly, ed., *Mary and the Wrongs of Woman*, 225, n. 1.

26   Wollstonecraft, *Wrongs of Woman*, 98. In *Proper Lady* Poovey argues that
     while the narrator is aware that 'romantic expectations often do not
     correspond to real possibilities,' she nevertheless 'harbours the hope
     that such romantic expectations might be fulfilled' (97).
         For an alternate view, see Laurie Langbauer, who in 'An Early Ro-
     mance: Motherhood and Women's Writing in Mary Wollstonecraft's
     Novels,' in *Romanticism and Feminism*, ed. Anne K. Mellor (Blooming-
     ton: Indiana University Press 1988), 208–19, argues that romance is
     aligned with the maternal rather than the paternal and that this move
     'undercuts the distinctions between mother and father, literature and
     life, other and self' (218).

27   Poovey, *The Proper Lady*, 107

28   In his *Memoirs of the Author of a Vindication of the Rights of Woman* (Lon-
     don: J. Johnson 1798) William Godwin pointed out that while all other
     works were produced with rapidity by Wollstonecraft, *Wrongs of Woman*
     'was written slowly and with mature consideration ... She wrote many
     parts of the work again and again' (172). Similarly, Eleanor Flexner, in
     Mary Wollstonecraft: A Biography (New York: Coward, McCann and
     Geoghegan, Inc. 1972), says that Wollstonecraft was 'clearly aware that
     something was wrong with her novel,' as she discussed it with Godwin
     and sent the first fourteen chapters of it to George Dyson (250).

29   Poovey, *Proper Lady*, 109

30   Luce Irigaray, 'This Sex Which Is Not One,' trans. Ann Liddle, in *New
     French Feminisms: An Anthology*, ed. Elaine Marks and Isabelle de
     Courtivron (New York: Schoken Books 1981), 103

CHAPTER 2 Breaking the 'Magic Circle'

1 Mary Hays, *Memoirs of Emma Courtney* (1796), introd. Sally Cline (London: Pandora 1987), xvii. Subsequent page references are to this edition.

2 See Janet Todd, *Sensibility: An Introduction* (London: Methuen 1986), 1–6 for a description of sentimental literature and the cult of sensibility.

3 Mary Hays, *An Appeal to the Men of Great Britain in Behalf of Women*, introd. Gina Luria (New York: Garland 1974), 97

4 Katharine M. Rogers, in 'The Contribution of Mary Hays,' *Prose Studies* 10, no. 2 (Sept. 1987) 131–42, compares Wollstonecraft's prose style and arguments to those of Hays and notes that Wollstonecraft's approach was more theoretical.

5 Mary Kays, *Letters and Essays, Moral and Miscellaneous*, ed. Gina Luria (New York: Garland 1974), 19–20

6 See William Godwin, *Enquiry Concerning Political Justice*, ed. and abridged K. Codell Carter (Oxford: Clarendon 1971), 28.

7 Katharine Rogers points out that Hays's tone reflects the choice of the title of the *Appeal.* Hays's attitude is 'less adversarial than Wollstonecraft's, more good-natured and easy going' ('The Contribution of Mary Hays,' 138).

8 Luce Irigaray, *Speculum of the Other Woman*, trans. Gillian C. Gill (Ithaca, NY: Cornell University Press 1985), 142

9 Luce Irigaray, *This Sex Which Is Not One*, trans. Catherine Porter (Ithaca, NY: Cornell University Press 1985), 136

10 Janet Todd, *The Sign of Angellica: Women, Writing and Fiction, 1660–1800* (London: Virago 1989), 245

11 In *Women, Power, and Subversion: Social Strategies in British Fiction 1778–1860* (Athens: University of Georgia Press 1981), 14–22, Judith Lowder Newton discusses the effects of industrialization on middle-class women and its manifestations in literature. While industrialization meant rising economic and social power for middle-class men, women were increasingly being allocated to the domestic sphere.

12 Janet Todd points out that this 'magic circle' is probably from a 'Wollstonecraftian feminist context' and echoes the 'enchanted circle' of Mary Astell (*The Sign of Angellica*, 246).

13 In 'Ideology and Ideological State Apparatuses' Louis Althusser includes literature among the 'ideological apparatuses which contribute to the process of *reproducing* the *relations of production*, the social relationships which are the necessary condition for the existence and

perpetuation of the capitalist mode of production.' See Catherine Belsey's summary of his, Roland Barthes's, and Jacques Lacan's theories of subjectivity in *Critical Practice* (London: Methuen 1980), 56–84.

14 In *The Sign of Angellica* Janet Todd emphasizes the self-pitying aspects of Emma Courtney and Wollstonecraft's Mary (237, 245). While Emma does tend to ask her readers to sympathize with her at the beginning, the ending shows a strengthening of her fortitude and a sense of her resignation, if not acceptance of her lot.

15 Gina Luria, 'Mary Hays: A Critical Biography' (PHD diss., New York University, 1972), 297

16 In *The Unsex'd Females,* introd. by Gina Luria (New York: Garland 1974) Richard Polwhele included Hays in Wollstonecraft's band of 'Gallic freaks' who mixed 'corporeal struggles' with 'mental strife' (7, 21). See also Felicity A. Nussbaum, *The Brink of All We Hate: English Satires on Women 1660–1750* (Lexington: University Press of Kentucky 1984), 4ff, for a discussion of the learned lady as a frequent target of satire.

17 Michel Foucault, *The History of Sexuality: An Introduction,* vol. 1, trans. Robert Hurley (New York: Vintage 1990), 103

18 Samuel Taylor Coleridge, *Collected Letters,* 4 vols, ed. Earl Leslie Griggs (Oxford: Clarendon 1956–66), 1:563

19 In *Jane Austen and the War of Ideas* (Oxford: Clarendon 1976), 109, Marilyn Butler says that this relationship bears more resemblance to Mary Wollstonecraft's affair with Gilbert Imlay. However, Lady Gertrude Sinclair's many passages verbatim from *Emma Courtney,* documented with footnotes, suggest that the target was more likely Hays. See Charles Lloyd, *Edmund Oliver,* 2 vols (Bristol: J. Cottle 1798).

20 Julia Kristeva, 'From One Identity to an Other,' in her *Desire in Language: A Semiotic Approach to Literature and Art,* ed. Leon S. Roudiez, trans. Thomas Gora, Alice Jardine, and Leon Roudiez (New York: Columbia University Press 1980), 136, 138

21 Patricia Elliot, *From Mastery to Analysis: Theories of Gender in Psychoanalytic Feminism* (Ithaca, NY: Cornell University Press 1991), 213

22 Belsey, *Critical Practice,* 85

CHAPTER 3 The Mother and Daughter

1 Jane Spencer, *The Rise of the Woman Novelist: From Aphra Behn to Jane Austen* (Oxford: Basil Blackwell 1986), 132

2 In *Jane Austen and the War of Ideas* (Oxford: Clarendon Press 1975), Marilyn Butler says that 'it is still possible to draw a critical divide

where [Richard] Whately puts it: between the advocates of a Christian conservatism on the one hand, with their pessimistic view of man's nature, and their belief in external authority; on the other hand, progressives, sentimentalists, revolutionaries, with their optimism about man, and their preference for spontaneous personal impulse against rules imposed from without' (164–5). Hays is clearly of the latter camp, as she believes in individual worth, rather than the judgment of external authority.

3 Mary Hays, *The Victim of Prejudice*, 2 vols (London: J. Johnson 1799), 1:i. Subsequent page references are to this edition.

4 Mary Hays, *An Appeal to the Men of Great Britain in Behalf of Women*, introd. Gina Luria (New York: Garland 1974), 287

5 Extrapolating from the theories of Klein, Horney, and Deutsch, Marianne Hirsch, in *The Mother/Daughter Plot: Narrative, Psychoanalysis, Feminism* (Bloomington: Indiana University Press 1989), suggests that narratives of female development 'would not be linear or teleological but would reflect the oscillations between maternal and paternal attachments as well as the multiple repressions of the female developmental course.' (102).

6 One instance of 'bearing the word' that Margaret Homans discusses occurs when the text 'performs linguistic operations – translation, transmission, copying' of the language of other authors (*Bearing the Word* [Chicago: University of Chicago Press 1986], 31). Here Hays does not actually 'bear the word' of another, but she does replicate her own story or fears.

7 For example, Charlotte Smith's *Emmeline; or, The Orphan of the Castle* (1788), Ann Radcliffe's *The Mysteries of Udolpho* (1794), and Elizabeth Inchbald's *A Simple Story* (1791) featured abducted maidens. However, in these novels the heroines escape before they are actually violated.

8 M.H. 'On Novel Writing,' *Monthly Magazine* (Sept. 1797), 180

9 See Homans, *Bearing the Word*, 4ff.

10 See, for example, William Godwin, *Things As They Are; or, The Adventures of Caleb Williams,* ed. David McCrachen (London: Oxford University Press 1970), vol. 3, chapters 8–10; and Mary Wollstonecraft, *Mary and the Wrongs of Woman,* ed. Gary Kelly (Oxford: World's Classics 1976), 178.

11 Mary Hays, *Letters and Essays, Moral and Miscellaneous,* ed. Gina Luria (New York: Garland 1974), 84

12 In Radcliffe's *Mysteries of Udolpho* Signore Montoni attempts to coerce both his wife and Emily to sign over their properties to him. Emily's

lawful possession of the estates and her refusal to give them up are her means of asserting the little power she has at Udolpho (see vol. 3, chap. 5).

13 Luce Irigaray, *This Sex Which Is Not One*, trans. Catherine Porter (Ithaca, NY: Cornell University Press 1985), 159

14 Luce Irigaray, *Speculum of the Other Woman*, trans. Gillian C. Gill (Ithaca, NY: Cornell University Press 1985), 165

CHAPTER 4 Resisting the Phallic

1 Helen Maria Williams, *Letters from France*, 2 vols, introd. Janet M. Todd (Delmar, NY: Scholars' Facsimiles and Reprints 1975), 1:123

2 Helen Maria Williams, *Julia*, 2 vols, introd. Gina Luria (New York: Garland 1974), 2:221. Subsequent page references are to this edition.

3 Mary Wollstonecraft, Review of *Julia*, *Analytical Review* 7, (May–Aug. 1790), reprinted in *A Wollstonecraft Anthology* ed. Janet M. Todd (Bloomington: Indiana University Press 1977), 226

4 In 'Jane Austen and the English Novel of the 1790s,' in *Fetter'd or Free? British Women Novelists, 1670–1815*, ed. Mary Anne Schofield and Cecilia Macheski (Athens: Ohio University Press 1986), 291, Gary Kelly points out that both the English Jacobin and the anti-Jacobin novel tend 'to mount consistent satire on social conventions and social institutions of certain kinds, and on "Society" or fashionable life in particular.' While the attack is not original, what I see as singular and particularly feminist in Williams's work is her way of resolving the problem.

5 Kelly, 'Jane Austen and the English Novel of the 1790s,' 293

6 Nancy Chodorow, *The Reproduction of Mothering: Psychoanalysis and the Sociology of Gender* (Berkeley: University of California Press 1978), 177

7 Carol Gilligan, *In a Different Voice: Psychological Theory and Women's Development* (Cambridge: Harvard University Press 1982), 17

8 Ibid., 32

9 Ibid., 63

10 John Gregory, *A Father's Legacy to His Daughters* (1774), reprinted, in part, in *Women in the Eighteenth Century: Constructions of Femininity*, ed. Vivien Jones (London: Routledge 1990), 49

11 J.M.S. Tompkins, *The Popular Novel in England 1770–1800* (London: Constable 1932), 145–6

12 Ruth Perry, 'Interrupted Friendships in Jane Austen's *Emma*,' *Tulsa Studies in Women's Literature* 5, no. 2 (Fall 1986), 185

13 Ibid., 186

14 Ibid., 188

15 Luce Irigaray, *Speculum of the Other Woman,* trans. Gillian Gill (Ithaca,
    NY: Cornell University Press 1985), 22
16 Chodorow and Gilligan would argue that the qualities of separation,
    competitiveness, and self-assertion are more frequently associated with
    men than women, who because of their psychic maturation 'grow up
    and remain more connected to others' (Chodorow, 177). This notion
    is in keeping with my earlier contention that Williams is attempting a
    mode of resolving the love triangle based on a female ethos.
17 In such poems as 'Edwin and Eltruda' and 'An American Tale' Wil-
    liams similarly argues against war and violence by depicting in affect-
    ing terms those bereaved by war. I am indebted to Deborah Kennedy's
    paper '"Storms of Sorrow": The Poetry of Helen Maria Williams,' *Man
    and Nature: Proceedings of the Canadian Society for Eighteenth Century
    Studies* 10 (1991), 77–91, for this information.
18 In *The Popular Novel in England 1770–1800,* 96–105, J.M.S. Tompkins
    discusses the importance of 'tears' and 'distress' at this time: 'It be-
    came the fashion to conclude a novel with a funeral. "The heroes and
    heroines must all be buried," said the *Monthly* in 1787' (103).
19 Janet Todd, *The Sign of Angellica: Women, Writing and Fiction, 1660–1800*
    (London: Virago 1989), 231
20 Rachel Blau Duplessis, *Writing beyond the Ending: Narrative Strategies of
    Twentieth-Century Women Writers* (Bloomington: Indiana University Press
    1985), 20

CHAPTER 5 Disruption and Containment

 1 Gary Kelly, *The English Jacobin Novel 1780–1805* (Oxford: Clarendon
    Press 1976), 65
 2 Luce Irigaray, *This Sex Which Is Not One,* trans. Catherine Porter
    (Ithaca, NY: Cornell University Press 1985), 29
 3 Ibid., 29
 4 Terry Castle, *Masquerade and Civilization: The Carnivalesque in Eighteenth-
    Century English Culture and Fiction* (Stanford: Stanford University Press
    1986), 325
 5 Julia Kristeva, *The Kristeva Reader,* ed. Toril Moi (New York: Columbia
    University Press 1986), 91
 6 I am greatly influenced by Margaret Homans's reading of Emily
    Brontë's *Wuthering Heights,* another story in two generations. See Mar-
    garet Homans, *Bearing the Word: Language and Female Experience in Nine-
    teenth-Century Women's Writing* (Chicago: University Press 1986), espe-
    cially chapter 3, 68ff.

7 Elizabeth Inchbald, *A Simple Story*, ed. and introd. J.M.S. Tompkins (London: Oxford University Press 1967), 338. Subsequent page references are to this edition. The novel is also available unedited in Pandora Press's Mothers of the Novel series.

8 Robert Palfrey Utter and Gwendolyn Bridges Needham, *Pamela's Daughters* (New York: Macmillan 1937), 389

9 Kelly, *The English Jacobin Novel*, 88, 90

10 Ibid., 90, 73

11 Mary Wollstonecraft, *A Wollstonecraft Anthology*, ed. Janet Todd (Bloomington: Indiana University Press 1977), 226–7

12 Biographical information on Inchbald is found in Roger Manvell, *Elizabeth Inchbald: England's Principal Woman Dramatist and Independent Woman of Letters in Eighteenth Century London* (Lanham: University Press of America 1987); Samuel R. Littlewood, *Elizabeth Inchbald and Her Circle* (London: Daniel O'Connor 1921); and in J.M.S. Tompkins's introduction to *A Simple Story* (London: Oxford University Press 1967).

13 Elizabeth Inchbald, *Wives As They Were and Maids As They Are*, in *Selected Comedies*, introd. and notes by Roger Manvell (Lanham: University Press of America 1987), 1.1 [p. 12]

14 Castle, *Masquerade and Civilization*, 294

15 See Julia Kristeva, 'The Semiotic and the Symbolic,' in her *Revolution in Poetic Language*, trans. Margaret Waller, introd. Leon S. Roudiez (New York: Columbia University Press 1984), 19–90.

16 As paraphrased by Toril Moi, *Sexual/Textual Politics: Feminist Literary Theory* (London: Methuen 1985), 162

17 John Lechte, *Julia Kristeva* (London: Routledge 1990), 129

18 In *Speculum of the Other Woman* (Ithaca, NY: Cornell University Press 1985) Luce Irigaray points out that woman 'remains in unrealized potentiality' (165) because she is required to be the mirror or specular object of man. Similarly, in *A Room of One's Own* (Harmondsworth: Penguin 1945), Virginia Woolf notes that 'women have served all these centuries as looking-glasses possessing the magic and delicious power of reflecting the figure of man at twice its natural size' (37).

19 In *Masquerade and Civilization* Terry Castle makes a slightly different point about male education. She says that male characters 'learn to forgo austerity and emotional detachment for a new life of passion and adhesiveness. Dorriforth must yield, as it were, to the impure power of eros. Thus he enacts the familiar story of metamorphosis – from chastity to sexuality, from celibate to lover' (305).

20 Judith Butler, *Gender Trouble: Feminism and the Subversion of Identity* (New York: Routledge 1990), 80

21 Katherine Sobba Green, *The Courtship Novel, 1740–1820: A Feminized Genre* (Lexington: University Press of Kentucky 1991), 145

22 Castle, *Masquerade and Civilization*, 291

23 Only the first part of this novel is reprinted in paperback form at present: Frances Sheridan, *Memoirs of Miss Sidney Bidulph*, introd. Sue Townsend (London: Pandora Press 1987).

24 Michel Foucault, in *Discipline and Punish: The Birth of the Prison*, trans. Alan Sheridan (New York: Vintage 1979) and *The History of Sexuality*, vol. 1, trans. Robert Hurley (New York: Vintage 1990), argues that the eighteenth century invented the techniques of discipline and examination. Individuals are involved in the social system of power and discipline since they are part of its mechanism (*Discipline*, 225, 217). 'Power is not an institution, and not a structure; neither is it a certain strength we are endowed with; it is the name that one attributes to a complex strategical situation in a particular society' (*Sexuality*, 93).

25 In *The History of Sexuality*, vol. 1, Foucault notes: 'It is worth remembering that the first figure to be invested by the deployment of sexuality, one of the first to be "sexualized," was the "idle" woman. She inhabited the outer edge of the "world," in which she always had to appear as a value, and of the family, where she was assigned a new destiny charged with conjugal and parental obligations' (121). By her indiscretion with the Duke of Avon, Lady Elmwood fails to fulfil her conjugal and parental obligations. A woman's sexual fidelity was particularly important because of the eighteenth-century practice of primogeniture.

26 Even though her association of the Mother with the literal and nature does not exactly figure in this case, I am here using Margaret Homans's phrasing and much of her theories formulated in *Bearing the Word*, 72, 74, and 75ff.

27 Homans, *Bearing the Word*, 74, 75

28 Kelly, *The English Jacobin Novel*, 85

29 See Kate Ferguson Ellis, *The Contested Castle: Gothic Novels and the Subversion of Domestic Ideology* (Urbana: University of Illinois Press 1989).

30 Cynthia Griffin Wolff, in 'The Radcliffean Gothic Model: A Form for Feminine Sexuality,' in *The Female Gothic*, ed. Juliann E. Fleenor (Montreal: Eden Press 1983), 207–26, points out that in Gothic novels there is often a pairing of 'villain,' a demon lover who is a powerful authority figure, and a 'hero.' Though the heroine declares her preference for the hero early on in the novel, she is not indifferent to the compelling presence of the dark villain, who can be an 'uncle, a stepfather, sometimes the biological father himself' creating a 'spectre of incest' (213–14).

31   Foucault, *Discipline and Punish*, 227

CHAPTER 6   Resisting the Symbolic

1   Gary Kelly, *The English Jacobin Novel 1780–1805* (Oxford: Clarendon Press 1976), 99, 85
2   Ibid., 94
3   The novel's title when first completed, according to James Boaden, *Memoirs of Mrs. Inchbald* (London 1833), i, 328, as noted by Kelly, *English Jacobin Novel*, 94
4   Elizabeth Inchbald, *Nature and Art*, 2 vols (London: G.G. & J. Robinson 1796), 1:55, 56: Subsequent page references are to this edition.
5   See Lawrence Stone, *The Family, Sex and Marriage in England 1500–1800* (New York: Harper and Row 1977), 414–15. Stone points out that in general there was a shift from a more formal address of parents by their children in the seventeenth century to an increasing 'relaxation of manner' in the late eighteenth century.
6   Kelly, *English Jacobin Novel*, 105
7   In some editions her name is Agnes Primrose.
8   Mona Scheuermann, *Social Protest in the Eighteenth-Century English Novel* (Columbus: Ohio State University Press 1985), 189
9   Luce Irigaray, *This Sex Which Is Not One*, trans. Catherine Porter (Ithaca, NY: Cornell University Press 1985), 84
10   See Stone, *Family, Sex and Marriage*, chapter 8.
11   Ibid., 392
12   Katherine Sobba Green, *The Courtship Novel, 1740–1820: A Feminized Genre* (Lexington: University Press of Kentucky 1991), 14
13   Ibid., 161
14   Kelly, *English Jacobin Novel*, 267
15   Ibid., 267
16   Soon after her seduction by William, Hannah goes to London with her child to seek employment and to be nearer to William. Here she attempts first to earn a living toiling 'from morning till night' in a dismal kitchen (2:103); then is enticed into prostitution through necessity.
17   See also Stone, *Family, Sex and Marriage*, 331–2, where he emphasizes that 'women could acquire nothing which did not automatically become their husbands' (331).
18   Scheuermann, *Social Protest in the Eighteenth-Century English Novel*, 194
19   Ibid., 10, 195, 197.
20   Kelly, *English Jacobin Novel*, 111, 112

21 Ibid., 112
22 See ibid., 101, 110.

CHAPTER 7 Contradictory Narratives

1 The celebrated English critic, George Stevens, severely censured Smith for her choice of an immoral work. He believed that the passion in *Manon Lescaut* was an apology for licentiousness and ought to be condemned. As a result of this outcry Smith withdrew the work. See Florence Hilbish, 'Charlotte Smith, Poet and Novelist (1749–1806)' (PHD diss., University of Pennsylvania, 1941), 118–19.

2 As quoted by Anne Henry Ehrenpreis, 'Introduction,' *Emmeline; or, The Orphan of the Castle,* by Charlotte Smith (London: Oxford University Press 1971), vii. Subsequent page references are to this edition.

3 As quoted by Hilbish, 'Charlotte Smith, Poet and Novelist,' 131

4 Jane Spencer, 'Charlotte Smith,' in *A Dictionary of British and American Women Writers 1600–1800,* ed. Janet Todd (London: Methuen 1984), 289

5 Mary Anne Schofield, *Masking and Unmasking the Female Mind: Disguising Romances in Feminine Fiction, 1713–1799* (Newark: University of Delaware Press 1990), 150

6 M.M. Bakhtin, *The Dialogic Imagination: Four Essays,* ed. Michael Holquist, trans. Caryl Emerson and Michael Holquist (Austin: University of Texas Press 1981), 324

7 As quoted by Elaine Showalter, 'Feminist Criticism in the Wilderness,' in *The New Feminist Criticism,* ed. Elaine Showalter (New York: Pantheon 1985), 266

8 This plot summary fits a number of novels written in the eighteenth century, including, for example, Samuel Richardson's *Pamela,* Frances Burney's *Evelina,* and Jane Austen's *Emma* and *Mansfield Park.*

9 Egerton Brydges, *Imaginative Biography* (1834), 2:95–6, as quoted by Anne Henry Ehrenpreis, 'Introduction,' *Northanger Abbey,* by Jane Austen (Harmondsworth: Penguin 1972), 14

10 See Catherine Belsey, *Critical Practice* (New York: Methuen 1980), especially chapter 3, 'Addressing the Subject,' for a further discussion of this topic.

11 Several critics have noted that Catherine Morland is a parody of Smith's Emmeline, among them, Anne Henry Ehrenpreis, in her 'Introduction' to *Emmeline,* xi; and Mary Lascelles, *Jane Austen and Her Art* (Oxford: Oxford University Press 1939), 60–3.

12 See the first chapter of *Northanger Abbey.*

13   Linda Hutcheon suggests that 'parody is a form of serious art criticism' and 'has the advantage of being both a re-creation and a creation, making criticism into a kind of active exploration of form' (*A Theory of Parody: The Teachings of Twentieth Century Art Forms* [New York: Methuen 1985], 51).

14   See, for example, Kenneth L. Moler, *Jane Austen's Art of Allusion* (Lincoln: University of Nebraska Press 1968); Frank W. Bradbrook, *Jane Austen and Her Predecessors* (Cambridge: Cambridge University Press 1966); Marilyn Butler, *Jane Austen and the War of Ideas* (Oxford: Oxford University Press 1975); William H. Magee, 'The Happy Marriage: The Influence of Charlotte Smith on Jane Austen,' *Studies in the Novel,* 7, no. 1 (Spring 1975), 120–32; and Eleanor Ty, 'Ridding Unwanted Suitors: Jane Austen's *Mansfield Park* and Charlotte Smith's *Emmeline,*' *Tulsa Studies in Women's Literature* 5, no. 2 (Fall 1986), 327–29.

15   Virginia Woolf, 'Professions for Women,' reprinted in *Virginia Woolf: Women and Writing,* ed. Michèle Barrett (London: Women's Press 1979), 59

16   Ibid., 59, 60

17   According to Nancy Chodorow, 'a girl usually turns to her father as an object of primary interest from the exclusivity of the relationship to her mother, but this libidinal turning to her father does not substitute for her attachment to her mother. Instead, a girl retains her preoedipal tie to her mother ... and builds oedipal attachments to both her mother and father' (*The Reproduction of Mothering: Psychoanalysis and the Sociology of Gender* [Berkeley: University of California Press 1978], 192–3). On the basis of Chodorow's theories Mary Poovey suggests that 'it may well be the case that woman's psychological relation to authority may involve accommodation rather than confrontation; in other words, it may be more in keeping with her psychological development to identify with and accept a number of role models instead of trying to usurp the place of her authoritative forebears' (*The Proper Lady and the Woman Writer* [Chicago: University of Chicago Press 1984], 254).

18   Hayley was quoted as observing that *Emmeline,* 'considering the situation of the author, is the most wonderful production he ever saw, and not inferior, in his opinion, to any book in that fascinating species of composition.' Hayley is quoted in a letter of J.C. Walker to Bishop Percy, 16 September 1788, in John Nichols, *Illustrations of the Literary History of the Eighteenth Century* (1848), 708, as noted by Ehrenpreis, 'Introduction,' *Emmeline,* vii.

19   See the first chapter of Poovey, *The Proper Lady and the Woman Writer.*

20   Jane Spencer, in *The Rise of the Woman Novelist: From Aphra Behn to Jane*

Austen (Oxford: Basil Blackwell 1986), says that 'Adelina proves herself not really ruined by this one error by the extravagance of her repentance' (128).

21 Eva Figes, who sees similarities between Smith's *Emmeline* and Frances Burney's *Cecilia*, points out that the incident with Adelina illustrates the difference between Smith's and Burney's fictional worlds. Figes observes: '... no Burney woman would have been allowed to be friends with a pregnant woman ... Smith's heroines constantly express active sympathy for women in distress' (*Sex and Subterfuge: Women Novelists to 1850* [London: Macmillan 1982], 64).

22 The kind of feminist criticism that seeks to identify stereotypical portraits of women has been labelled 'feminist critique' by Elaine Showalter in 'Toward a Feminist Poetics' and 'Feminist Criticism in the Wilderness,' both reprinted in Showalter, ed. *The New Feminist Criticism.* One early example of this type of feminist criticism is Mary Ellmann's *Thinking about Women* (New York: Harcourt 1968).

23 One classic case is Defoe's Moll Flanders, who is seduced by an older brother, but marries the younger brother, Robin. Moll subsequently becomes a prostitute and thief. In Inchbald's *A Simple Story* Miss Milner is unfaithful to Dorriforth and is exiled to die unloved and alone in Scotland. In Smith's *Emmeline* another adulterous figure, Lady Frances, who, because of vanity and boredom, embarks openly on an affair with Chevalier de Bellozane, is disciplined for her indiscriminate actions by a '*lettre de cachet*, which confined her during pleasure to a convent' (525).

24 Edwin Hood, *The Age and Its Architects,* as quoted by Poovey, *The Proper Lady and the Woman Writer,* 247

25 See, for example, the first chapter, 'Formative Influences,' of F. Hilbish's 'Charlotte Smith, Poet and Novelists,' where she cites Mr and Mrs Stafford's 'history' as the experience of Benjamin and Charlotte Smith (88–91, 95–9).

26 Quoted by Ehrenpreis, 'Introduction,' *Emmeline*, viii

27 Mary Wollstonecraft, *Analytical Review* 1 (1788), 333

28 See, for example, J.M.S. Tompkins, *The Popular Novel in England 1770–1800* (London: Constable 1932), 266, 375, who first pointed out that Radcliffe was profoundly indebted to Smith. Similar views are expressed in James R. Foster, 'Charlotte Smith, Pre-Romantic Novelist,' *PMLA* 43 (June 1928), 463–75; and Ehrenpreis, 'Introduction,' *Emmeline*, xi.

29 Spencer, *The Rise of the Woman Novelist,* 194

30 Kate Ferguson Ellis, *The Contested Castle: Gothic Novels and the Subversion*

of Domestic Ideology (Urbana: University of Illinois Press 1989), 86

31 Luce Irigaray, *Speculum of the Other Woman*, trans. Gillian Gill (Ithaca, NY: Cornell University Press 1985), 191

32 David Morse, in *Romanticism: A Structural Analysis* (Totowa, NJ: Barnes and Noble 1982), argues that 'the gothic is a field of discourse saturated with political connotations and addressing itself to issues raised in the work of Godwin and Paine: the incompatibility of reason and humanity with a society based on domination and fear; the critique of secrecy and the insistence that healthy society must be based on frankness, openness and sincerity; the suggestion that in a society governed by despotism and permeated by religious hypocrisy and bigotry natural human impulses will become warped and distorted; the conviction that relationships between individuals on any basis other than that of freedom and equality must necessarily be alienating, even for ... those who coerce and manipulate' (3).

CHAPTER 8 Revolutionary Politics

1 Charlotte Smith, 'Preface,' *Desmond, a Novel,* 3 vols, introd. Gina Luria (New York: Garland 1974), 1:i. Subsequent page references are to this edition.

2 Diana Bowstead, 'Charlotte Smith's *Desmond:* The Epistolary Novel as Ideological Argument,' in *Fetter'd or Free? British Women Novelists, 1670–1815,* ed. Mary Anne Schofield and Cecilia Macheski (Athens: Ohio University Press 1986), 237

3 Sir Walter Scott, *The Journal of Sir Walter Scott* (Edinburgh 1891), 1:156, as quoted by Rufus P. Turner, 'Charlotte Smith (1749–1806): New Light on Her Life and Literary Career,' (PHD diss., University of Southern California, 1966), 118

4 Leigh Hunt, *Men, Women and Books* (London 1847), 2:135, as quoted by Turner, 'Charlotte Smith,' 118

5 In the 'Author's Preface' Richardson notes that 'all the letters are written while the hearts of the writers must be supposed to be wholly engaged in their subjects ... so that they abound not only with critical situations, but with what may be called instantaneous descriptions and reflections' (*Clarissa; or, The History of a Young Lady,* introd. John Butt [New York: Dutton, Everyman 1962], xiv). See also George Sherburn, 'Writing to the Moment: One Aspect,' in *Samuel Richardson: A Collection of Critical Essays,* ed. John Carroll (Englewood Cliffs, NJ: Prentice-Hall 1969), 152–60.

6 Janet Gurkin Altman, *Epistolarity: Approaches to a Form* (Columbus: Ohio University Press 1982), 19

7 Ibid., 14–15

8 Altman points out that the epistolary form is 'is unique among first person forms in its aptitude for portraying the experience of reading. In letter narrative we not only see correspondents struggle with pen, ink, paper; we also see their messages being read and interpreted by their intended or unintended recipients. The epistolary form is unique in making the reader (narratée) almost as important an agent in the narrative as the writer (narrator)' (ibid., 88).

9 The so-called Black Act of 1723 extended the death penalty to cover crimes against property as trivial as cutting down young trees or deerstalking in disguise. E.P. Thompson, in *Whigs and Hunters* (London: Allen Lane 1975), 254–5, points out that there was humane, enlightened opposition to ferocious legislation like the Black Act in literature; for example, in Fielding's *Joseph Andrews*. See also John Richetti, 'Representing an Under Class: Servants and Proletarians in Fielding and Smollett,' in *The New Eighteenth Century: Theory, Politics, English Literature*, ed. Felicity Nussbaum and Laura Brown (New York: Methuen 1987), 84–98.

10 Luce Irigaray, *This Sex Which Is Not One*, trans. Catherine Porter (Ithaca, NY: Cornell University Press 1985), 192

11 In *The Madwoman in the Attic: The Woman Writer and the Nineteenth-Century Literary Imagination* (New Haven: Yale University Press 1979), Sandra Gilbert and Susan Gubar use the trope of the madwoman to designate the repressed desires of the female.

12 In 'Jane Austen and the English Novel of the 1790s' in Schofield and Macheski, eds., *Fetter'd or Free?* 285–306, Gary Kelly writes about the debate of the 'progressive bourgeois ideology' and its manifestations in the writings of both the Jacobin and the anti-Jacobin novelists of the 1790s.

13 Mary Poovey, *The Proper Lady and the Woman Writer* (Chicago: University of Chicago Press 1984), 44. Poovey talks about doubling and parody as an expression of accommodation, as the desire to 'retain *both* the inherited and the revised genre' (44).

CHAPTER 9 Celebrating the Ex-Centric

1 Allene Gregory, *The French Revolution and the English Novel* (New York: Putnam's Sons 1915), 222

2 Charlotte Smith, *The Young Philosopher*, 4 vols, introd. Gina Luria (New York: Garland 1974), 1:iii–iv. Subsequent page references are to this edition.

3 Charlotte Smith, *Marchmont, a Novel,* 4 vols (London: Sampson Low 1796), 2:215

4 Mark S. Madoff, 'Inside, Outside, and the Gothic Locked-Room Mystery,' in *Gothic Fictions: Prohibition/Transgression,* ed. Kenneth W. Graham (New York: AMS Press 1989), 51

5 Nancy Chodorow, in *The Reproduction of Mothering: Psychoanalysis and the Sociology of Gender* (Berkeley: University of California Press 1978), and Carol Gilligan, in *In a Different Voice: Psychological Theory and Women's Development* (Cambridge: Harvard University Press 1982), both stress that female development encourages bonding, relationships, and connection, whereas the male maturation process tends to emphasize competition, separation, and confrontation.

CONCLUSION

1 Roland Barthes, *S/Z,* trans. Richard Miller (New York: Hill and Wang 1974). See also Kaja Silverman, *The Subject of Semiotics* (New York: Oxford University Press 1983), chapter 6.

Index